The Rhetoric of Interpretation

and the Interpretation of Rhetoric

Edited by Paul Hernadi

Duke University Press   Durham and London   1989

The text of this book was originally published, in slightly different form and
without the present index, as Volume 9, number 2 of *Poetics Today*.
Copyright © 1989 The Porter Institute for Poetics and Semiotics
Printed in the United States of America
on acid-free paper ∞
Library of Congress Cataloging-in-Publication Data
The Rhetoric of interpretation and the interpretation of rhetoric /
Paul Hernadi, editor.
p.   cm.
Bibliography: p.
Includes index.
ISBN 0-8223-0934-3
1. Criticism. 2. Literature—Philosophy. 3. Hermeneutics.
4. Rhetoric.   I. Hernadi, Paul, 1936–   .
PN81.R45   1989
801′.95—dc20   89-7924

Contents

Acknowledgments

Most of the essays collected in this volume were first presented in the framework of six conferences sponsored by the Interpretive Studies Colloquium of the University of California at Santa Barbara. Each conference had its particular theme—"Interpretation and Knowledge," "The Interpreter's Eye," and "The Social Contexts of Textual Interpretation," for example. Taken together, however, the twenty or so papers delivered by prominent visiting scholars between November 1986 and May 1988 turn out to have traced much of the horizon of current thinking about interpretation in half a dozen humanistic disciplines.

With the present volume in mind, some authors substituted a more fitting essay for the talk delivered in Santa Barbara and several others have revised their original papers in response to the lively exchange of views that occurred at each of the six conferences. It seems appropriate, therefore, to acknowledge here the indirect contribution to this book of those speakers whose own papers had already been committed for publication elsewhere: Arthur Danto, Stanley Fish, Michael Fried, David Hoy, Oscar Kenshur, Sandra Gilbert, Mary Louise Pratt, Robert Scholes, Susan Suleiman, and Jane Tompkins. By helping to shape the profile of discussion sessions, many expert and alert local participants had comparable impact on the pages that follow. Special thanks are due, however, to three colleagues (Richard Comstock, Bert O. States, and Everett Zimmerman) for their willingness to serve on the organizing committee. I am also grateful to two doctoral students (James Egan and Jill Widdicombe) for their assistance, respectively, in running the conferences and preparing the manuscript for publication.

Our collection of twelve essays first appeared as a special issue of *Poetics Today*, whose founding editor Benjamin Harshav of Yale University enthusiastically supported the project from the outset. In the final stages of proofing the special issue and in eventually turning it into the present book with a new introduction and index, I was helped by Randi Glick and Diane Dussler, two staff members of the new Inter-disciplinary Humanities Center at the University of California, Santa Barbara. It is in the larger framework of this Center that the activities of the Interpretive Studies Colloquium continue.

Paul Hernadi
Santa Barbara, January 3, 1989

Editor's Introduction

Paul Hernadi

Early versions of most of the ensuing essays were designed to fit a common framework of six interrelated conferences. As described in the foregoing "Acknowledgments," this framework obliged the participants to reflect on the interpretive dimension of their respective disciplines. Such reflection tends to reveal that all interpretation takes place for a particular audience and within a specific historical horizon. Searching questions about interpretation thus elicit no less searching questions about rhetoric and ideology as well. Small wonder, then, if the present volume strongly suggests that the principles and operations of interpretation invite being studied in conjunction with those of rhetoric and those informing descriptions and critiques of ideology.

By and large, the individual essays highlight three types of contacts between interpretation, rhetoric, and ideology. Accordingly, it seemed appropriate to divide the book into three sections: "The Rhetoric of Interpretation," "Interpretation, Rhetoric, Ideology," and "Interpreting Rhetoric." In the first section, Hayden White, Jonathan Culler, Edward Pechter, and Martin Jay explore various types of rhetorical strategy embodied in modern interpretive theory and practice. In the second section, Terry Eagleton, Houston Baker, Richard Ohmann, and Dominick LaCapra make us see interpretation and rhetoric as mediated through various modes of ideology. In the third section, Susan Handelman, Renato Rosaldo, Robert Berkhofer, and Michael Holquist interpret various kinds of discourse—philosophical, anthropological, historical, and literary—from the respective points of view of their particular rhetoric. Needless to say, such a bird's-eye view of the book's contents does not begin to do justice to the thematic, methodological, and stylistic diversity of the individual contributions. Even the following rapid survey of the twelve essays is intended merely for the reader's initial orientation amidst complex polyphonic arguments.

In "The Rhetoric of Interpretation," Hayden White uses a passage from Proust to illustrate how both expository and narrative interpretations can gain rhetorical coherence by passing through four "dominant modalities of figuration": metaphor, metonymy, synecdoche, and irony (6). The "figurative coherence" achieved by completing the rhetorical cycle of four tropes is different in kind from both the grammatical coherence of the sentence and the logical coherence of explicit argument (19). But it emerges just as clearly when rhetorically successful interpreters proceed (not necessarily in this typical sequence) "from a metaphorical apprehension of the *interpretandum,* through a metonymic dispersion of its attributes and a synecdochic comprehension of its possible 'nature,' to an ironic distancing of the process of interpretation itself" (6). Readers seeking more information about White's appropriation of Giambattista Vico's and Kenneth Burke's "four master tropes" may consult the Introduction to his *Metahistory* (1973) and several essays collected in his *Tropics of Discourse* (1978).

Jonathan Culler's "Interpretations: Data or Goals?" takes Baudelaire's famous sonnet titled "Correspondances" as its point of departure. Having surveyed some earlier interpretations of the poem, Culler adds his own reading, in large part to demonstrate that a positive answer is possible to his initial question, "Can one interpret a poem without making interpretation the overriding goal?" (27). Culler prefers theoretical to "practical," interpretive criticism for the following reason. Taking interpretations (including their own) as data, critics of poetry can "move toward an elucidation of the interpretive processes associated with lyric" and "show how genres, such as the lyric, are sets of reading strategies for making sense of language" (36–37). Such a dis-placement of the present goal of most literary critics ("the production of new interpretations of literary texts") should lead to increased understanding of language and genre by way of carefully "interpreting readings themselves." The theoretical rhetoric proper to this kind of interpretation of interpretations—a rhetoric of systematic poetics—might in turn "discourage the impression" that what literary scholars offer as knowledge is "in fact just an endless series of ingenious interpretations" (37).

Edward Pechter also contrasts two approaches to interpretation, each displaying its own kind of legitimating rhetoric. His essay, "Of Ants and Grasshoppers: Two Ways (or More) to Link Texts and Power," turns the familiar fable about socially responsible and individualistically pleasure-seeking creatures into a contrastive allegory of politically and aesthetically motivated critics. Quotations of different weight and length from such varied sources as *Doctor Faustus, The Duchess of*

Malfi, Oscar Wilde, Roland Barthes, Lenny Bruce, and Woody Allen help Pechter make his grasshopperish case for following the "energies" of a text or performance beyond the interpreter's own "consciously understood ideological agendas" (50). Pechter argues that such an "aesthetic" approach is more likely to bring about truly significant social change than a self-constraining political approach might. Thus, he claims, "grasshoppers make the best ants" (51).

In "The Rise of Hermeneutics and the Crisis of Ocularcentrism," Martin Jay juxtaposes the respective demands implied by the visual rhetoric of enlightened empirical science (we should *see* things for ourselves) and by the auditory rhetoric of romantic and post-romantic hermeneutics (we should *listen* to voices from within and from the past). Having considered some earlier controversies involving, for instance, the spiritual superiority of the word over the image, Jay warns against "essentializing sight, hearing, or any other sense"; after all, "different cultures at different moments have stressed some over others" (61). As for the present, Jay follows Habermas in assuming that we continue to "live in a society without the immediacy, transparency, and communicative rationality of perfect intersubjectivity." Even in the human sciences, therefore, hermeneutic understanding of the interpreted other cannot fully replace explanatory distanciation from one's objects of study. Jay concludes that "without the tension between explanation and interpretation—sight and hearing, if you will—there can be no genuine critique of the mixed quality of our society. Each is a necessary check to the totalizing pretensions of the other" (68).

The first essay in the second group, "The Ideology of the Aesthetic," offers a radical socialist critique of what Terry Eagleton takes to be the ideological predecessor of hermeneutics: eighteenth-century aesthetics as a newly emergent "discourse of the body" (75). Eagleton applauds the materialistic and utopian strains in the pertinent opinions of Baumgarten, Shaftesbury, Kant, Schiller, and other thinkers. On the whole, however, he considers all philosophies of the aesthetic as more or less successful attempts to seduce both the sensuous body and the working classes into willing submission to the hegemony of oppressive reason and an exploitative social order. In Hume, to be sure, Eagleton detects an anticipation of what will happen in the mid-nineteenth century and after: "Reason, having spun off the subaltern discourse of aesthetics, now finds itself threatened with being swallowed up by it" (84). Yet only Marx and Freud, "the two greatest aestheticians," will try to "think everything through again, this time from the basis of the body: . . . Marx with the laboring body, Freud with the desiring one" (85).

It is with the laboring and desiring—but also enchained, beaten, and violated—African body that Houston Baker is concerned in "The

Promised Body: Reflections on Canon in an Afro-American Context."
The late eighteenth-century publication of the life stories of former
slaves like Ukawsaw Gronniosaw and Olaudah Equiano is roughly con-
temporaneous with the high tide of aesthetic discourse in Europe and,
more pertinent for Baker, with some celebrated American avowals of
man's (white man's?) natural right to freedom. From Baker's essay a
painfully stark black and white image of the age emerges, threatening to pale our colorized ideas and ideologies of enlightened human
nature, religious and political tolerance, as well as the potentially lib-
erating aesthetic appreciation of spirit sublime and body beautiful.

Richard Ohmann's "History and Literary History: The Case of
Mass Culture" links literature to a more subtle kind of trade with
reified human beings. Ohmann credits Frank Munsey, the nineteenth-
century inventor of the mass circulation magazine that sells for less
than the cost of its production, with paving the way to the current
advertising practice of radio stations and television networks: they
help to sell the advertised products by first selling "us"—the captive
attention of large quantities of commodified potential consumers—to
"monopoly capital." Ohmann notes the homogenizing effect of com-
mercially supported mass culture in the October 1895 issue of *Munsey's
Magazine*. He suggests that an almost identical voice—impersonal yet
familiar and, above all, unproblematically self-confident—speaks to
readers through two seemingly disparate channels: a highly conventional love story with the requisite happy end and an advertisement
praising as pure, sweet, and wholesome the box of Quaker Oats cereal
that a pictured Quaker of visibly robust health and wealth offers to
the viewer. Ohmann argues that the formulas of mass culture reduce
"dense historical understandings" to "comfortable ideology," thereby
channelling our anxieties "into smaller concerns like the need for a
healthy breakfast or for a laundry soap that won't shrink clothes—
worries that may be allayed by purchasing commodities" (121).

Mass culture is only one of several formations discussed by Dominick
LaCapra in "Culture and Ideology: From Geertz to Marx"; others
include official, elite, and popular culture. None of these should be
equated with ideology because, LaCapra insists, each can contain both
ideological and nonideological ingredients. Unlike Geertz, LaCapra
follows Marx and especially Gramsci in ascribing to ideology five negative characteristics: ideology mystifies; it illegitimately generalizes a
particular group's partial interests; it naturalizes and essentializes the
historical; it promotes consent to hegemonic rule; and it wishfully
reads coherence into chaos. Yet LaCapra also stresses that ideology
"need not be construed one-dimensionally as 'false consciousness' and
placed (as sometimes by Marx himself) in a binary opposition with
absolute truth (itself often equated with positive science)" (139–40).

While disclosing what ideology mystifies, critique remains "recurrently subject to self-mystification and never entirely transcends this possibility in a realm of absolute truth or pure, value-neutral theory and method." Since LaCapra proposes to situate critique "in a discursive and argumentative context which itself has no absolute or ultimate grounds" (140), he seems to assign the crucial task of distinguishing between ideological and critical aspects of a particular cultural formation to open-ended interpretive and rhetorical activity.

The last four essays of the volume are allied in attempting to interpret the rhetoric of different kinds of discursive endeavors. In "Parodic Play and Prophetic Reason: Two Interpretations of Interpretation," Susan Handelman juxtaposes "two outcomes of the radical critique of philosophy in our era": the deconstructive "demystification of oppressive ideologies" through the revelation of their status as constructs (144) and the ethical self-questioning of a displaced subjectivity that knows itself responsible to the equally vulnerable Other. Jacques Derrida stands for the former alternative; his admired predecessor and interlocutor, Emmanuel Levinas, for the latter. Since Derrida's ideas are better known today, Handelman concentrates on representative passages culled from Levinas's writings, most of which appear equally embedded in the traditions of Greek and Jewish thought. Indeed, both the human law of the *polis* and the divine law of Judaism can help evolve an interpretive rhetoric that is based not on "difference" as an anonymous function of language but on the decentered self's "non-indifference to the other" (153). For Levinas's ethical politics and hermeneutics alike, "equality of all is born by my inequality, the surplus of my duties over my rights" (158).

A similar ethical concern for vulnerable persons motivates Renato Rosaldo's essay on "Death in the Ethnographic Present." Rosaldo criticizes ethnographers who "ignore the cultural practices and lived experiences characterized by improvisation, subjectivity, and particularity" in order to find "the lowest common denominators that make all funerals not different from one another but the same." Along with the subjective testimony of some other mourners, Rosaldo quotes a few of his own diary entries about symptoms of bereavement after his first wife's accidental death. It is clear that most anthropologists do not pay this kind of close interpretive attention to the behavior of their "subjects." At any rate, their published research tends to exhibit the altogether different rhetoric of ostensibly noninterpretive observation so that it is "characterized by formality, externality, and generality" (173). Rosaldo pleads for what he calls a metonymic rather than metaphoric view of culture. In such a view, a funeral should be studied not as a self-contained whole that is similar to other such wholes but "like a busy intersection through which a number of different processes hap-

pen to pass" (180). Rosaldo's "metonymic" anthropologist would investigate large complexes of spatially and temporally contiguous events
in order to find out "how things work out for the participants over
the long run, not simply during the confines of any particular ritual"
(181).

In "The Challenge of Poetics to (Normal) Historical Practice,"
Robert Berkhofer follows Louis Mink in suggesting that historians
tend to presuppose that the narrative structure of their histories faith-
fully mirrors the original structure of events surveyed by them. In
other words, "normal" historians assume that all that ever happened
could, in principle, be captured by the Great Story of a total history
and that this Great Story would stand in the relation of perfect structural homology to the untold Great Past of the world. The "poetics"
implied by recent critical theories of textuality is opposed to such assumptions. It refuses to equate representational coherence with referential correspondence and raises the stakes, therefore, of the dispute
as to whether history is an art or a science. Berkhofer used to hold
the contrary view but seems now fully persuaded that the historian's
quasi-scientific claim to realistic representation is based on the rhetorical concealment of the art of interpretive historytelling: "Realism
enters historical practice to the extent that historians try to make their
structure of factuality seem to be its own organizational structure and
therefore conceal that it is structured by interpretation represented as
(f)actuality" (194).

In the final essay of the volume, "The Inevitability of Stereotype:
Colonialism in *The Great Gatsby*," Michael Holquist suggests that language as a necessary means of each individual's "subjectification" (206)
forces all subjects mutually to stereotype and thus "colonize each
other." Far from being unique to "colonial discourse" in the literal,
imperialistic sense of the phrase, stereotyping is for Holquist "a universal strategy for seizing the other" (208), both in perception and
in verbal communication. The struggle against racist or sexist stereotypes should not make us forget, Holquist argues, that stereotyping
is a psychological and linguistic necessity of subject formation and as
such "cannot be extirpated; its effects can only be ameliorated" (210).
To illustrate some of the theoretical points made in the first half of the
essay, Holquist proceeds to interpret the narrative rhetoric of F. Scott
Fitzgerald's *The Great Gatsby* as a novel that "textualizes its own stereotyping with the clarity of a paradigm: in large measure it is 'about'
the suppression of difference and change required to maintain the
(stereotypical) illusion of identity and stasis" (211).

The most intriguing questions raised in the twelve essays are, of
course, too large to be laid to rest by a single set of answers. Debates
about the rhetoric of interpretation cannot be reduced, for example,

to a particular interpretation of rhetoric. Those siamese twins will not even permit themselves to be neatly separated: our "readings" of texts and of the world strive to be persuasive, and there is an interpretive, hermeneutic dimension to all "saying," whether it takes the form of speech, writing, or silent deliberation. I find it tempting to say that rhetoric concerns the active beginning of communication and interpretation concerns its productive end, while ideology has to do with the mental middle: whatever goes on inside the brain and the nervous system between the listening ear and the speaking tongue or between the reading eye and the typing fingers. Yet such talk fails to account for the fact that both verbal communication and other kinds of interactions among human beings are multi-layered and continuous. Our attempts to analyze the unholy trinity of rhetoric, hermeneutics, and ideology into detachable components can serve useful purposes in the study of speech and writing, listening and reading, consciousness and the unconscious. But the constant interplay of rhetorical, hermeneutic, and ideological processes must not be ignored. It profoundly connects what speaking, writing, and thinking individuals do, make, and mean with what their traditions and societies do to, make of, and mean for them.[1]

---

1. See my "Doing, Making, Meaning: Toward a Theory of Verbal Practice," *PMLA* 103 (October 1988), 749–58.

The Rhetoric of Interpretation

The Rhetoric
of Interpretation

Hayden White

Contemporary thought about the nature of interpretation, especially in the human and social sciences, tends to stress the ways it differs from simple description, on the one hand, and from explanation on the other. This is not to suggest that interpretation, description and explanation are in any way mutually exclusive operations; indeed, we could well characterize description and explanation as different kinds of interpretation or, conversely, regard interpretation itself as a kind of explanation which features description over formal argument or demonstration as its *modus operandi*. But if we do wish to stress the differences between interpretation on the one side and both description and explanation on the other, we would have to insist on the propaedeutic and heuristic aspects, the pre-classificatory and pre-explanatory functions of interpretation. We might wish to say that interpretation is what we do when we are uncertain how properly to describe some object or situation in which we have an interest and unsure about which of several available analytical methods should be used to explain it. As thus envisaged, interpretation is a product of thought in the preliminary stage of grasping an object by consciousness, thought in the effort of deciding, not only *how* to describe and explain such an object, but *whether* it can be adequately described or explained at all.

Because interpretation typically entertains different ways of describing and explaining some object or situation deemed worthy of the effort to comprehend it, its own modality of discursive articulation is characteristically more *tropical* than logical in nature. In this feature it will differ from any technical description, carried out in conformity with the procedures of a given taxonomic system, and from any explanation provided by a specific analytical method. In interpretative discourse, thought moves by turns which are unpredictable prior to their actualization in speech or writing and the relations among which need not bear any relationship of strict deducibility of any one from any other. Because interpretation is systemically doubtful as to the nature of its object of interest, the terminology best suited to the description thereof, and the most appropriate way to explain it, it can only proceed by departing from whatever passes for literal (or technical) language and stereotypical conceptualizations of possible objects of perception and giving itself over to techniques of figuration by which to fix its referent in consciousness and thereby constitute it as a possible object of cognition. It is this process of *pre-figuring* a referent, to constitute it as a *possible* object of cognition, that distinguishes interpretation from both description and explanation alike. And this is why rhetoric, considered less as a theory of persuasive speech than as the theory of the tropological bases of speech, discourse and textuality provides one promising way of comprehending what goes on in interpretative discourse in general.

Because interpretation is a predominantly tropical manner of discourse, it resembles narration which, in fact, is a discursive tactic often utilized in interpretative discourse. Typically, the successive events that constitute the story-line of a narrative are only retrospectively comprehensible, after the plot-structure of which they are functions has become perceivable; but even then they are hardly deducible one from another in the manner of the component terms of a syllogism. So, too, the sequence of turns taken in interpretative discourse resembles more the path traversed in the *search* for a plot-structure adequate to the configuration of a diachronic series of events into a paradigmatic structure of relationships, than it does the progressive accommodation of a set of perceptions to the exigencies of a nomological-deductive demonstration.

The similarities between interpretation and narration argue for the essentially figurative nature of the discourses in which they are typically represented in speech or writing. Which is not to say that interpretation, any more than narration, has no literalist dimension to its characteristic mode of articulation. On the contrary, like narration, interpretation does its work or achieves its peculiar effect of providing a kind of "understanding" of the objects of which it speaks precisely by virtue of its problematization of the relation between literalist and figurative speech. Although an interpretation typically wishes to speak the literal truth about its objects of interest, it is generated by a fundamental sense of the inadequacy of any convention of literalness to the representation of those objects. This is why all genuinely interpretative discourse must always appear as both a play of possible figurations of its objects of interest and an allegorization of the act of interpreting itself. Just as all narratives are also, at some level, more or less explicitly articulated meta-narratives (discourses as much about narration as about their ostensible, extra-discursive referents), so too all genuine interpretations are meta-interpretations (discourses as much about interpretation as about their ostensible primary objects of interest). And while in both descriptive and explanatory discourses, the meta-levels of their articulation can be identified by a combination of grammatical and logical analysis, in interpretative discourse the discernment of the meta-level requires analysis by methods more distinctly rhetorical in nature.

Considerations such as these argue for a reconceptualization of the traditional notion of the relation between the form and the content of interpretative discourse. If we conceive of interpretation as a prefiguration of a given object of interest, then the sequence of turns from one modality of figuration to another must be considered less as an aspect of the form of the discourse than as one of its contents. This does not mean that it is impossible to distinguish between the form and the content of interpretative discourse, that its referential or conceptual content is indeterminable or that the form of an interpretation *is* its content. For indeed it is not only meaningful but useful to discriminate between the linguistic and generic features of any given interpretative discourse, on the one side and its referential and explicitly conceptual elements, on the other. But we must also count among the contents of the specifically interpretative discourse the structure of the modalities of figuration utilized in the process of transforming the referent from an object of perception into a possible object of cognition. It is the structure of the modalities of figuration that provides the basis for the equivalent of emplotment in narrative. It is the modalities of figuration which effect the correlation of the linguistic, generic, referential and conceptual levels of the discourse on its paradigmatic axis, on the one hand; and it is the sequence of these modalities of figuration which presides over the transfers from the paradigmatic to the syntagmatic axes of its articulation, on the other. At any rate, this is one way of conceptualizing what a rhetorical approach to the analysis of interpretative discourse might consist of.

It is now time to present an example of the kind of interpretative discourse I have been talking about thus far and to test the utility of these generalizations as an instrument for analyzing or rather interpreting interpretation itself.

I have chosen as an example of interpretative discourse a passage taken from the volume *Sodome et Gomorrhe* of Proust's *À la recherche du temps perdu*. The passage consists of what appears to be a purely "descriptive pause" in the main action of the first chapter of the work, which tells of Marcel's attendance at a *soirée* of the Princesse de Guermantes. This interlude comes just after Marcel has finally succeeded, with much difficulty, in getting himself introduced to the Prince de Guermantes and has immediately thereafter witnessed the Prince's violent expulsion of his friend Swann from the gathering. It consists of a paragraph relating Marcel's contemplation of Hubert Robert's fountain in the garden of the Guermantes' palace.

The paragraph represents a scene of interpretation because it describes the effort of the protagonist to grasp by consciousness an object, a work of art, whose beauty is taken for granted but the nature of the fascination of which is presumed to be unfathomable. I have marked the places at which the narrative "turns" from one characterization of the fountain to succeeding ones:

Dans une clairière réservée par des beaux arbres dont plusieurs étaient aussi anciens que lui, planté a l'écart, on le voyait de loin, svelte, immobile, durci, ne laissant par la brise que la retombée plus légère de son panache pâle et frémissant. Le XVIIIe siècle avait épuré l'élégance de ses lignes, mais, fixant le style du jet, semblait en avoir arrêté la vie; *à cette distance* on avait l'impression de l'art plutôt que la sensation de l'eau. Le nuage humide lui-même qui s'amoncelait perpétuellement à son faîte gardait le caractère de l'époque comme ceux qui dans le ciel s'assemblent autour des palais de Versailles. *Mais de près* on se rendait compte que tout en respectant, comme les pierres d'un palais antique, le dessin préalablement tracé, c'était des eaux toujours nouvelles qui, s'élançant et voulant obéir aux ordres anciens de l'architecte, ne les accomplissaient exactement qu'en paraissant les violer, leurs mille bonds épars pouvant seuls donner à distance l'impression d'un unique élan. Celui-ci était en réalité aussi souvent interrompu que l'éparpillement de la chute, alors que, de loin, il m'avait paru infléchissable, dense, d'une continuité sans lacune. *D'un peu près*, on voyait que cette continuité, en apparence toute linéaire, était assuré à tous les points de l'ascension du jet, partout où il aurait dû se briser, par l'entrée en ligne, par la reprise latérale d'un jet parallèle qui montait plus haute que le premier et était lui-même, à une plus grande hauteur, mais déjà fatigante pour lui, relevé par un troisième. *De près*, des gouttes sans force retombaient de la colonne d'eau en croisant au passage leurs soeurs montantes, et parfois, déchirées, saisies dans un remous de l'air troublé par ce jaillissement sans trêve, flottaient avant d'être chavirées dans le bassin. Elles contrariaient de leurs hésitations, de leur trajet en sens inverse, et estompaient de leur molle vapeur la rectitude et la tension de cette tige, portant au-dessus de soi un nuage oblong fait de mille gouttelettes, mais en apparence peint en brun doré et immuable, qui montait, infrangible, immobile, élancé et rapide, s'ajouter aux nuage du ciel. Malheureusement un coup de vent suffisait à l'envoyer obliquement sur la terre; parfois même un simple jet désobéissant divergeait et, si elle ne s'était pas tenue à une distance respecteuse, aurait mouillé jusqu'aux moelles la foule imprudente et contemplative.   (1954: 656–657)

The scene appears at first glance to be a pure description of an object which, because it is a work of art, can only be interpreted rather than explained. The interpretation itself, however, consists of four successive characterizations of the object, given at different points in Marcel's movement toward the fountain. It is this *movement* of the speaking subject through space and time, in what appears to be an *activity* directed at the effort of "recognizing and identifying" the object, which permits us, following the lead of Gérard Genette, to view this scene as a genuine narrative. Indeed, rather than being a "descriptive pause," this scene can be regarded as a small narrative within the larger narrative that recounts the events of Marcel's re-entry into that society from which he had been absent for some ten years. If we accept this characterization of the scene in question, we can then proceed to inquire into its structure as a kind of narrative interpretation, on the one side, and its metanarrational function (as a narrative "interference" of the larger narrative of which it is a part), on the other.

In his commentary on the scene of Marcel's "interpretation" of Robert's fountain, Genette simply reproduces the text and marks the terms that indicate its duration and the activity of the protagonist as a "*travail* de la perception" and "du discernement." It is an example, he says, of a typically Proustian description-as-narrative: "toute une précoce éducation de l'art de voir, de dépasser les faux semblants, de discerner les vraies identités, . . ." (1972: 186). If, however, we attend to the modalities of figuration in which the successive characterizations of the fountain are cast, we can note two features of this narrative interpretation of the "jet d'eau." One is the tropological structure of the passage which endows it with a signified quite distinct from the thematic content observed by Genette ("l'activité perceptive du personnage contemplant, de ses impressions, découvertes progressives, changements de distance et de perspective, erreurs et corrections, enthousiasmes et déceptions, etc." (1972: 186). In fact, the four successive characterizations of the fountain are cast respectively in the modes of metaphor, metonymy, synecdoche and irony. This tells us something about the narrative "logic" of the passage and provides us with a way of characterizing the relation between narration and description in Proustian interpretation if not in interpretation in general.

The other feature of the passage has to do with its structural resemblance to the three discernable scenes of interpretation which precede it in the larger narrative account which it seems to interrupt. These three units consist of: 1) the first chapter of *Sodome et Gomorrhe*, which recounts the narrator's observation, from a hidden vantagepoint, of a scene of homosexual seduction, his reflection on the nature of the "descendants of the inhabitants of Sodom" and his classification of the genera and species thereof. For the moment I will note only that the taxonomy provided features successive descriptions or characterizations of four species of the genus male homosexual. 2) This preface is then followed by the chapter which relates Marcel's efforts to "recognize and identify" the various personnages he encounters on the way to his presentation to the Prince. Here too there are four extended descriptions, this time in the manner of a taxonomy of types of hangers-on of noble society: Marcel's successive descriptions of Professor E——, M. de Vaugoubert, Mme. d'Arpajon and M. de Bréauté, who actually presents Marcel to the Prince. And, finally, 3) we have the brief scene with the Prince himself, in which Marcel is represented as achieving an illuminating insight into the differences between genuine nobility of character and its hypocritical imitation. This scene, too, is structured as a succession of four distinct perceptions as recognitions.

Each of these three scenes of interpretation features a distinct *interpretandum*, which we may distinguish as male homosexuality, certain marginalized social types, and nobility respectively. The specific interpretations provided consist of narrative accounts of the narrator's efforts to "recognize and identify" the nature and kinds of the objects contemplated. Each of these narrations, in turn, takes the form of four successive descriptions of the object in question and each description is cast in a distinctive figurative mode. Each narration consists of an account of the narrator's passage among the dominant modalities of figuration, a passage which consists typically, though not exclusively, of a movement from a metaphorical apprehension of the *interpretandum*, through a metonymic dispersion of its attributes and a synecdochic comprehension of its possible "nature," to an ironic distancing of the process of interpretation itself.

It is this pattern, common to all three of the scenes of interpretation preceding that in which the fountain of Hubert Robert is described, that serves as the principal signified of the fountain scene itself. And it is the identification of this signified that permits us to comprehend both the placement of the description of the fountain in the larger narrative of which it is a part and its metanarrational function. Its placement in the fourth position of successive scenes of interpretation allows us, on the basis of our understanding of the fourfold structure of the preceding scenes, to regard it as an ironic commentary on the process of interpretation itself; and the fact that it explicitly takes interpretation as its referent permits us to regard it as Proust's own instruction on how to read or interpret the scenes preceding and following it. It is this feature of the scene that permits us to consider it as a condensed model of Proustian interpretation in general, for narrative interpretation specifically, and for the interpretation of the larger narrative of which it is a unit in particular.

I must now, however briefly and inadequately, interpret the scene in which the fountain of Hubert Robert is interpreted by Marcel. I note that this scene is framed by two figures of "deviation," one social, the other natural. The passage *ends* with an act of "désobéissance" by one of the jets of the fountain, which results in the inundation of Mme. d'Arpajon, to the general (somewhat vicious) merriment of the assembled company. It *begins* just after Marcel's conversation with the Prince, when he observes this newly revealed paragon of "consideration" sweeping Swann, "avec la puissance d'une pompe aspirante, . . . au fond du jardin," to "show him the door."[1] It is this event that leads Marcel to remark on the depths of his absorption in the company, from which he seeks to recover "quelque faculté d'attention à la pensée d'aller voir le célèbre jet d'eau d'Hubert Robert." The four descriptions of this celebrated work of art then follow.

The first description is introduced by a report of the appearance of the fountain made from afar: ". . . on le voyait *de loin,* svelte, immobile, durci, ne laissant agiter par la brise que la retombée plus légère de son panache pâle et frémissant." It is an impression captured by or condensed into the image of the "pale and quivering plume." The description itself consists of a specification of the image, as giving "l'impression de l'art, and features the figures of speech of synec-

1. Swann explains why the Prince intercepted him and whisked him off for a private conversation later on in the chapter. The Prince had wished to inform him of his own conversion to the Dreyfusard cause. Swann professes to be unsurprised by the conversion, viewing it as virtually inevitable, given the Prince's "nature si droite." (1954: 712). Marcel notes that, "Swann oubliait que, dans l'après-midi, il m'avait dit au contraire que les opinions en cette affaire Dreyfus étaient commandées par l'atavisme." Whereas Swann had attributed Saint-Loup's conversion to Dreyfus's cause to "intelligence," he attributes that of the Prince to his "droiture du coeur," something like that "simplicity" Marcel had perceived as the secret of the Prince's nobility of character during his conversation with him. But this perception of the Prince's nobility of character is brought into question in Marcel's comment on Swann's recognition of the Prince's "straightforwardness." "En réalité, nous découvrons toujours après coup que nos adversaires avaient une raison d'être du parti où ils sont et que ne tient pas à ce qu'il peut y avoir de juste dans ce parti, et que ceux qui pensent comme nous, c'est que l'intelligence, si leur nature morale est trop basse pour être invoquée, ou leur droiture, si leur pénétration est faible, les y a contraints" (Ibid.: 712).

doche ("Le XVIIIe siècle"), pun ("style"), two metaphors ("nuage" and "faite"), and a simile ("comme ceux qui"), all of which are advanced in the interest of suggesting the contrast between the "impression" of the image as "l'art" and the mere "sensation" that one might have had of it as "eau."

Marcel (or Proust), having figuratively characterized the fountain in the mode of metaphor, might very well have let the matter rest there but instead he presses on to a second description, cast in an altogether different mode of figuration, that of metonymy. From a closer view ("Mais de près"), it was possible, apparently, to realize that ("on se rendait compte que"), while seeming to respect ("tout en respectant"), like the stones of an ancient palace, the design traced out for it beforehand ("comme les pierres d'un palais antique, le dessin préalablement tracé"), the spray of the jet was able to produce the "impression d'un unique élan" only by sending forth ever new streams of water which, "springing upwards and wishing to obey the ancient orders of the architect, carried them out to the letter ("les accomplissaient exactement") only by seeming ("qu'en paraissant") to infringe them ("les violer"). The "single flow" of which one had originally had an impression is now revealed to be "in reality as often interrupted as the scattering of the fall, whereas from a distance it had appeared to me unyielding, solid, unbroken in its continuity."

This is a remarkable passage for my purposes in many ways. First, the passage features two contrasts: one between an original "impression" from a distance and the kinds of perceptions made from closer on that yield insights into the "reality" of the object in question and another between an artist's designs and the realization of them in the work of art itself. But, secondly, it posits a complex relationship between the traditional rules of artistic composition ("ordres anciens de l'architecte") and the transgression of those rules that appears to be necessary for the creation of any work of art. Indeed, not only do these two sentences tell us much about Proust's notion of the difference between appearance and reality in any object seeming to be whole, solid, unbroken in its continuity, etc., they tell us even more about his notion of the role of figuration in the production of literalness itself.

I wish to call the mode of figuration of this passage metonymic for two reasons. First, it *reduces* the "aesthetic" appearance of the jet to the material thing it is; it thereby substitutes the material cause of the appearance for its visual effect. This reduction is suggested figuratively in the simile which likens the fluid elements of the waterplay to the rigid "stones of an ancient palace." Secondly, the passage explicitly *reduces* the appearance of orderliness of the spray to the reality of the necessity of appearing to "violate" the principles governing its composition. These reductions provide insights into both the nature of artistic creativity, on the one side and the ways in which the products thereof are to be interpreted, on the other.

But Marcel (or Proust) does not leave us with these reductions. He presses on to yet another description of the fountain, "D'un peu près," a description which I wish to call synecdochic because it consists of nothing less than a characterization of the actual structure, what might be called the structural secret, of the "jet d'eau." This passage is cast in the most literalist language of all of the four descriptions provided; there is very little in it that might be called metaphorical in the common meaning of the term. Specifically, the passage consists of an explanation of how the effect of a "continuité sans lacune, . . . en apparence toute linéaire" was produced by the architect's setting of the styles of the jets. It is possible actually to draw a diagram of the paths of the jets and of the relationships among them on the basis of this characterization of its structure, in a manner that one could not possibly do with any of the other descriptions.

At the same time, the sense of this passage, perhaps because it is so literalist, so barren of figures of speech, is the most difficult to grasp in a single quick reading. It seems difficult to form an "impression" of it because it is less *about* the "impressions" of the narrator than it is *about* the actual structure of the "jet d'eau" itself. Here Marcel asserts that "one *saw*" ("on voyait") how the "uninterrupted continuity of the jet" was assured ("était assurée") by the structure of its design, which he then proceeds to sketch out. The passage is not reductive, as the previous passage is but rather *essentializing:* what we have is a representation of the relationships among the elements of the spray such that it is impossible to distinguish between its "form" and its "content." In the manner of a synecdoche, the spray is "grasped together" as a whole indistinguishable from the parts that constitute it. Moreover, this description of the structure of the spray replicates the structure of the paragraph itself: the continuity of the paragraph—like the continuity of the jet it describes—is assured by the "entering into line," by the "lateral incorporation" of a succession of descriptions, each in a different mode, which "mount[s] higher than the first and [is] itself, at an altitude greater but already a strain upon its endurance, relieved by a third." Thus, the third description of the fountain is a synecdoche, not only of the "jet d'eau" but also of the paragraph which describes the fountain in a fourfold manner.

It might seem that, after so totalizing a description of the object, the interpretation would have been completed. But not so. We still have not had a description from "close at hand" ("De près"). This, the fourth description of the fountain, is cast in yet another mode, which I wish to characterize as ironic—not only because, in the extravagance of its figurative technique, it draws attention to the arbitrariness of the figurative modes of the three descriptions that precede it but also and above all because it is internally ironic, consisting as it does of a virtual personification of the "jet d'eau" in its first two sentences followed by an abrupt reversal of this process, which returns the fountain to the status of a banal stream of water, in the third and final sentence.

In this last description, no speaking subject is overtly posited. There is no "on voyait," "on avait l'impression de," "on se rendait compte que" or "il m'avait paru" of the kind met with in the other descriptions. The passage begins "De près, des gouttes sans force . . ." Scott Moncrieff translates this phrase: "Seen close at hand, drops without strength . . . ," and this is certainly a plausible rendering of its sense (1970: 43). But the French does not say "*Vu* de près" or "De près, on *voyait* . . ." Indeed why should it, since this has nothing of the aspect of a report of a perception or of an impression about it? It is in fact a hypotypotic or pragmatographic representation, shot through with metaphorical figures of speech but cast in a tone so different from the first description as to belie the adequacy of its dominant mode of figuration to its referent.

In fact, the referent of this passage is neither the spray as a whole, the "bursts" of water emanating from the jets nor the structure of their relationships but the myriads of "gouttes" and "gouttelettes" which, now personified ("Elles contrariaient") and gendered ("leurs soeurs"), are depicted as actants in a spectacle as chaotic and senseless as the stream of life of which it is an image. The casualties of the process, those "gouttes sans force," who "fall back and float for a while" and "tease with their hesitations" before "being drowned in the basin," are given the positive function of "blurring" "la rectitude et la tension" of the jet's central stem—positive because the verb used is "estompaient," which suggests the artist's toning down or softening of a line. The connotation of this figure is carried over to the characterization of the "oblong cloud" that crowns the stem ("tige," with its connotation both of arboreality and of phallic erection). This cloud, although in reality "composed of a thousand tiny drops," presents the appearance of having been *painted* ("en apparence peint") and painted, moreover, in an "unchanging golden brown" ("en brun doré et immuable"). But the image of this cloud, which apparently rises, "unbreakable, constant, urgent, swift, to mingle with the clouds of the sky," is abruptly dispossessed of its attributes of immutability, constancy, infrangibility, and urgency by the reminder that, "Unfortunately, a gust of wind was enough to scatter it ("l'envoyer") obliquely on the ground"; and a report that, "at times indeed a single disobedient jet swerved ("divergeait") and, had they not kept a respectful distance, would have drenched to their skins the incautious crowd of gazers."

It seems to me that this fourth description, which is by turns lyricalelegaic and playful in tone, is at once ironical in its structure and radically revisionary with respect to all three of the preceding descriptions of the fountain. Its revisionary relationship to the first description, cast in the mode of metaphor, is especially striking. While it replicates the metaphorical *mode* of the first description, it substitutes images of mobility, change, and evanescence for those of immobility, stiffness, and continuity given in the original "impression." So too, the personification of the elements of the "jet d'eau" in the fourth description stands in direct contrast to the assimilation of the qualities of the fountain to those of "nobility" suggested by the figures of speech used in the first description: "panache," "art," and "Versailles." While the fourth description metaleptically retrieves the metaphorical *mode* of the first description, it both radically alters the semantic domain from which its figures of speech are drawn and abruptly, almost violently, undercuts the very impulse to metaphorize by its reminder that the fountain is, after all, *only* a fountain ("Unfortunately, a gust of wind was enough to scatter it obliquely on the ground; . . .").

As for the relationship of the fourth description to the second and third descriptions, it can be said that it revises in a significant way the figurative contents of both of the latter. First, the "rising," "falling," "crossing" movement assigned to the "gouttes" and "gouttelettes" picks up the images of "infringement" and "scattering" of the second description and confirms the metonymic mode in which it is cast even as it effectively denies it by way of its personification of the elements of the spray. Secondly, this personification of the drops of the spray stands in direct opposition, not to say negation, of the essentializing schematism of the third or synecdochic description, in which the structure of the "jet d'eau" is set forth.

It is not that the fourth description is to be apprehended as the most precise, correct, comprehensive or appropriate, in comparison with which the others that make up the set are to be adjudged in some way inferior. The fourth description is given from the point of observation *closest* to the object being described but it is no more precise than those launched from the other points further away. Nor is the fourth description to be accorded the status of the kind of revelation or *anagnorisis* that is supposed to attend the completion of a well-made plot in the conventional narrative. The fountain has not been *better* comprehended in the fourth description than it was in any of the three preceding descriptions. It is not that we *now* comprehend the nature of the fountain in the way that we seem to comprehend the successive events of a story as we near its end and are given the crucial bit of information that allows us suddenly to grasp "the point of it all."

True, by the time we have registered the fourth description, in the full consciousness of its overtly ironical mode of figuration, we are permitted to discern something like the kind of "plot" that permits a retrospective correlation of the events of this "story" as a story of a particular kind—a specifically "ironic" story. But what we have been permitted to comprehend is less the nature of the "jet d'eau" than that of the nature of figuration itself. It was by the provision of this exercise in figuration that Proust has set before us a model for comprehending the other passages of description-by-narration in which the passage in question is embedded and which it only *seems* to "interrupt."

I say "seems" to interrupt, because actually the passage in which the fountain is described in four successive modalities of figuration bears the same relationship to the three much longer and more extended scenes of interpretation that the fourth description of the passage bears to its three preceding parts. Recall that the fountain scene is the fourth of three successive narrative segments in which Marcel "interprets," by the same process of fourfold figuration, the subjects of male homosexuality, types of social hangers-on, and nobility (in the person of the Prince de Guermantes). I will not try the reader's capacities of toleration for pedantry (which have no doubt been strained to the maximum already) by trying to demonstrate that these three preceding scenes of interpretation have substantially the same structure as the fountain scene. But a cursory re-reading of the brief scene in which Marcel is finally introduced to the Prince, the scene immediately preceding the interpretation of the fountain, will suggest the ways in which the latter is related to those preceding it in the larger narrative.[2]

First, there is no causal or logical connection between the scene in

2. "Autant l'accueil du duc de Guermantes était, quand il le voulait, aimable, empreint de camaraderie, cordial et familier, autant *je trouvai* celui du Prince compassé, solennel, hautain. Il me sourit à peine, m'appela gravement: 'Monsieur'. J'avais souvent entendu le duc se moquer de la morgue de son cousin. Mais aux premiers mots qu'il me dit et qui, par leur froideur et leur sérieux faisaient le plus entier contraste avec le langage de bon camarade de Basin, *je compris* tout de suite que l'homme foncièrement dédaigneux était le duc qui vous parlait dès la première visite de 'pair à compagnon', et que, des deux cousins, celui qui était vraiment simple c'était le Prince. *Je trouvai* dans sa réserve un sentiment plus grand, je ne dirai pas d'égalité, car ce n'eût pas été concevable pour lui, au moins de la considération qu'on peut accorder à un inférieur, comme il arrive dans tous les milieux fortement hiérarchisés, au Palais par example, dans une Faculté, ou un procureur général ou un 'doyen', conscients de leur haute charge, cachent peut-être plus de simplicité réelle et, quand on les connaît davantage, plus de bonté, de cordialité, dans leur hauteur traditionnelle que de plus modernes dans l'affectation de la camaraderie badine. 'Est-ce que vous comptez suivre la carrière de Monsieur votre père?' me dit-il d'un air distant, mais d'intérêt. Je repondis sommairement à sa question, *comprenant* qu'il ne l'avait posée que par bonne grâce, et je m'éloignai pour le laisser accueillir les nouveaux arrivants." (1954: 655) I have italicized the verbs indicating the four successive "recognitions" of the Prince's nature.

which the Prince's "nobility" is interpreted and that in which the fountain is interpreted. The relationship between them is tropical only. After having exchanged a few words with the Prince, Marcel simply "moved away" ("je m'éloignai"). He then catches a glimpse of the Prince expelling Swann, "with the force of a suction pump," from the party. And he reports how his absorption in the company ("Tellement distrait dans le monde . . .") had all but occluded his powers of perception (". . . que je n'appris que le surlendemain, par les journaux, qu'un orchestre tchèque avait joué toute la soirée et que, de minute en minute, s'étaient succédés les feux de Bengale. . ."). It is in response to *this* absorption "dans le monde" that he decides to seek to recover "some power of attention with the idea of going to look at the celebrated fountain of Hubert Robert." A causal connection is implied between the decision to seek to recover some power of attention by going to contemplate Robert's masterpiece and the contemplation of it which follows but not between the scene of the meeting with the Prince and that of the interpretation of the fountain.

Nor is there any logical connection between the two latter scenes: there are no conceivable grounds on which the scene describing the fountain can be "deduced" from the scene describing the meeting with the Prince as a logical consequence. The relation between the scene of the encounter with the Prince and that in which the fountain is described is only tropical, which is to say that it is unpredictable, unnecessary, undeducible, arbitrary and so on but, at the same time, functionally effective and retrodictable as a narrative unit *once its tropical relationship to what comes before (and what comes after) it is discerned.*

It will be noticed that the Prince scene, like the fountain scene, is clearly marked by a succession of four distinct "recognitions": "je *trouvai* [l'accueil] du Prince compassé, solennel, hautain . . ."; "je *compris* tout de suite que [le Prince était] vraiment simple . . ."; "je *trouvai* dans sa réserve un sentiment . . . de la considération . . ."; and "*comprenant* qu'il ne l'avait posée [sa question] que par de bonne grâce, . . ." What is interpreted in this scene is the significance of the words and bearing of the Prince for the comprehension of the nature of noble "consideration" in comparison with the merely feigned camaraderie of those members of the aristocracy who speak to their social inferiors from the first as "man to man." The interpretation consists of successive characterizations of the Prince's manner of greeting, the style of his address, the tone of his words, and an example of his speech.

Like the fountain viewed from a distance, *at first sight* the Prince appears "stiff (*compassé*), solemn, haughty," quite in contrast to the "greeting of the Duc de Guermantes [the Prince's cousin]," which was, "when he chose, friendly, instinct with good fellowship, cordial and familiar." The Prince "barely smiled at me, addressed me gravely as 'Sir,'" in the manner in which Marcel had, he says, "often heard the Duke make fun of. . . ."

But then, "from the first words" *spoken* by the Prince to Marcel, the latter realizes that "the fundamentally disdainful man was the Duke, . . . and that, of the two cousins, the one who was really simple was the Prince."

Marcel *then* reports "I found in his reserve a stronger feeling, I do not say of equality, . . . but at least of the consideration which one may show for an inferior, such as may be found in all strongly hierarchical societies, . . ."

Finally, Marcel relates the question asked him by the Prince ("Do you intend to follow the career of Monsieur, your father?") and his realization that, since "he had asked it only out of politeness," it required no answer and that it remained to him only to move away "to allow him to greet the fresh arrivals."

The sequence of modes of figuration of this set of apprehensions and comprehensions follows the same pattern as the fountain scene. First, there are the two metaphorical apprehensions of the Prince's manner as *seemingly* "stiff, solemn, haughty" and that of his cousin the Duke's as *seemingly* "friendly, instinct with good fellowship, cordial and familiar." These apprehensions are immediately reduced, however, in the manner of a metonymy, to the status of masks of two kinds of character (exactly as the "impression de l'art" is reduced to the status of a "sensation de l'eau" in the second description of the fountain), the one "vraiment simple" and the other "foncièrement dédaigneux." In the third characterization of the Prince's manner, its aspects are, as it were, grasped together in the synecdoche of "un sentiment plus grand, . . . de la considération qu'on peut accorder à un inférieur, comme il arrive dans tous les milieux fortement hiérarchisés'" and the identification of the "hauteur traditionelle" of the representatives of such "milieux" with a "simplicité réelle" utterly lacking in their more modern brethren "dans l'affectation de la camaraderie badine."

But this comprehension of the Prince's "consideration" is forthwith sublimated into an apprehension of the mere "politeness" of his question to Marcel: "'Est-ce que vous comptez suivre la carrière de Monsieur votre père?' me dit-il d'un air distant, mais d'intérêt." Moreover, the comprehension of the Prince's true nature is immediately belied by the Prince's comportment, reported in the paragraph immediately following. Instead of "waiting where he was" to receive the greeting of "fresh arrivals," the Prince goes to intercept Swann and rudely carries him off, "with the force of a suction pump, . . . in order . . . to show him the door." This act of social rupture exactly parallels the swerve of that "single disobedient jet" which inundates Mme. d'Arpajon reported at the end of the fountain scene. The action of the Prince has the effect, not so much of cancelling out as of putting under question the set of apprehensions and comprehensions related in the scene of greeting, just as the "unpleasant" ("désagréable") swerve of the "disobedient" jet of water distances and problematizes the fourfold description of the fountain in the scene in which it is reported. To be sure, later in the chapter it will be revealed that the Prince had intercepted Swann to tell him of his (the Prince's) conversion to the party of the Dreyfusards. But this revelation confirms less the Prince's authenticity of character than the contingency of the events that had led to his conversion.[3]

Granted the two scenes analyzed do possess the common structural features I have ascribed to them, we can then proceed to specify the nature of their relationship considered as narrational units. I suggest that the scene describing the "work of art" bears the same figurative relationship to that describing the Prince's "nobility of character" that the fourth description of the fountain (in the ironic mode) bears to the third description of it (in the synecdochic mode). In a word, the paragraph describing the fountain provides an ironic commentary on the purported identification of the true "nature" of the Prince's character in the paragraph containing it. Being about perception-as-interpretation and more precisely about the interpretation of an object (a work of art) that is in principle uninterpretable, the fountain scene can be read as calling into question the interpretation of the nature of the Prince provided in the scene immediately preceding it. The predominantly ironic structure of the fountain scene reinforces the ironic distantiation of the interpretation of the Prince's "simple" and "considerate" character already given in the recognition of that nature as being only seemingly "de bonne grâce" by the perception of the Prince's rude comportment vis-à-vis Swann. The irony informing the fountain scene is thus doubled, being directed as it is not only at Marcel's efforts to interpret the fountain but also at the effort to interpret anything having the fascination of a "work of art"—which would include not only the "nobility" figuratively represented in the third scene of interpretation but also the representations of social hangers-on and of "male homosexuality" presented respectively in the second and first scenes of interpretation as well.

That the fountain scene is intended to serve the function of ironically distantiating the description of the Prince's seemingly noble nature given in the preceding scene is suggested by the figurative content of the first description of the fountain—as seen "from afar." Recall that the first description of the fountain utilizes three images to spec-

3. See above, note 1.

ify its nature as a "work of art": "panache," "Le XVIIIe siècle," and "Versailles," all three of which are associated metonymically with the "nobility" of the ancien regime. The successive refigurations of the fountain given in the three descriptions that follow this first characterization have the effect of at once filling out and specifying the "content" of this attributed impression of "nobility" and of bringing it under question as an adequate characterization of the "work of art" itself. Especially the fourth description of the fountain, which purports to reveal the chaos and insubstantiality of the "jet d'eau" when viewed from "de près," has the effect of both affirming and modifying the "nobility" attributed to the object in the first description.

Coming as it does, as the fourth of four successive scenes of interpretation, Marcel's efforts to interpret the "work of art" casts its shadow back across the scene immediately preceding it in the narrative, that in which the nobility of the Prince is described. And its relationship to that scene, I suggest, is structurally homologous with the relationship of the fourth description of the fountain (in the mode of irony) to the third description of it (in the mode of synecdoche). Once this relationship is recognized, it becomes possible to see the fountain scene as a "fulfillment" of the "figure" of noble character given in the Prince scene. The figure of the Prince, a "synecdoche of nobility," is fulfilled in the figure of the "work of art," which is to say that it is sublated in the irony with which both "nobility" and "art" are treated in the fountain scene.

I would now like to suggest that, on this reading of the text, we are in a position to comprehend the relation of both the fountain scene and the scene with the Prince to the other two scenes of interpretation which precede them in the narrative: that is, the scenes that interpret male homosexuality and the types of social hangers-on respectively. If the fountain scene provides the reader with a model for interpreting all objects which, like the work of art, are presumed to be by nature uninterpretable and if the signified or implicit referent of the scene is indeed the fourfold refiguration of the object I have attributed to it, then we are authorized, it seems to me, in looking at the first and second scenes of interpretation—those of male homosexuality and of social hangers-on—in terms of what must be taken as *their* predominant modes of figuration. And we are permitted, I would further argue, to inquire into the ways in which these earlier scenes may be related to one another and to the sequence of scenes of which they are units in a similar structure of figure and fulfillment.[4]

4. I hope that I shall not be understood as using the notion of figure and fulfillment in any theological sense. As I conceive it, a figure is "fulfilled" when the full tropological range of a metaphorical characterization of a thing, person, process,

On this reading, the four subjects of interpretation—male homosexuality, social hangers-on, nobility, and a work of art—can be seen to constitute a series in which the first term (male homosexuality) serves as a "figure" that is progressively filled out and (provisionally) "fulfilled" in the fourth (art). "Fulfillment" is not of course to be construed in the manner of medieval Biblical exegetes, for whom, for example, the Moses of the Hebrew Bible was a "figure" finally "fulfilled" in the Jesus of the New Testament but rather more as Dante used the notion as a structural principle of his *Commedia*, in which a life lived here on earth is treated as a figure of an immanent "meaning" finally made manifest only in a future (beyond time and space, after death). In the case of Dante, the "fulfillment" of the life "figured" here on earth consisted of the revelation of the fourfold order of significance of the actions that constitute (the story of) that life: literal, figurative, moral, and mystical. Of course, for Dante, the fulfillment of a figure constituted a genuine revelation of its true meaning, so that the fulfillment of a figure results in a repetition of it but now with its "content" revealed and its manifest meaning revealed to be only a "container" or sensory vehicle of its latent meaning, in short, *only* a figure.

For Proust, the absence of any ground for the revelation of the kind of ultimate meaning Dante took for granted reduces all meaning to nothing but "figuration." This is why it is legitimate to read Proust's narrative as an allegory of figuration itself, with the modalities of figuration as he construed them serving as the basic units of his strategies for "emplotting" the drama of consciousness which is its manifest subject-matter.

The plausibility of this reading can be supported by a number of remarks inserted into his text in the passages I have been considering: "Until then, because I had not understood, I had not seen" (1970: 12). "It is the explanation that opens our eyes; the dispelling of an error

---

institution, etc., is worked through in a discourse. In the case of Proust, as I seek to demonstrate, what are originally given as metaphorical apprehensions of things are always progressively sublated, by way of metonymic and synecdochic characterizations, into ironic inversions of the original apperception. It is not a matter of one "thing" being a "fulfillment" of another but of a succession of figures of speech or thought progressively modifying, qualifying and ultimately either reinforcing or undoing the figure serving as the first term in the sequence. Thus, for example, in Marx's discussion of the "forms of value" in Chapter 1 of *Capital*, the last term, "the money form of value" can be said to "fulfill," in the sense of inverting and revealing the latent content of, the first term, "the Elementary form." The relation between the first term and the last of a given sequence of figurations of a thing should not be viewed as analogous to that governing the relation between a major premise and a conclusion of a syllogism. The only necessity governing the relations among a succession of figurations is tropical, that is, is given by the possible modalities of figuration itself, not logical in nature.

gives us an additional sense" (1970: 12). ". . . [A]nd here the word fertilise must be understood in a moral sense, since in the physical sense the union of male with male must be sterile, . . ." (1970: 22). "But sometimes the future is latent within us without our knowledge, and our words which we suppose to be false forecast an imminent reality" (1970: 31). And, finally, with respect to M. de Charlus:

> Now the abstraction had become materialised, the creature at last discerned had lost its power of remaining invisible, and the transformation of M. de Charlus into a new person was so complete that not only the contrasts of his face, of his voice, but, in retrospect, the very ups and downs of his relations with myself, everything that hitherto had seemed to my mind incoherent, became intelligible, brought itself into evidence, just as a sentence which presents no meaning so long as it remains broken up in letters and scattered at random upon a table, expresses, if these letters be rearranged in proper order (*dans l'ordre qu'il faut*), a thought which one can never afterwards forget. (1970: 12–13)

If it could be shown that the four successive scenes of interpretation which open this part of Proust's novel describe the same tropological sequence—from metaphor through metonymy and synecdoche to irony—as that described in the culminating fourth (the fountain) scene, this would provide important insights into the nature of interpretation in general and of interpretation by narration specifically. Specifically, it would yield some understanding of the "paralogic" of narrative, on the one hand, and of the extra-logical dimensions of interpretative discourse, on the other.

What I want to suggest is that interpretative discourse is governed by the same principles of "configuration" (I borrow the term from Paul Ricoeur) as those used in narration to endow the events that comprise the "story" being told with the structural coherency of a "plot."[5] In other words, interpretative discourse tells a story—a story in which the interpreter is both the protagonist and the narrator and whose characteristic themes are the processes of search, discovery, loss and retrieval of meaning, recognition and misrecognition, identification and misidentification, naming and misnaming, explanation and obfuscation, illumination and mystification, and so on. The coherence of this story is the coherence of the plot-structure or congeries of plot-structures by which the story-elements are fashioned into an identifiable story-type (epic, romance, comedy, tragedy, satura, farce, etc.), what Frye has called an "archetypal" story (1973: 131ff). But, if this is a possible way of construing what goes on in interpretative discourse, it is not a matter of the interpreter simply *imposing* the pattern of a given plot-type on the elements of the story being told, any more than, in a novel,

5. On "configuration," see Paul Ricoeur (1984 II: 64ff).

it would be a matter of mechanically fitting the events that constitute the story into the form of a comedy, tragedy, etc. The plot or congeries of plots has to appear to emerge gradually and, as it were, "naturally" from the events reported on the story-level of the discourse, just as the "tragic" nature of a play like Hamlet becomes comprehensible over the course of the play's unfolding as what appears to be merely a series of contingent events.

What, then, are the transformational principles by which a story can be progressively endowed with the structural coherence of a given plot-type or, since I am arguing for the formal similarities between narration and interpretation, by which an interpretation can be endowed with a coherence quite other than the kinds of coherence it may possess at the level of the sentence (grammatical coherence) and at the level of demonstration or explicit argument (logical coherence)? Obviously, my answer to this question is "figurative coherence," the coherence of the activity of (linguistic) figuration itself.

This having been said, however, we are still left with the task of specifying how figurative coherence is *produced* in discourse. In my view, we have in the pattern of progressive figuration, refiguration, and what (following de Man)[6] we may call "disfiguration" held up to us in Proust's "descriptive pause" in his narrative as the very model of what such a pattern consists of. In a word, in the sequence of tropological modes which leads from an original metaphorical characterization of an *interpretandum,* through a metonymic reduction and a synecdochic identification, to an ironic apprehension of the figurality of the whole sequence, we have something like the plot of all possible emplotments—the meaning of which is nothing but the process of linguistic figuration itself. This is not the only content of a narrative, to be sure, but it is the one without which neither any story can be told nor any plot constructed.

The fact that the four descriptions of the fountain are cast in different modes of figuration and that they have a distinct (and, indeed, even conventional) order of succession permits us to view this passage as Proust's model of what interpretation considered as figuration might consist of. The successive descriptions bear no logical relationship to one another, at least, no relationship that could be mapped out according to the logic of identity and non-contradiction. There is no *argument* about the nature of the fountain and hardly anything that might be considered a predication about it. The predications in the

---

6. Paul de Man (1984: 93ff). But recall the words Proust places in the mouth of Charlus who, when commenting on Bréauté's futile efforts to improve on Robert's fountain by placing lights around it, remarks: "C'est beaucoup plus difficile de défigurer un chef-d'oeuvre que de le créer." (1954: 659)

passage are for the most part about what "one" saw, the impressions "one" had or what "one" realized. Only the fourth description contains direct predications about the spray: "drops . . . fell . . . and . . . floated," "they teased . . . and blurred," "a single jet . . . swerved" and so on. Insofar as the passage has a referent, it is less the "jet d'eau" (which is both never really quite described and over-described) than the process of translating attentive seeing into language, with language itself, rather than perception, providing the categories of whatever interpretative matter the passage itself may contain.

The meta-narrational and metainterpretative functions of the passage can now be specified. Considered as a *narrational unit,* the paragraph containing the fourfold description of the fountain is related to the three scenes of interpretation that precede it by the four figurative modes which constitute the substance of its own form. It is figuratively related to the scene of the Prince's greeting by contiguity, formal similitude, structural homology, and parodistic repetition, that is, metonymically, metaphorically, synecdochally, and ironically. Considered as a *model of interpretation* itself, the fountain scene provides a paradigm of how to read the three more extensive scenes of interpretation that precede it: those in which male homosexuality, society, and nobility are interpreted. If we return to these preceding scenes and re-read them in the light of this paradigm, we can apprehend the ways in which these scenes are to be taken *as* interpretations.

Each of the four subjects successively marked out for contemplation in the opening pages of *Sodome et Gommorhe*—male homosexuality, the social types, an exemplar of high nobility, and a work of art—appears as an enigma resistant to both adequate description and definitive explanation. Each is interpreted, however, and interpreted in the same way, that is, submitted to successive characterizations in the four modes of metaphor, metonymy, synecdoche, and irony. This sequence of modes of figuration can be said to constitute something like an equivalent for interpretation to what is commonly called "plot" in narrative representation.

An *emplotment* (what Ricoeur calls a *mise en intrigue* [1984: 155–168]) of a set of events or, as in the case under examination, of observations, recognitions, identifications, characterizations, etc., does not constitute an explanation of the sort typically provided by "technical thinking, of an algorithmic nature 'founded on objective modal necessity,' . . ." (Greimas 1987: xxxix). Emplotment, rather, provides (or wishes to appear to provide) what hermeneutic theory calls an "understanding" of a referent and it does so by what Ricoeur calls "configuration," a term that might legitimately be used to translate the Greek "synecdoche" ("to grasp together," "com-prehend," Latin: "subintellectio"). This understanding, in turn, is composed of a twofold order of signification: a manifest one, in which the object of interest (a referent) is submitted to a succession of descriptions, and a latent one, of which the activity and effects of figuration itself are the referents. If this can be said of the relationship between any two or more successive passages of an interpretative discourse, it can be said of interpretative discourse as a whole.

How is the scene of the contemplation of the fountain related to the scene of the contemplation of nobility of character which immediately precedes it and of these two scenes to the scenes of contemplation of social types and of male homosexuality preceding them in the narrative sequence? If we say: "figuratively," we shall mean not only that they replicate the kinds and sequences of the modes of figuration employed in their respective emplotments but that each scene is a "fulfillment" of the "figures" of the scenes that precede it. As thus envisaged, the fountain scene gathers up, fulfills, and realizes the figure of the scene of nobility, just as this latter does with respect to that of society and this scene that of male homosexuality. Each of the subjects of the sequence—male homosexuality, the social types, nobility, and art—is an interpretation of the subjects that precede it in the manner of a fulfillment of the figures contained therein.

It could be fairly asked whether there is any extratextual evidence for this argument. In response it could be pointed out that, if the *fountain* described in the scene is purely fictive, the artist credited with its creation, Hubert Robert, was a real human being, a painter and architect whose career spanned the period of the French Revolution. Moreover, Robert was an artist fascinated with the subject of ruins, those caused by natural disruptions, such as floods, earthquakes, fires, and disuetude and by political acts, such as rebellions, revolutions, jacqueries, sacking, looting, and so on. He not only painted real ruins but imagined ruins—such as his well-known canvases of the Grand Gallery of the Louvre in ruins. So obsessed was Robert with ruins that he earned the nickname of "Robert des ruines," by which he is still known today. Is it too much to suggest that, in choosing to posit as the object of Marcel's effort to recover "some power of attention," the "celebrated fountain of Hubert Robert," Proust was suggesting, by this act of nomination alone, his interest in the relation between art and ruination, the achieved form of a thing and its immanent deliquescence, its impression of solidity and beauty and its real nature as a chaos as senseless as the "jet d'eau" of Hubert Robert when viewed "close at hand"?

References

De Man, Paul
1984 *The Rhetoric of Romanticism* (New York: Columbia University Press).

Frye, Northrop
  1973 *Anatomy of Criticism: Four Essays* (Princeton: Princeton University Press).
Genette, Gérard
  1972 *Figures III* (Paris: Seuil).
Greimas, A. J.
  1987 *On Meaning: Selected Writings in Semiotic Theory* (Minneapolis: University of Minnesota Press).
Proust, Marcel
  1954 *À la recherche du temps perdu*, edited by Pierre Clarac and André Ferré (Paris: Gallimard).
  1970 *Cities of the Plain*, translated by C. K. Scott Moncrieff (New York: Vintage Books).
Ricoeur, Paul
  1984 *Time and Narrative*, translated by Kathleen McLaughlin and David Pellauer (Chicago: University of Chicago Press).

Interpretations: Data or Goals?

Jonathan Culler

One way to think about intellectual activities and disciplines is to inquire about the organization of knowledge, to ask what counts as knowledge in a particular domain—and indeed the history of disciplines is in large measure a history of the organization of knowledge, as Michel Foucault's archeology suggests. From this perspective, it seems evident that there have been significant changes in the field of literary criticism in the twentieth century in the United States. In the earlier part of the century one might have distinguished a realm of taste and a realm of knowledge: the first the domain of public critics; the second that of scholars in the university, where knowledge consisted of historical and philological information of various sorts. In the 1930s and 1940s, as the New Criticism began to invade the universities, the single most common argument against its approach was that what the New Critics wrote did not count as knowledge but was simply an exercise of ingenuity at the expense of authors and their works. In his famous MLA Presidential address of 1948, "The New Criticism: Some Old-Fashioned Queries," Douglas Bush accused New Critics of inventing "unhistorical theories" and reading "modern attitudes and ideas into the past": "when complexity and ambiguity have become a fetish, there seems to be no check on interpretive irresponsibility except the limits of the critic's fancy"(1949: 138–150). Arthur Mizener, a New Critic fired by Yale in 1940, reports a senior colleague asking "Do you think that a scholar, who is committed to the ideal of objectivity, ought to write for something called *The Partisan Review?*" (Kunitz 1955: 679)

The success of the New Criticism, however—first as a pedagogical technique, second as a way of talking about refractory modernist poetry—brought a shift in what counted as knowledge. Formerly the distinction between scholarship and criticism had divided genuine knowledge from subjective evaluation or ingenious interpretation but this began to change as supporters of the New Criticism such as René Wellek, deeply versed in literary history and scholarship, sought to persuade their colleagues that, on the contrary, the products of scholarly inquiry counted as genuine knowledge of literature only when they contributed to the task of interpretation.[1] Chapter six of Wellek and Warren's *Theory of Literature*, entitled "The Ordering and Establishment of Evidence," illustrates vividly the transformation of literary studies that was underway. "One of the first tasks of scholarship," Wellek begins,

> is the assembly of its materials, the careful undoing of the effects of time, the examination as to authorship, authenticity, and date. Enormous acumen and diligence have gone into the solution of these problems; yet the literary student will have to realize that these labours are preliminary to the ultimate task of scholarship. Often the importance of these operations is particularly great, since without them critical analysis and historical understanding would be hopelessly handicapped. This is true in the case of a half-buried literary tradition such as that of Anglo-Saxon literature; but for the student of most modern literatures, concerned with the literary meaning of the works, the importance of these studies should not be overrated. (1956: 57)

Although in theory these "Preliminary Operations," as the title of *Theory of Literature*'s Part Two calls them, are preliminary both to critical analysis and to historical explanation, Wellek's formulations here suggest that concern with the meaning of works is the appropriate focus of the student of literature and that historical and textual scholarship is important insofar as it contributes to critical understanding. The concessions to "extrinsic approaches to the study of literature" are frequently framed in these terms: "Nobody can deny that much light has been thrown on literature by a proper knowledge of the conditions under which it has been produced," Wellek and Warren declare; "the exegetical value of such a study seems indubitable. Yet it is clear that

---

1. The conflicts between scholarship and criticism can be followed in MLA presidential addresses, published annually in *PMLA*. Two early instances occur in the addresses of 1929 and 1930 (*PMLA* 44 & 45). For useful discussion, see Grant Webster, *The Republic of Letters* (Baltimore: Johns Hopkins University Press, 1979), especially pp. 113–19; and Gerald Graff, *Professing Literature: An Institutional History* (Chicago: University of Chicago Press, 1987), chapters 8–11.

causal study can never dispose of problems of description, analysis, and evaluation of an object such as a work of literary art" (1956: 93). On the one hand, extrinsic approaches are supposed to have a special purpose of their own, causal explanation; but on the other hand when extrinsic scholarship is praised for its indubitable exegetical value, the game seems to have been given to interpretation. Extrinsic approaches are seen as providing mere information, which becomes knowledge only when relevant to the interpretation of the work itself. More specifically, for example, proscription of the intentional fallacy did not in itself make biographical investigation a marginal activity; that happens when the principle that questions about meaning are not resolved by investigation of the author is joined to the presumption that elucidation of the meaning of a work is the goal of critical activity. With this shift, interpretation—one's own interpretations of literary works and familiarity with prior interpretations—became the central concern of literary studies. In effect, the New Criticism created a new type of knowledge: to produce interpretations of poems is to make a contribution to knowledge; and periodicals such as *The Explicator* were founded precisely to record this knowledge. The scholar could even be attacked precisely for lacking the relevant knowledge, as in Cleanth Brooks's complaint that the scholar "has little or no knowledge of the inner structure of a poem or drama . . . he is ignorant of its architecture; in short, he often does not know how to *read*" (1940: 405). Since the 1950's, one might say, the test of scholarly endeavors seems to have become their contribution to critical interpretation.[2]

Indeed, here is where the New Criticism's greatest triumph occurred. The most widespread legacy of the New Criticism is the assumption, which to a considerable extent still holds sway, that the test of any critical activity—including textual criticism and historical scholarship—is whether it helps us to produce richer, more compelling interpretations of particular literary works. We are now beginning to see some changes in this configuration of knowledge. In particular, during the last few years understanding of a range of difficult theoretical discourses has come to count as knowledge in the domain of criticism. Literature departments increasingly expect such knowledge of new Ph.D.s they hire. But for the most part, these theoretical

2. The result, however, seems to have been a curious overlay. While scholarship is deemed relevant to the extent that it contributes to criticism, nevertheless the field of literary studies remains organized, for the most part, according to the historical periods identified by traditional scholarship. These persistent institutional arrangements exert considerable pressure on criticism, encouraging teachers to engage in historical projects and substantially modifying the triumph of the New Criticism, which nevertheless persists in the assumption that interpretations are the goals of literary study and literary research.

discourses are seen as critical approaches and thus as methods of inter-pretation, so that the notion of interpretation or interpretations as the goal of literary studies remains very strong. And post-structuralist theory, maintaining that theoretical frameworks or metalinguistic dis-courses are simply further interpretations, has if anything strength-ened the presumption that interpretations are what we seek to pro-duce. Deconstruction, precisely because it can be taken as a method of interpretation, has succeeded in America in ways that structuralism and Marxism, which urged other sorts of critical projects, never did.[3]

This state of affairs seems peculiar to literary studies and we might well expect, in a conference on interpretation and knowledge, that comparisons with other disciplines would illuminate its situation. The practitioners of other disciplines in the humanities interpret, of course, but frequently they are interpreting data to explain something else: anthropologists interpret information about the behavior of a group to work out the system of categories through which it makes sense of the world; historians interpret documents and other information to reconstruct the political forces of a period and determine why things happened as they did. Now one could say straight away that one would not wish literary criticism to adopt this model—at least as I have de-scribed it: one of the signal virtues of literary criticism is that it does not deem its texts to be simply data about something else. If we study literature, it is because literary works and their complexities are of in-terest in themselves. The question of whether interpretation is, then, necessarily the goal seems to me to have been raised in a pertinent way by the mutual incomprehension that arises when linguists and literary critics seek to cooperate, as they frequently did in the 1960s and 1970s, when the generic dialogue ran something like this:

> Critic: So how can linguistics help us with this poem?
> Linguist: What do you want to do?
> Critic: To understand it.

Linguists find it hard to help because linguistics does not provide new interpretations of English sentences. Rather the interpretations of na-tive speakers are data it seeks to explain. This, of course, is the model of a poetics or semiotics seeking to understand the processes of literary signification, but in American literary studies at least, the interpretive teleology has been so strong that any attempt at poetics is immedi-ately treated as a method of interpretation. Northrop Frye's ambitious *Anatomy* was scarcely ignored but led to—what?—myth criticism. The justification most frequently offered when one criticizes this result is

---

3. For further discussion of these issues see the opening chapter, optimistically entitled "Beyond Interpretation," of Jonathan Culler, *The Pursuit of Signs* (Ithaca: Cornell University Press, 1981).

that to describe works at all is to interpret them, so that any incipient poetics becomes a practice of interpretation, especially as it attends to how works outplay the categories and conventions to which one seeks to attribute their meaning.

In the past I have sought to challenge the primacy of interpretation without much success—particularly in an essay optimistically entitled "Beyond Interpretation"—by discussing the issue theoretically. Here I would like to attempt another approach, exploring the possible relationships between making interpretations one's data and interpretation one's goal by engaging interpretation and interpretations directly. Can one interpret a poem without making interpretation the overriding goal?

My text is a poem much interpreted in discussions of Baudelaire and the modern poetic tradition—a poem whose conflicting interpretations provide data for reflecting on the stakes of literary interpretation and the conceptions of poetic language and poetic structure on which conceptions of literary history and the practice of reading rely. Baudelaire's "Correspondances" has frequently been treated as a central document for the study of his poetics. Jean Pommier used it as the key to *La Mystique de Baudelaire*. Cherix's *Commentaire des Fleurs du Mal* identifies it as "la pièce maitresse de la doctrine esthétique de Baudelaire" and Lloyd Austin's *L'Univers poétique de Baudelaire* "takes as its point of departure the doctrine of correspondences. The best Baudelairiens have not failed to grant a capital importance to the set of theories that Baudelaire constituted around this word" (1956: 51).

Correspondances

La Nature est un temple où de vivants piliers
Laissent parfois sortir de confuses paroles;
L'homme y passe à travers des forêts de symboles
Qui l'observent avec des regards familiers.

Comme de longs échos qui de loin se confondent
Dans une ténébreuse et profonde unité
Vaste comme la nuit et comme la clarté,
Les parfums, les couleurs et les sons se répondent.

Il est des parfums frais comme des chairs d'enfants,
Doux comme les hautbois, verts comme les prairies,
—Et d'autres, corrompus, riches et triomphants,

Ayant l'expansion des choses infinies,
Comme l'ambre, le musc, le benjoin et l'encens,
Qui chantent les transports de l'esprit et des sens.

[Nature is a temple where living pillars
Sometimes let emerge confused words;
Man passes there through forests of symbols
Which observe him with familiar looks.

Like long echoes which from far merge
In a shadowy and profound unity,
As vast as night and as luminosity,
Smells, colors, and sounds answer each other.

There are smells which are fresh like babies' skin,
Soft like oboes, green like meadows,
—And others, corrupt, rich, triumphant,

With the expansion of things infinite,
Like amber, musk, benjamin, incense,
Which sing the transports of the mind and senses.]

In undertaking a reading of this poem, I am interested in eluci-
dating the stakes of readings, the assumptions and investments of the
multifarious discussions of this poem and the methodological issues
they raise. The two ground rules I set myself are, first, not to hold back
from interpretation but to propose alternative readings as corrections
or supplements to the interpretations of others—providing the best
interpretations I can—and second, to take my own interpretations as
data as well, even though structurally I cannot account for them.

A good deal of the scholarly energy devoted to this poem has
worked to constitute an intertextual space for it that includes passages
from Swedenborg, Schelling, Mme de Stael, Hoffmann, Balzac, Es-
quiros, Sainte-Beuve, Constant, and Gautier, not to mention Hugo
and Lamartine. The first quatrain in particular, is seen as echoing
a romantic topos: the visible forms of the universe are signs of an
invisible spiritual reality. Citing texts which Baudelaire might have
seen prior to 1846, Antoine Adam concludes, with a declaration in
which he no doubt failed to see the humor, that "Le poète des *Fleurs
du Mal* ne pouvait donc ignorer, dès cette époque, l'idée qui forme
le premier mouvement de son sonnet" (1961: 271). [The poet of the
Fleurs du Mal therefore could not have been ignorant at this time of
the idea that forms the first movement of his sonnet.] This is the idea
of vertical correspondence: relations between material signifiers and
spiritual signifieds or what Baudelaire calls "cet admirable, cet immor-
tel instinct du Beau qui nous fait considérer la terre et ses spectacles
comme un aperçu, comme une correspondance du Ciel" (1975: II,
334) [this admirable, immortal instinct of beauty, which makes us consider the earth and its spectacles as a glimpse or correspondence of
heaven].

Interpretations adduce parallels to the poem's opening statement,
"La nature est un temple," from Hugo and Lamartine for instance.
Here is Hugo:

C'est Dieu qui remplit tout. Le monde, c'est son temple.
Oeuvre vivante, où tout l'écoute et le contemple!
Tout lui parle et le chante.   (1972: 345)

Here is Lamartine:

> Dieu caché, disais-tu, la nature est ton temple!
> L'esprit te voit partout quand notre oeil la contemple.
>   (1968: 20)

And again:

> L'univers est le temple, et la terre est l'autel.
>   .   .   .
> Mais ce temple est sans voix. Où sont les saints concerts?
>   .   .   .
> Tout se tait: mon coeur seul parle dans ce silence.
> La voix de l'univers, c'est mon intelligence.   (1968: 68–69)

Correspondances echoes these passages but there is a question about the meaning of such echoes or correspondences, which can be taken as reiteration and affirmation or as ironic repetition. In Baudelaire's temple, living pillars—are these people or trees?—"laissent *parfois sortir* de confuses paroles." It is as though in compromising between Hugo's version, in which everything speaks and sings, and Lamartine's version, where "Tout se tait," Baudelaire had let things speak *sometimes,* giving us, if not a compromise that parodies the alternatives, at least an undermining of the continuous, authoritative signifying relation that seemed the basis of any doctrine of correspondences.

The symbolic relation is confused and intermittent, and while commentators identify here as the underlying image Chateaubriand's comparison of the forest to a cathedral, it is not clear that we are in fact in a forest: we are told that man passes not through forests that are symbolic but through "des forêts de symboles," forests of symbols. "*Forest*" may be a figure not of spirituality but of enumeration and confusion (in the "Salon de 1859" Baudelaire evokes the possibility of being "perdu dans une forêt d'originalités" [lost in a forest of originalities]) (1975: II, 608).

Interpretations focusing on the first stanza have generally emphasized the forceful articulation of a doctrine of vertical correspondences, though the intermittent symbolic relation raises enough questions to suggest that this reading may owe a good deal to the premise of continuity that sustains source-hunting. In recent years, however, readings of the sonnet have shifted attention from the vertical correspondences to the so-called horizontal correspondences of the remaining quatrain and tercets. Leo Bersani's *Baudelaire and Freud* provides a vigorous example.

> Readers of this poem have frequently been misled by the reference to Nature as containing "forests of symbols" in the first stanza. This presumably refers to a system of vertical correspondences: the "temple" of Nature is replete with symbols of spiritual reality. In fact, the metaphysical suggestiveness of the first four verses is *simply dropped* in the second and third

stanzas. We move from vertical transcendence to horizontal "unity." "Les parfums, les couleurs et les sons se répondent": that is, stimuli ordinarily associated with one of our senses can produce sensations "belonging" to another sense. Baudelaire asserts, and in the third stanza illustrates, the reality of these analogies (certain perfumes, for example, are "green as fields"). "Correspondances" does present itself as a doctrinaire poem (thus the countless critical efforts to extract the doctrine, to find its sources in nineteenth-century esthetics, philosophy, and psychology), and the doctrine which the poem espouses and vaguely outlines has much less to do with symbolism in Nature than with a metaphorical unity within Nature. Comparisons using the word *comme* occur six times in the two middle stanzas, and we might think of this as a stylistic demonstration of those "echoes" of a distant likeness which the poet asks us to hear in each of our experiences. (1977: 32)

Baudelaire's notion of a "keyboard of correspondences" suggests that the poet's task might be to construct melodies out of the metaphorical equivalents between sensations of various sorts. The last four lines move from tropes that relate one sensory experience to another to the more general claim that certain sensations effect a spiritualization, that they explicitly thematize the movement beyond sense suggested by synesthesias: they "chantent les transports de l'esprit et des sens."

We have here, it seems, a notable poetic adumbration of a symbolist aesthetics but such a reading of this "doctrinaire poem" depends on an understanding of another set of intertextual relations, correspondences between the verse text and various prose texts which it echoes: the theoretical statements about analogies, correspondences, colors, smells and sounds, etc. Here a problem arises. Antoine Adam writes,

Il est notable, pourtant, que s'il existe un texte de Baudelaire qui offre des analogies de pensée et d'expression avec le sonnet, c'est bien moins le *Salon de 1846* que l'article sur *L'Exposition Universelle de 1855*. Le mot de *correspondance* s'y trouve, et dans une phrase qui est comme le commentaire du sonnet: le professeur d'esthétique est un barbare "qui a oublié la couleur du ciel, la forme du végétal, le mouvement et l'odeur de l'animalité, et dont les doigts crispés, paralysés par la plume, ne peuvent plus courir avec agilité sur l'immense clavier des correspondances." (1961: 272)

[It is striking, though, that if there exists a text by Baudelaire that offers analogies of thought and expression with the sonnet, it is less the *Salon de 1846* than the article on the *Exposition Universelle de 1855*. The word *correspondance* appears there and in a sentence that is like a commentary on the sonnet: the professor of aesthetics is a barbarian "who has forgotten the color of the sky, the form of the vegetal, the movement and scent of animality and whose clenched fingers, paralyzed by the pen, can no longer play with agility on the immense keyboard of correspondences."]

One might note the initial complication that the passage of aesthetic writing which Adam calls "*comme* le *comme*ntaire du sonnet" is about the inability of a professeur d'esthétique to play with and appreciate correspondences. When the piece of aesthetic writing that offers the best "analogie de pensée et d'expression avec le sonnet" concerns the incompatibility of works of art and aesthetic doctrine, this at least raises a question about the relation of correspondence critics must take for granted in discussing a *doctrine* of correspondences.

The prose text continues more explicitly to address this question.

> Tout le monde conçoit sans peine que si les hommes chargés d'exprimer le beau se conformaient aux règles des professeurs-jurés, le beau lui-même disparaitrait de la terre, puisque tous les types, toutes les idées, toutes les sensations se confondraient dans une vaste unité, monotone et imperson-nelle, immense comme l'ennui et le néant. (1975: 578)

> [Everyone easily conceives that if the men charged with expressing the beautiful obeyed the rules of the professor-judges, beauty itself would disappear from the earth, since all types, all ideas, all sensations, would blend in a vast unity, monotonous and impersonal, as immense as boredom and nothingness.]

There are striking echoes here.

Prose	Poem
Se confondrait	se confondent,
dans une vaste unité	dans une ténébreuse et profonde unité
vaste unité, immense comme l'ennui	unité vaste comme la nuit

There is an exchange of letters involved (*l'ennui, la nuit*), if not a correspondence. Antoine Adam declares categorically that "*la ténébreuse et profonde unité* of which the sonnet speaks is unrelated to (*sans rapport avec*) the *monotone et impersonnelle* unity of which the article on the Exposition universelle speaks" (1961: 276).

The critic's position here is not an altogether comfortable one. At stake for Adam is the doctrine of correspondences, which he seeks to maintain by denying the correspondence between these passages: "He believes in the metaphysical reality of correspondences in the firmest way, and it is inconceivable that one could maintain the contrary" (Ibid.: 275). One could, however, maintain the inconceivable position, contesting the absolute firmness of Baudelaire's commitment to the metaphysical doctrine, by exploiting the correspondence between these texts, insisting on the relevance to one another of the echoing descriptions of unity.

In both Baudelaire's prose text and his poem, for instance, unity results from the failure to distinguish: professors have forgotten the distinctiveness of each thing and thus everything is confused in this vast monotonous unity. In the poem, echoes heard from afar blend into a unity—*vaste comme la nuit et comme la clarté*—a nuit, perhaps, *où tous les chats sont noirs* (night and luminosity share the property of making it difficult to distinguish). Nor are these texts exceptional. "De la couleur" in the *Salon of 1846*, which cites Hoffmann on correspondences and celebrates vibration of color, describes the unity of nature like this: "et comme la vapeur de la saison,—hiver ou été,—baigne, adoucit, ou engloutit les contours, la nature ressemble à un tonton qui, mû par une vitesse accélérée, nous apparaît gris, bien qu'il résume en lui toutes les couleurs" (1975: II, 423). [And since the vapor of the season—winter or summer—bathes, softens or engulfs all contours, nature resembles a top which, spinning swiftly, appears to us gray, although it has all the colors on it.] Unity is the result of confusion, the effacement of difference. Generally, every description of unity is based on tropes that suppress difference and this creates a certain ambivalence, as the alternation of values between these corresponding texts shows.

A reading treating unity as a tropological product would doubtless go on to examine what is asserted in the tercets: first, the ability of certain stimuli to evoke sensations belonging to other senses and second the indeterminate signifying possibilities of certain "parfums." The poem links synthesia with verbal art by asserting links between sensations that seem to rely on verbal echoes or relays, whether semantic or phonological: *chairs* connects with *doux* by a pun that is close to the surface in *chairs d'enfants* ("chères enfants"); the *bois* of *hautbois* helps to justify *verts*, in *verts comme des prairies*, where *verts* itself is echoed in the first syllable of *prairies*.

> Il est des parfums frais comme des chairs d'enfants,
> Doux comme les hautbois, verts commes les prairies. . . .

But the tercets also distinguish the regular, specifiable relations between sweet or innocent smells and the corresponding sounds and colors from the indeterminate signifying possibilities of corrupt, rich and triumphant smells.

Why smells, one wants to know? If the point is, as Leo Bersani claimed in the passage I quoted earlier, to assert the metaphorical unity of the universe, to present a stylistic demonstration of "the echoes of a distant likeness which the poet asks us to hear in each of our experiences," why should smells have been selected as the case in point? The answer might be that of all sensations smells are the most inextricably linked with tropological, specifically metonymical operations. Other sensations may have literal names. Smells mnemonically generate chains of metonymical associations: to name a smell is to metonymially describe its cause or the circumstances in which one first smelled it (unlike colors, which have names of their own), so that smells hold the attention to reorient it toward what surrounds them, in the poetic (discursive and descriptive) movement evoked in Baude-laire's "Parfum exotique" or "La Chevelure" or the prose poem, "Une hémisphere dans une chevelure." Smell is the sensation where *il n'y a pas de propre* and which joins the mnemonic power of recognition to the discursive exfoliation of a metonymical imagination.

I have here outlined two kinds of intertextual explorations whose methodological compatibility should not be taken for granted but which do, taken together, generate a plausible reading of the poem. The first placed the sonnet in the intertextual space of possible sources, a persistent prior discourse about nature and temples, and sought to treat the poem either as an affirmation or as an ironic repetition or transformation of this language. If one feels no loyalty to the doctrine of vertical correspondences and thinks that lyric poetry can better be explained and justified in other ways, then one will no doubt find the second, ironic possibility more attractive and productive, since taking the poem to undermine the transcendental claims it cites and modifies prepares the way for the second quatrain.

The second approach (for the second quatrain), emphasizing verbal echoes or repetitions within the Baudelairian corpus, sought to make the so-called doctrine of horizontal correspondences more textual and tropological. Bringing thematically distinct texts closer to each other, suggesting that in their repetition they infect one another, showing that unity might be viewed as a tropological effect, foregrounding the ambiguity of "se confondent," one reinstated "Correspondance" as an *art poétique*.

Combining these procedures, which seem to work in different direc-tions and on different principles, nevertheless generates a reading of the poem, according to which the ironic treatment of doctrines in the first two quatrains sets the stage for the assertion of tropological rela-tions in the tercets. These assertions are cast in terms that suggest, on the one hand, that supposedly natural or inherent equivalences of sensory qualities may depend on verbal links and second, that what is most valued is the process (epitomized by smell) of metonymical ex-trapolation from sensation—quite literal "transports de l'esprit et des sens." "Correspondances," often thought to declare that the natural is a sign of the divine, by this reading in fact celebrates the poetic process whereby the smell of hair evokes or generates a hemisphere.

Briefly and schematically, the various interpretations suggest that "Correspondances" has been an important poem for three reasons. First, because its definition of our encounter with the world as a pas-sage through "des forêts de symboles" has seemed aesthetically pro-ductive: the world as a forest of signs accessible to poets and vision-aries. "Correspondances" seems to be the economical enunciation of principles of aesthetic signification at work in Baudelaire's *oeuvre*, as it explores correspondences between *le mal* and *la beauté* or *la boue* et *l'or,* for example.

Second, the poem is important because it echoes numerous statements of Baudelaire's prose writings—about *correspondances, analogie universelle*—and in so doing works to confirm the possibility of a correspondence between poems and prose accounts of aesthetic principles. If critics make much of "Correspondances," it is partly because criticism relies on the possibility of a correspondence between poems and poetics. As a poem based on what Lloyd Austin calls the "doctrine of correspondences," "Correspondances" confirms the vital possibility of a close, signifying relation between poems and critical statements.

Third, "Correspondances" is essential to any attempt to situate Baudelaire in a story of modern poetry because of its echoes of a range of romantic sources, not to speak of the echoes of it in the later poetic tradition. Marcel Raymond, for example, makes it the point of departure for the trajectory summed up by his title, *De Baudelaire au surréalisme.* More recently, in an essay entitled "Anthropomorphism and Trope in the Lyric" in *The Rhetoric of Romanticism,* Paul de Man declares of "Correspondances" that "it, and it alone, contains, implies, produces, generates, permits (or whatever aberrant verbal metaphor one wishes to choose) the entire possibility of the lyric" (1984: 261–2).

What seems to be at stake in all these interpretive possibilities is the preservation of "Correspondances" as a key, doctrinal poem: both a Baudelairian *art poétique* and a key poem for any literary history that wants to integrate Baudelaire in a story of post-Enlightenment poetry. Even contradictory interpretations seem to leave intact the notion of "Correspondances" as at once the culmination of the Romantic doctrine of vertical correspondences, the adumbration of a symbolist aesthetic, and the point of departure for surrealism. The poem, that is, brings about a change of direction, echoing romantic doctrine but, with an ironic twist, sending things off in a new direction; through its ironic repetition, making correspondence no longer a one-to-one divinely sanctioned relation but rather a metonymical exfoliation such as is set off by the recognition of a smell. The romantic line runs into this poem; the modernist line runs out of it. The change from one line to another takes place at the Baudelaire correspondence.

These interpretive convergences, the very plausibility of a synthetic interpretive overview that transcends major disagreements—about the presence or absence of irony, the value of unity, whether we are in a forest or in the city—may tell us a good deal about our conceptions of lyric and demands on lyric. To encourage the project of treating our interpretations as data to be explained, I should like to note a couple of objections to this satisfying convergence—objections which might encourage us to see it as the product of conventional and generic demands.

The first bears on the notion that this poem is a Baudelairian *art poétique*. As Sandro Genovali observes in *Baudelaire, O della dissonanza*, there are actually very few synesthesias in Baudelaire—"des parfums verts" is not a familiar kind of image in Baudelaire but, on the contrary, very rare (1971: 137–147). There are poems that talk about synesthesia—"j'aime à la fureur/ Les choses où le son se mêle à la lumière" (Les Bijoux)—but it is not a major poetic technique. So an initial problem is that if "Correspondances" is about poetry, it is not describing what this poetry does.

Still, one might answer this valid objection by conceding that Baudelaire is not interested in synesthesia, as the first tercet suggests, so much as in sensations as stimuli to reverie, memory, imagination: the other smells

> corrompus, riches, et triomphants
> Ayant l'expansion des choses infinies, . . .
> Qui chantent les transports de l'esprit et des sens.

This exfoliation is both the subject of poetry and the process of poetic production, and in taking "Correspondances" as an *art poétique* one can bracket the first two lines of the tercets while concentrating on the last four.

This defense, however, only increases the pertinence of the second objection, which bears on the interpretation of the tercets as glorifying tropological relations—specifically on such claims as Leo Bersani's that comparisons using the word *comme* demonstrate the relations we are invited to perceive in nature. Paul de Man notes of the final *comme* in the poem ("Et d'autres, *comme* l'ombre, le musc, le benjoin et l'encens"), "Ce comme n'est pas un 'comme' comme les autres." It is not comparative, bringing together different sorts of sensations, bridging gaps in a metaphorical transfer of properties or fusion involving analogy ("des parfums frais *comme* des chairs d'enfants"). It is a *comme* of enumeration—smells *such as* a, b, c—opening a list which can go on without getting us anywhere else. De Man writes,

> Considered from the perspective of the "thesis" or of the symbolist ideology of the text, such a use of "comme" is aberrant. For although the burden of totalizing expansion seems to be attributed to these particular scents rather than the others, the logic of "comme" restricts the semantic field of "parfums" and confines it to a tautology: "Il est des parfums . . . / Comme (des parfums)." Instead of analogy, we have enumeration, and an enumeration which never moves beyond the confines of a set of particulars: . . . the enumeration could be continued at will without ceasing to be a repetition, without ceasing to be an obsession rather than a metamorphosis, let alone

a rebirth. One wonders if the evil connotations of these corrupt scents do not stem from the syntax rather than from the Turkish bath or black mass atmosphere one would otherwise have to conjure up. For what could be more perverse or corruptive for a metaphor aspiring to transcendental totality than remaining stuck in an enumeration that never goes anywhere? . . . Enumerative repetition disrupts the chain of tropological substitution at the crucial moment when the poem promises, by way of these very substitutions, to reconcile the pleasures of the mind with those of the senses and to unite aesthetics with epistemology. That the very word on which these substitutions depend would just then lose its syntactical and semantic univocity is too striking a coincidence not to be, like pure chance, beyond the control of author and reader. (1984: 249–250)

This shift to a *comme* of enumeration does rather disrupt the synthesis that takes the tercets as a celebration of the tropological productivity of poetic imagination and memory (poetry as the exploitation of a clavier de correspondances). The question, then, is what does one do with this significant textual detail, whose very flatness and negativity make it extremely seductive. The hermeneutic imperative, which seeks to transmute negatives into positives, tempts us to make this the basis for a new interpretation of the poem. There would be a strong temptation, then, to make a further interpretive move and take the poem to be *about* the disruption of tropological substitution and its totalizing goals by the sheer materiality of language and thus ultimately to read "Correspondances" as a poem that demystifies lyric. Such moves are tempting because of our assumption that to produce a new interpretation of a major literary work is the goal of the critical endeavor but I wish to resist it and to ask whether resistance makes any difference. Would it make any difference, that is, to think that instead of working at a new reading of the poem one were in fact attempting to move toward an elucidation of the interpretive processes associated with lyric? De Man remarks, suggestively, that "The lyric is not a genre but one name among several to designate a defensive motion of understanding, the possibility of a future hermeneutics" (Ibid.: 261). The lyric seems to consist of patterns of anthropomorphism and naturalization that guarantee the intelligibility of tropes. Here, in readings of a poem that has long been taken as exemplary not of the lyric but of a poetics of the lyric, we have observed among other things the use of the notion of intertextuality as a fundamentally recuperative strategy, ultimately a strategy for making sense of sheer repetition. My two approaches to Baudelairian intertextuality in effect recuperated intertextual echoes as a potential attitude of consciousness—what at the thematic or psychological level we call "irony." Study of the interpretive moves illustrated in both the tradition and our response to that tradition would show how genres, such as lyric, are sets of reading strategies for making sense of language, ways of convincing ourselves not only that language is meaningful, that it will give rise to an intuition or understanding, as would be amply illustrated by our interpretive examples, but also that this is an understanding of the world.

To take interpretations as data rather than goals does not mean an end to interpretation but rather a displacement of our present goal: the production of new interpretations of literary texts as the aim and the test of literary study. Encouraging an understanding of language and genre, which now often have to be achieved by interpreting works as allegories of reading rather than by interpreting readings themselves, this would give us a more capacious, differently articulated domain of knowledge and might also discourage the impression so many of our colleagues in other fields seem to have gained, that what we in literary studies think of as knowledge is in fact just an endless series of ingenious interpretations.

References

Adam, Antoine, ed.
  1961 *Les Fleurs du Mal*, by Charles Baudelaire (Paris: Garnier).
Austin, Lloyd
  1956 *L'Univers poétique de Baudelaire* (Paris: Mercure de France).
Baudelaire, Charles
  1975 *Oeuvres complètes*, 2 vols., edited by Claude Pichois (Paris: Gallimard).
Bersani, Leo
  1977 *Baudelaire and Freud* (Berkeley: University of California Press).
Brooks, Cleanth
  1940 "Literary History Versus Criticism," *Kenyon Review* 2: 403–412.
Bush, Douglas
  1949 "The New Criticism: Some Old-Fashioned Queries," *PMLA* 64 (March), Supp. pt. 2: 138–150.
Cherix, Robert Benoit
  1949 *Commentaire des Fleurs du Mal* (Geneva: P. Cailler).
Culler, Jonathan
  1981 *The Pursuit of Signs* (Ithaca: Cornell University Press).
De Man, Paul
  1984 *The Rhetoric of Romanticism* (New York: Columbia University Press).
Genovali, Sandro
  1971 *Baudelaire, o della dissonanza* (Florence: La Nuova Italia).
Graff, Gerald
  1987 *Professing Literature: An Institutional History* (Chicago: University of Chicago Press).
Hugo, Victor
  1972 *Poésies*, vol. 1 (Paris: Seuil).
Kunitz, Stanley, ed.
  1955 *Twentieth Century American Authors: First Supplement* (New York: H.W. Wilson).

Lamartine, Alphonse de
 1968 *Méditations*, edited by F. Letessier (Paris: Garnier).
Nitze, William Albert
 1929 "'Horizons':—The Presidential Address," *PMLA* 44, Supp.: iii–xi.
Pommier, Jean
 1967 *La Mystique de Baudelaire* (Geneva: Slatkine Reprints).
Raymond, Marcel
 1952 *De Baudelaire au surréalisme* (Paris: J. Corti).
Tupper, Frederick
 1930 "'Authors and Arts: A Mediaeval Instance':—The Presidential Address,"
  PMLA 45, Supp.: iii–xviii.
Webster, Grant
 1979 *The Republic of Letters* (Baltimore: Johns Hopkins University Press).
Wellek, René and Austin Warren
 1956 *Theory of Literature* (New York: Harcourt Brace).

Of Ants and Grasshoppers: Two Ways (or More) to Link Texts and Power

Edward Pechter

Every man is born an Aristotelian or a Platonist. I do not think it possible that any one born an Aristotelian can become a Platonist; and I am sure no born Platonist can ever change into an Aristotelian. They are two classes of men, besides which it is next to impossible to conceive a third.—Samuel Taylor Coleridge, Table-Talk, *2 July 1830*

Canada est omnis divisa in partes duo: all Canada is divided into two parts. We used to have Upper and Lower Canada but, with the settling of the plains beyond Ontario, this division is now expressed as East and West. There's also North and South and lots of divisions not based on geography: a political division between the Provincial and Federal Governments; an economic one between the have and have-not provinces; a sectorial one between industrial regions and agricultural; a linguistic and cultural one between English and French. And so on. These divisions are divisive. Eastern and Western Canada don't like each other and on down the line to French and English Canada. Canadians like to say that as a result of all our differences Canada is ungovernable but all nation-states are ungovernable—abstractions into which an enormous variety of meaning is overloaded. These differences, moreover, can be seen not so much as a resistance to government but as a form of government, since they give shape to something. After all, how you can divide something unless you can first of all conceive of the thing to be divided? These divisions, then, don't represent something that's already there; they constitute that something in the sense of packaging it in a way that allows us to see it; and what these divisions shape or package—namely, all Canada—would be hard to see *except* for the packaging.

Maybe I can make this point clearer if I switch from Canadiana to Americana. At the end of his book, Huck Finn reckons he's "got to light out for the Territory." The Territory is empty space; it can be defined only negatively. It's the place where there's no Aunt Polly trying "to adopt me and sivilize me"—that is, no social constraints, no legal fictions; and no Tom Sawyer who had "his bullet around his neck on a watch-guard for a watch, and is always seeing what time it is"—that is, no history, no hypocrisy, no scars, no guilt. The freedom of this Territory is pure negativity; it is no place, Utopia. Gertrude Stein's phrase is truer about the Territory than it is about Oakland: "there's no there there."

If Huck heads due west in search of the Territory, we can place him in Oklahoma, Rodgers-and-Hammerstein style: "Territory folks should stick together/Territory folks should all be pals/Farmers dance with the ranchers' daughters/Ranchers dance with the farmers' gals." There's an appeal here to a transcendental ideal, shared existence in the Territory but the Territory no longer exists. Or rather it only now does exist: all the Territory is divided into two parts, farmers and ranchers. The two parts constitute the Territory but also divide it. The farmers want to build fences and grow cash crops, the ranchers want to keep the range open for the cattle to graze so they can sell beef. The Territory has become land, property. Utopia has become filled with the topics of invention. Empty space has become a place and a place of contestation. However this dispute was settled, we may be sure it involved coercion. Moreover, any resolution between farmers and ranchers was bound to be only temporary, because it failed to resolve or even acknowledge another kind of difference. No one bothered to ask the ranchers' daughters and the farmers' gals how they felt about such arrangements. We never even asked them whether they wanted to dance.

Though it's hard to say what the Territory or Canada is as a God- or nature-given fact, it's easy to say that they are words. If I say *only* words, though, I'm reproducing the metaphysical ideas I have been trying to dispute. The thing about words is that they have real power; they can be used to regulate human behavior; in fact they are the best way to do so. The word Canada can be used to regulate quite a lot of behavior: more than dog or Uruguay, less than reason, Lenin or the United States. People sometimes say dismissively that a particular dispute is "*only* semantic" but all disputes seem to go back to different claims about the meanings of words and seem to be resolved—at least temporarily—by means of the same kinds of claims.

Coleridge thought we were born Platonists or Aristotelians and unlikely or unable to change; in other words, that all critical activity is divided into two parts. In this context it should come as no surprise if I assert that the field of interpretation and power, as I see it, is both made up of and contested by two exemplary claims upon our belief. In one, interpretation is understood to be a tightly controlled activity, governed by the powerful institutions of collective life; and as serious, responsible critics we should be focusing on these institutions, seeing how they work, how they work on us, how we can change them. In the other view, interpretation is located in the power of the text or rather in a random responsiveness that allows texts to turn into experiences of energy, freedom, and pleasure. I will call the holders of these two exemplary positions the ants and the grasshoppers. I shall first define what it means to be an ant or a grasshopper. I don't pretend to be describing them from above; I am a grasshopper advocate because I think the position is a good one and deserves better representation than it tends to get these days. But beyond such advocacy, I will consider at least a bit at the end whether this particular division is a good one, whether it enhances our projects more than it blocks them, whether other stories, potentially more useful, might be available.

First the ants. Consider the case of Lenny Bruce, a comic who made a career of transgression; he acknowledges as much in the title of his autobiography, *How to Talk Dirty and Influence People*. By talking dirty, Lenny Bruce not only influenced people, he got in trouble with the law. He was repeatedly charged with various legal offenses, all of which added up to talking dirty. As his law cases multiplied and dragged on, dirty Lenny, as he called himself, became obsessed with the law and this obsession changed his act. In his last years his night club performances harped on his legal situation. He entertained audiences with the history of his arrests and court battles, sometimes reading from the legal transcripts: "On the aforementioned occasion, the said Mr. Bruce did twice use the word ——, and four times the word ——." The only time I saw Lenny Bruce, shortly before his death, he had already been obsessed with the law for years and the performance of the history of his arrests had itself acquired a narrative history with meaning and consequences, which he described to us: after reading from the official transcripts in his act, he would be arrested and charged again for saying the same dirty words, even though these words were part of the transcript. How, dirty Lenny wondered, could it be illegal to read a legal document?

This question gets us to the center of interpretation and power. First of all, interpretation is contextualization. The same text looks different, means different things, in different contexts. Lenny Bruce used this point repeatedly in his defenses. The dirty word that got him in trouble when he uttered it in a nightclub performance is clean in the mouth of a peace officer in a police station. But this is where power comes in. If the interpretive act of determining a context is what gives shape and meaning to the text, then who has the power to determine the context? Dirty Lenny's statement that he was quoting a legal document as part of a legal argument claimed the right to establish a certain context for his speech. But his claim had no force when confronted with the entrenched, institutionalized power of the police and their claim that he was trying to talk dirty and influence people.

We can expand on this point with reference to someone else who talked dirty and influenced people, Christopher Marlowe. In the Baines document, Marlowe skeptically analyzes religion as pie in the sky, a purely human institution invented as a means to social control:

> Moyses made the Jewes to travell xl yeares in the wildernes, (which Jorney might haue bin done in lesse then one yeare) to thintent that those who were privy to most of his subtilties might perish and so an everlasting superstition Remain in the hartes of the people. . . . the first beginning of Religioun was only to keep men in awe.   (MacLure 1979: 37)[1]

It is easy to connect this sort of thing with the plays. "I think hell's a fable," says Doctor Faustus, "trifles and mere old wives' tales." "But," says Mephostophilis, "I am an instance to prove the contrary, / For I tell thee I am damn'd, and now in hell" (1962: scene v). But is he —*really*? Isn't he an actor, performing in a theatrical fable? Just how do we interpret this exchange; that is, what's the context?

If religion is the controlling context, then this exchange centers on a moral choice with real consequences—salvation or damnation. But then, maybe theater is the controlling context, religion a form of theater. This is just what the Baines document says: "that if there be any god or any good Religion, then it is in the papistes because the service of god is performed with more Cerimonies, as Elevation of the mass, organs, singing men, Shaven Crownes &cta" (MacLure, 1979: 37). From this perspective, the exchange between Faustus and Mephostophilis has no consequences. Plays are play, free play; the price of admission is the only one exacted. A lot of *Doctor Faustus* can be seen in this context—the whole clown plot and much of the Faustus plot itself. Heads are cut off but they are only false heads; Faustus's leg is pulled off but it grows back. Faustus is only "slain-unslain," to use Kenneth Burke's phrase about Cinna the Poet in *Julius Caesar*, "like a

---

1. I am rather blandly assuming that the Baines document represents Marlowe's statements but recent work by John Manningham and Constance Kuriyama have inclined people to be less skeptical about Baines. See Kuriyama's summary (1987: 10).

clown hit by cannon balls" (Burke 1973: 343). In the theater nobody dies.

This sort of argument—that theatrical performance has a special status outside the normalizing sanctions of cultural power—is one that occurred to Lenny Bruce, who noted that an amendment was added to the statute under which he was charged "which *excludes from arrest* stagehands, spectators, musicians and *actors*" (Bruce 1963: 195). But dirty Lenny never got anywhere with this argument and a seventeenth-century story about a production of *Doctor Faustus* suggests that it won't work with Marlowe's play either:

> Certaine Players at Exeter, acting upon the stage the tragical storie of Dr. Faustus the Conjurer; as a certain nomber of Devels kept everie one his circle there, and as Faustus was busie in his magicall invocations, on a sudden they were all dasht, every one harkning other in the eare, for they were all perswaded, there was one devell too many amongst them; and so after a little pause desired the people to pardon them, they could go no further with this matter; the people also understanding the thing as it was, every man hastened to be first out of dores. The players (as I heard it) contrarye to their custome spending the night in reading and in prayer got them out of the town the next morning.   (Chambers 1951: 424)

The "magicall invocations" must be Faustus's Latin speech in the third scene of the play, abjuring Jehovah and summoning Mephostophilis. These are perhaps the dirtiest words imaginable in Marlowe's culture and, though uttered in a play, they are not sanitized by that context, for the presumably free space of theatrical representation is seen to be occupied by a real devil—real in its power to effect belief, to suspend any temporary suspension of disbelief.

Like Lenny Bruce's bust for quoting a legal document, the extra devil at *Doctor Faustus* suggests the controlling power of cultural institutions in determining the context and therefore interpreting the text. The stories, though, aren't the same. It would be easy to understand the Lenny Bruce story as a conflict between the heroically transgressive individual and the repressive forces of the state. But the *Faustus* story seems to mean something less simple and less flattering since the extra devil is observed by the actors themselves. The devil invades their own consciousness and conscience, which turn out to be no more free than the physical space of theatrical representation. "The individual," Michel Foucault says, is "not a *vis-à-vis* of power; it is . . . one of its effects" (1980: 98). "The individual," Morse Peckham tells us, is "a mere cultural precipitate" (1979: xviii). And so it seems with the individual actors at Exeter. They have internalized the official version of cultural authority—convinced into feeling their own guilt, cooperating in their own conviction.

But let's leave them for the moment and with them the interpretive ants, presumably hard at work contemplating those powerful institutions which shape and constrain all discursive possibility; let's consider instead how things might look from the grasshoppers' point of view. Here is a grasshopper story about a man called Orazio Busino. Busino, who served as chaplain to the Venetian ambassador in London in the early seventeenth century, kept a kind of diary, and in his entry for February 7, 1618, he refers to a theatrical performance apparently of Webster's *Duchess of Malfi*.[2] Although the entry is too confused to tell us much about the production practices of Jacobean public drama, it does tell us a good deal about the interpretive activity of Jacobean audiences—or at least about Busino's interpretive activity in a theater on February 7, 1618.

What it tells us seems at first perfectly consistent with the Bruce and Marlowe stories. Busino comes to the theater as a Catholic with connections to the Venetian ruling class. From this culturally derived perspective, the first thing Busino sees is that "the English scoff at our religion" and theater is experienced within this context: "they never put on any public show whatever, be it tragedy or satire or comedy, into which they do not insert some Catholic churchman's vices and wickednesses, making mock and scorn of him, according to their taste, but to the dismay of good men." This same position is reaffirmed at the end of the entry: "all this was acted in condemnation of the . . . church, which they despise . . . in this kingdom." Everything in the middle, then, is merely example and could have been drawn as well from other, non-theatrical sources—a royal decree, an anti-Spanish uprising of London apprentices, whatever. From this subjective space, plays are seen as political moves, strategic deployments in the power struggles of seventeenth-century Europe. Theater itself, as we might put it, doesn't seem to exist for Busino. Neither does genre as a purely formal category. Though Busino mentions genre right at the beginning, "be it tragedy or satire or comedy," his point is merely that anti-Papism is all-pervasive and comes in plays of all kinds. He might as well have said: "be it at the Whitefriars or the Swan or the Red Bull." Genre as such isn't important to him. A literary or a theatrical response as such, as we might put it, doesn't seem to exist for Busino any more than literature or theater itself.

According to Stephen Greenblatt, such responses *couldn't* have existed; they were historically impossible. For the early modern period, Greenblatt tells us, "art does not pretend to autonomy; the writ-

2. The entry, in the same unattributed English translation, is conveniently available in the two recent collections of Webster criticism: *John Webster*, edited by the Hunters (1969: 31–32) and by Moore (1981: 34). The original choice Italian is extant in Chambers (1951: 511) and E. E. Stoll (1967: 29).

ten word is self-consciously embedded in specific communities, life situations, structures of power" (1980: 7). But in the long middle of Busino's diary entry things happen that should make us question such an assertion. We hear, for instance, about "a Franciscan friar [who] was seen by some of our countrymen introduced into a comedy as a wily character . . . , as given over to avarice as to lust. And the whole thing turned out to be a tragedy, for he had his head cut off on open stage." If Busino's point is merely that it's not nice to make fun of good men like Franciscan friars, then why the details about the decapitation that made the whole thing turn out to be a tragedy? He seems to have shifted ground. From saying it's not right to show nasty friars, he says it's not decorous to mix genres, to turn comedy into tragedy. For a moment Busino reveals a surprising formalist side. Not that this contradicts Busino's subject position with relation to the structures of power. Educated Italians read Scaliger and liked to keep their genres separate. Nonetheless, as the passage goes on, Busino floods us with theatrical impressions, for instance, the cardinal "they showed . . . in all his grandeur, . . . splendid and rich, . . . organizing a procession," where the relation to genre or to religious and national allegiance is impossible to specify. Busino seems to have become absorbed in the spectacle of the performance in a way that is now independent of his original point of view. And finally this independence—this autonomy —seems absolute: "Moreover, [the cardinal] goes to war, first laying down his cardinal's habit on the altar, with the help of his chaplains, with great ceremoniousness; finally he has his sword bound on and dons the soldier's sash with so much panache you could not imagine it better done." Busino is not here objecting to the cardinal's transformation as a kind of anti-Catholic slur. Nor is he approving of the transformation, as he might. Rather, the transformation—this quintessentially theatrical action: donning new garments and finding a new mode of being in the world—seems to have become the object of Busino's delighted attention for its own sake: "with so much panache you could not imagine it better done."

This lasts only a moment. In the last sentence Busino remembers his point or indeed remembers himself, an Italian Catholic chaplain in an English public theater, a stranger in a strange land. But for that moment, those features ceased to matter; he forgot them, just as Christopher Sly forgot about Burton-heath and Marian Hacket, the fat ale-wife of Wincot, all those papers and badges and labels of culturally derived identity, when finally yielding to the power of theatrical illusion at the beginning of *The Taming of the Shrew*. In this moment, Busino becomes not only rapt in the pleasures of beholding transformation but absorbed in the experience of it. He becomes, in other words, a member of a theatrical audience. Invoking the power structures doesn't seem to work here. Peter Quince's astonished cry about Bottom serves as a better gloss for the condition of being a theatrical audience: Bless thee, Busino, bless thee! Thou art translated.

Now pretty clearly these stories seem to lead us to contradictory conclusions—or rather, I have led them there.[3] The Busino story suggests that the interpreting subject, far from being a precipitate of culture, can find space outside the ideological network, a position from which in this case the Catholic-Protestant division doesn't seem to exist. Further, the Busino story seems to offer a different direction for interpretive activity. Instead of fixing response onto the political institutions that are claimed to generate it, we are free to play with the text as a set of impressions that can lead anywhere. The interpreter is now a sovereign autonomous consumer in a free interpretive market, endowed with the inalienable right to pursue happiness, the pleasure of . the text. It seems as if we have come upon mutually exclusive concepts of interpretation and power, between which we have to choose. What I argue, though, is that they are not mutually exclusive and that the choice is unnecessary.

Consider first the question of sovereignty vs. cultural determination. Busino's response may seem culturally undetermined but this is only because *we* have determined culture in an unnecessarily coherent way. I grew up with an idea of Renaissance culture as a monological structure called The Elizabethan World Picture. We have since moved to more complex, duological models which enable us to understand the Renaissance as more actively political, including conflict and con-

---

3. I have called them ant and grasshopper stories, as though their meaning were textually embedded but, like all stories, they can be appropriated in different ways. Busino, for instance, could be turned into an ant story if, armed (say) with Virginia Woolf's discussion near the end of the first chapter of *Three Guineas*, you understand his diary entry in terms of gender politics and phallic aggression: men always like to dress up and play soldier. So we'd find ourselves not floating freely above power, but embedded in the *real* power relations screened by Catholic-and-Protestant—namely, male and female. (As always, I mean *"real"* in a positional rather than a metaphysical sense.) This might work the other way round for the Marlowe story; though I have given it an antish interpretation, grasshoppers could use it for their purposes. The move here would be to look a little more closely at all the versions in Chambers. Quite possibly, they all derive from Middleton's "Hee had a head of hayre like one of my Diuells in Dr. Faustus when the old Theater crackt and frighted the audience" (Chambers 1951: 423), in which the actors are themselves unafraid. If this is true, then the original story is generated from within the theater and testifies to the power of theatrical illusion and subsequent anti-theatrical revisions (the next version is Prynne's in *Histriomastix*) including the one I quoted, place the fear in the actors rather than the audience as a way of containing any such theatrical claims—thereby of course providing additional testimony to the power of such claims.

testation. Hence the religious schism allows us to consider Catholic-vs.-Protestant as one possible candidate for a Master Theme of the early modern period. But the Busino story suggests ways in which Catholic-vs.-Protestant is not a Master Theme; lots of other Renaissance interpreters escaped from its domination as well, the most notable being Montaigne, and some of these others even into a theatrical or a quasi-theatrical space.[4] We could then hunt out a new-and-improved Master Theme in other divisions: power vs. transgression, authority vs. subordination—these are the leading candidates. These will work but only for some of the people and only some of the time. Like Canada, culture is a word, and the divisions which constitute this word, make it present to the understanding, are bound to be unstable, and will always look arbitrary and incomplete from some positions.

One move here is to go beyond such divisions, from duology to trilogy, a move with much potential. Dividing into *three* parts is unconventional, maybe even transgressive, crossing a conceptual Rubicon. It's a dirty move that influences people's way of thinking or it could; but in the proposed trilogies I have seen, this innovative potential has not been realized. Consider Raymond Williams's analysis of culture in terms of "residual, dominant, and emergent" elements (1977: 121–127). These terms clearly correspond to past, present, and future. Expanded considerably by Fredric Jameson, this correspondence is even clearer:

> every social formation or historically existing society has in fact consisted in the overlay and structural coexistence of *several* modes of production all at once, including vestiges and survivals of older modes of production, now relegated to structurally dependent positions within the new, as well as anticipatory tendencies which are potentially inconsistent with the existing system but have not yet generated an autonomous space of their own. (1981: 95)

This is the Big Picture—"that long discourse," as Hamlet called it, "looking before and after"; the historical narrative, whose three parts are beginning, middle, and end. However, since it is the interconnection among these three parts that gives the historical narrative its explanatory power, they must be seen as parts of a whole, a totality radiating from a center. You can call the center "the godlike capability of reason," "the material mode of production" or whatever you want

---

4. We have already seen Marlowe's suggestion that religion is just a kind of theatre. Sir Thomas Browne said, without any evident irony, "I could never heare the *Ave-Marie* Bell without an elevation . . . At a solemne [Catholic] Procession I have wept abundantly, while my [Protestant] consorts, blinde with opposition and prejudice, have fallen into an accesse of scorne and laughter" (Endicott 1968: 9). Donne's theatricality at the end of the sonnet on the church and throughout the third satire might, with some hard arguing, be brought in here as well.

but the thing about centers—as we've learned these past twenty years —is that they can always be shown to be arbitrary and the structures of thought built upon them can always be deconstructed.

This is not to say that we should stop writing historical narratives, for what else is there? But the question is, how do we write them? For example: if we say that "art does not pretend to autonomy" in the Renaissance, we are saying something about Renaissance culture in the form of a narrative beginning. The middle of this narrative, chapter two, is Romanticism: imagination, stories floating randomly above power structures, responses generated out of a willing suspension of disbelief, the free play of the cognitive faculties for their own sake or for pleasure. It is no doubt fair to say that the Romantics invented Romanticism but only in the sense of combining a bunch of assumptions and beliefs in a way that made them into a newly visible subject. But if you say that the Busino story is impossible because it belongs in chapter one, then you're making a fetish out of your own narrative structure. We should write our historical narratives with some measure of respect for Jean-Luc Godard's statement that, yes, of course he believed in beginnings and middles and ends but not necessarily in that order (Pechter 1971: 246).

What about chapter three, though, the ending? In the ants' version of critical history, we awaken from the sleep of Romanticism, put away grasshopperish things and return to a Renaissance sense of the embeddedness of texts in the specific power relations. There may be other versions of the Renaissance and Romanticism but let's forget about the earlier chapters. The end crowns all. The end is a plan for the future, the expression of desire in the form of historical analysis. It answers the question, what is the function of criticism at the present time? And the answer according to ants is antism. If we interpret like ants, we have our best chance to live happily ever after.

Ant advocacy starts with the notion that all activity is purposive, with consequences in and for the world. Critical activity is therefore political activity and interpretation is power or a bid for power. From this position, ants argue against indulging in the pleasures of a text disembodied from its political matrix. In the name of free play, such grasshopper activity actually performs cultural work—namely, the diversion of energy from the political tasks at hand. In the name of an illusory free space outside the political, it disguises its own politics, which turn out to be conservative or reactionary.

Once again we are faced with an apparently absolute contradiction between the two exemplary positions I have been concerned with here. Once again I want to argue that they need not be seen as mutually exclusive, that you can start by accepting all antian assumptions about the political nature of interpretive activity (as I think we should) and nonetheless wind up at home among the grasshoppers.

Let's go back to Busino or to the play he apparently witnessed. *The Duchess of Malfi* is about male power and female transgression. By marrying her steward, Antonio, the Duchess violates the hierarchy of class but gender difference seems to be the main code here. She disobeys the commands of her brothers not to marry and she initiates the wooing with Antonio—plays the man's part, as the play emphasizes. This wooing scene is full of great tenderness but also highly charged with an erotic and anxious sense of risk. "Wish me good speed," says the Duchess in words that set up the scene, "For I am going into a wilderness / Where I shall find nor path, nor friendly clew / To be my guide" (Webster 1977: 1.1.358–361). We have to wait until the middle of the play to discover what it is the Duchess discovers in her dangerous journey, for it is not until then that the Duchess and Antonio are placed before us again in a domestic context. The scene (3.2) is one of quiet and relaxed intimacy. The Duchess brushes her hair, and they talk—or better, chat. In their casual and affectionate banter, the play systematically parades before us the topics of the wooing scene. All has changed; the anxiety is gone, any hint of the perverse; only the tenderness remains and the continued sexual delight the Duchess and Antonio take in each other, apparently unabated over the years. As a whole the scene is suffused with a sense of fulfilled desire. "I prithee," says the Duchess, "When were we so merry?—my hair tangles."

All that's left to complete what is for us a very familiar picture is the children. Children have been part of this picture since the wooing scene, in Antonio's answer to the Duchess's question how he feels about marriage:

> Say a man never marry, nor have children,
> What takes that from him? only the bare name
> Of being a father, or the weak delight
> To see the little wanton ride a-cock-horse
> Upon a painted stick, or hear him chatter
> Like a taught starling.

This is a man who wants children and in a way that apparently has nothing to do with inheritance or property or power. The Duchess seems to hear in this speech an echo of her own desire for children and a confirmation of her desire for him: her response is to give him her ring, a gesture from which there is no turning back. The children are often on stage during the play, never far from their thoughts, and indeed they appear in this middle scene, at least verbally, in the Duchess's playful "I'll assure you / You shall get no more children."

We can use Lawrence Stone's rubrics to describe this scene: The Closed Domesticated Nuclear Family, The Companionate Marriage, Child Rearing in the Affectionate Mode (1977). The scene may appear not only familiar to us but too familiar, like Rodgers and Hammerstein again, this time *Carousel*: "When the children are asleep we'll stop and dream / What every other / Dad and mother / Dream." But to Webster's audience, as Frank Whigham (1985: 173) and Susan Wells (1985: 64) point out, the scene must have looked not old-hat but new-fangled. Stone applies those rubrics to the period 1640–1800. Obviously dates are not exact but the example of Shakespeare leads to the same conclusion. There is nothing like this scene in Shakespeare. Marriage is an ending in Shakespeare, a generic closure beyond which the plays do not really seem interested to look. It's a social and economic arrangement, no more (and no less). Children sometimes appear in Shakespeare in a variety of contexts but hardly ever to arouse the strong delight of being a parent. (Maybe Kate and Hotspur are an exceptional couple, Leontes and Mamilius an exceptional parent and child but the rarity of such exceptions is my point.) Sometimes this absence in Shakespeare is interpreted as evidence for abnormality of some kind but "gentle" Shakespeare made a career out of seeming to be normal, giving his audiences what they would and giving it to them the way they liked it. It's Webster who shocks, perversely talking dirty.

For many of us, the Nuclear Family is a cultural investment that is no longer paying dividends; we look to divest. Gender politics is a large part of this but so is the sense that a retreat from the material life of society is an illusion; we want to go public. Nonetheless, the invention of the Nuclear Family at the end of the seventeenth century looks like a step forward. It offered a mode of existence that was more productive than the residues of an exhausted post-feudalism. Webster's pre-invention of the Nuclear Family might have helped to realize this social change, at least for those who knew how to look for it: audiences willing to follow the performance's energies outside of their own consciously understood ideological agendas: grasshopper audiences.

There are, of course, different approaches to Webster's play. In the age of Tillyard, the official view was that *The Duchess of Malfi* endorsed convention and ceremony, the sustainers of a fragile and valuable civility. By transgressing, the Duchess brought the house down. Recently Lisa Jardine has argued that the cultural work of Webster's play was in the Duchess's torture and death. This served to reassure an anxious patriarchy that strong and independent women would be punished (1983: 68–93). Jardine, a new historicist, reverses the old historicist polarity; from her point of view, the house should be brought down. This difference is real enough but it exists within a surprisingly shared ground, since in both versions the play is seen to be contained within the already understood structure of cultural authority.

If we approach the play this way, like the ants, in terms of the specific power relations, a number of things might happen. Our anxieties might be assuaged or maybe intensified, our grievances confirmed or maybe relieved. But these are all the same in a way. Our ideological agendas may lead us to affirm or contest the structure of cultural authority but so long as we restrict our understanding to the terms of these agendas, we are bound to reproduce the very structure we may wish to contest. Willy nilly, ant critics replicate the situation; they tell the same old story. On the other hand we can approach the play in a condition of random responsiveness to the incoherent variety of cultural phenomena that constitute us. This way, we might get anything out of *The Duchess of Malfi*; like its original audiences, if they knew how to look, we might even get a new story.[5]

According to Michael Ignatieff in *The Needs of Strangers*:

> The problem is that our language is not necessarily adequate to our needs. Language which has ceased to express felt needs is empty rhetoric. . . . Our task is to find a language for our need for belonging which is not just a way of expressing nostalgia, fear and estrangement from modernity . . . language adequate to the times we live in. We need to see how we live now and we can only see with words and images which leave us no escape into nostalgia for some other time and place.   (1985: 137–138, 139, 141)

Ignatieff too wants to see new stories. "It is the painters and writers," he adds, "not the politicians or the social scientists, who have been able to find a language for the joy of modern life, its fleeting and transient solidarity" (141). Maybe, but this sort of argument can lead too easily to a fetishizing of art or the theater or the literary text. I prefer to distinguish not between categories of text but between categories of response. New stories can exist in any text, so long as we know how to look for them. This is the grasshoppers' way of interpreting and it is the best source of power to enable social change. The moral is clear and no socially responsible and serious critic can afford to ignore it: we should interpret like grasshoppers, because grasshoppers make the best ants.

One thing that might happen here is that the ants among us, the scales having fallen from their eyes, will rush to join me on the grasshoppers' side. But this won't happen. Though I have managed to contain the ants' arguments, they would now be able to contain mine.

---

5. We can never see *The Duchess* as its original audiences might have; the play is always bound to seem different, historically strange. I have not tried to account for the special problems of historicization in interpretive activity, though I think I could. I would (of course) start from the proposition that all historical activity is divided into two parts and that grasshopper historicists are more useful than ant historicists because they allow for the possibility of an historical understanding that can displace us from our familiar subject positions. In short, I would want to argue that there are ways in which old stories can be appropriated as new stories.

It is in the nature of ants to build well-articulated structures of containment. They see as far as the ultimate horizons into which we are all absorbed. They have purpose and seriousness on their side and these motives have always controlled the language of controversy. As Muriel Bradbrook said about the Renaissance defenders of theater, "On the level of theoretical debate they stood no chance at all. The cards were in their opponent's hands" (1964: 76). Maybe not. Such defenselessness can serve as a defense or even an attack. "We play for advantage, but we play for pleasure, too," says Richard Lanham (1976: 4–5). Grasshoppers wink slyly at each other: they know the ants are fooling themselves, playing like us, only not having as much fun. Hence the moral at the end of Woody Allen's version of the fable: in winter the grasshopper went to Florida and the ant had chest pains. From this it is only an easy step to appropriate the rhetoric of antish high seriousness. We can claim priority—wasn't the rhetorical Gorgias there before the dialectical Plato, perhaps like the matriarchal societies overrun by the Hebrew patriarchs? With Huizinga, we can affirm that "play cannot be denied. You can deny, if you like, nearly all abstractions: justice, beauty, truth, goodness, mind, God. You can deny seriousness, but not play" (1955: 3).

In the capacity of each side to contain the other, maybe both win— but win what? Presumably the ability to keep the game going, which may be all we can reasonably expect. On the other hand, maybe we can expect more, if we could somehow get out of the structure of opposition that constitutes the game. "In all unimportant matters," according to Oscar Wilde, "style, not sincerity is the essential. In all important matters," he adds, "style, not sincerity, is the essential" (1970: 296). If this were merely grasshopper advocacy, Wilde could have been clearer. He could have said that style, not sincerity, is the essential in both unimportant and important matters. What he does say, however, seems for a moment to collapse the structure of opposition—between style and sincerity, important and unimportant.

This is similar to Barthes's project in *The Pleasure of the Text*:

> An entire minor mythology would have us believe that pleasure . . . is a rightist notion. On the right . . . everything abstract, boring, political, is shoved over to the left and pleasure is kept for oneself. . . . And on the left, because of morality (forgetting Marx's and Brecht's cigars), one suspects and disdains any "residue of hedonism." On the right, pleasure is championed *against* intellectuality, the clerisy: the old reactionary myth of heart against head, sensation against reasoning, (warm) "life" against (cold) "abstraction" . . . On the left, knowledge, method, commitment, combat are drawn up against "mere delectation." (1975: 22–23)

Barthes proposes a tertium quid that has nothing to do with the oppositions of the first two, "a drift," he calls it, that "does not depend on a logic of understanding and on sensation," something "both revo-lutionary and asocial." One thing that might happen here is that all of us, grasshoppers *and* ants, might see the light, renounce our errors and follow Barthes. This won't happen either; in fact it can't, because Barthes isn't going anywhere, he is just drifting. The space to which he points us is, in his word, "atopic"—that is, Utopian, the Territory that is not divided into two parts. We can't get there from here and maybe we shouldn't even try. For the time being, we have to make do with our "historical contradictions," as Barthes later calls this same mythology of difference (Ibid.: 38–39). But as we go on trapped in the repetitions of the same old story, at least we can keep our eyes and our ears open. We'll never see a place empty of contradictions but maybe we can see one where the contradictions are surprisingly new —a different mythology of difference. Maybe we can hear a new story.

References

Barthes, Roland
   1975 *The Pleasure of the Text*, translated by Richard Miller (New York: Hill and Wang).
Bradbrook, Muriel
   1964 *The Rise of the Common Player* (London: Chatto and Windus).
Bruce, Lenny
   1963 *How to Talk Dirty and Influence People: An Autobiography* (Chicago: The Play-boy Press).
Burke, Kenneth
   1973 *The Philosophy of Literary Form* (Berkeley: University of California Press).
Chambers, E. K.
   1951 [1923] *The Elizabethan Stage*, Vol. 3 (Oxford: Oxford University Press).
Endicott, Norman, ed.
   1968 *The Prose of Sir Thomas Browne* (New York: New York University Press).
Foucault, Michel
   1980 *Power/Knowledge: Selected Interviews and Other Writings, 1972–1977*, edited by Colin Gordon (New York: Random House).
Greenblatt, Stephen
   1980 *Renaissance Self-Fashioning: From More to Shakespeare* (Chicago: University of Chicago Press).
Huizinga, Johan
   1955 *Homo Ludens: A Study of the Play-Element in Culture* (Boston: The Beacon Press).
Hunter, G. K. and S. K. Hunter, eds.
   1969 *John Webster* (Harmondsworth: Penguin).
Ignatieff, Michael
   1985 *The Needs of Strangers* (New York: Viking-Elisabeth Sifton Books).
Jameson, Fredric
   1981 *The Political Unconscious: Narrative as a Socially Symbolic Act* (Ithaca: Cornell University Press).
Jardine, Lisa
   1983 *Still Harping on Daughters: Women and Drama in the Age of Shakespeare* (Brighton, Eng.: The Harvester Press).

54

Kuriyama, Constance
  1987 "Marlowe, Shakespeare, and Biographical Evidence," *Shakespeare Newsletter* 38: 10.
Lanham, Richard
  1976 *The Motives of Eloquence: Literary Rhetoric in the Renaissance* (New Haven: Yale University Press).
MacLure, Millar, ed.
  1979 *Marlowe: The Critical Heritage* (London: Routledge and Kegan Paul).
Marlowe, Christopher
  1962 *The Tragical History of the Life and Death of Doctor Faustus*, edited by John D. Jump (London: Methuen).
Moore, Don D., ed.
  1981 *Webster: The Critical Heritage* (London: Routledge and Kegan Paul).
Pechter, William S.
  1971 *Twenty-four Times a Second: Films and Film-makers* (New York: Harper and Row).
Peckham, Morse
  1979 *Explanation and Power: The Control of Human Behavior* (New York: The Seabury Press).
Stoll, E. E.
  1967 [1905] *John Webster: The Periods of His Work as Determined by His Relations to the Drama of His Day* (New York: Gordian Press).
Stone, Lawrence
  1977 [1964] *The Family, Sex and Marriage in England 1500–1800* (London: Weidenfeld and Nicolson).
Webster, John
  1977 *The Duchess of Malfi*, edited by John Russell Brown (Manchester: Manchester University Press).
Wells, Susan
  1985 *The Dialectics of Representation* (Baltimore: Johns Hopkins University Press).
Whigham, Frank
  1985 "Sexual and Social Mobility in *The Duchess of Malfi*." *PMLA* 100: 167–86.
Wilde, Oscar
  1970 "Phrases and Philosophies for the Use of the Young," in *"The Soul of Man Under Socialism" and Other Essays*, edited by Philip Rieff (New York: Harper and Row), 296–298.
Williams, Raymond
  1977 *Marxism and Literature* (Oxford: Oxford University Press).

The Rise of Hermeneutics and the Crisis of Ocularcentrism

Martin Jay

In one of the most recent of his many jeremiads, the French theologian Jacques Ellul unleashes his considerable wrath on what he claims is perhaps the major failing of our time: the humiliation of the word (1985). The culprit, as might be expected, is the privileging of vision, which Ellul traces as far back as the fourteenth-century Church's desperate resort to idolatry to maintain the faithful in a period of extreme crisis. Through subsequent advances in the technological means for reproducing and disseminating images—Ellul's animus against technology is well-known—the over-turning of the traditional primacy of the word has been solidified to the point of virtual irreversibility. The result, he concludes, is that we now live in an era of the "debauchery of images" (Ibid.: 119) in which a virulent hostility toward the word prevents us from accepting the truth of divine annunciation.

Ellul's contrast between idolatrous images and God's word is, of course, a time-honored one in the history of Western religion. Ellul himself traces it to such texts as the First Epistle of John with its condemnation of the "lust of the eyes" (Ibid.: 81). And he explicitly affirms what he calls "the contradiction between word and image in the Bible, contrary to the present-day tendency to meld them into one" (Ibid.: 48). Whereas some commentators contrast the Jewish taboo on graven images or seeing the face of God with the Christian toleration for the word made flesh in the incarnation, a toleration that supports the visible sacraments and the mimetic *imitatio Dei*,[1] Ellul staunchly asserts the iconoclastic impulse in both faiths. Not for him is the contention that Christianity contains both Hellenic and Hebraic impulses. Instead, he insists that like Judaism, it worships an invisible, non-theophanus God, a God who speaks to humans who only listen. Anything else, he insistently maintains, is an idolatry that culminates in what he calls, following the unlikely lead of the Situationist Guy Debord, our secularized "society of the spectacle" (Ibid.: 115; cf. Debord 1977).

Whether Ellul is fair to the complexities of the Christian attitude toward these issues I will leave to those better versed in its history and theology. How defensible his account of the fall into idolatry during the fourteenth century may be I must also permit others to decide, although it may be worth mentioning that recent readings of the balance between textuality and figurality in late medieval art have come to very different conclusions (Bryson 1981: 1ff.). Nor do I want to pause to consider the implications of Ellul's rigid distinction between the illusory "reality" presented to the eyes and a deeper "truth" known only through language, a dichotomy whose plausibility depends on a faith in divine annunciation I cannot claim to share.

What I prefer to emphasize is the paradoxical typicality of Ellul's self-described cry in the wilderness and its implications for the recent upsurge of interest in hermeneutics. For despite Ellul's apparent isolation, his diatribe against vision is itself merely an instance, perhaps more blatant and apocalyptic than some others, of a now widespread excoriation of what can be called the sins of ocularcentrism. Although Ellul does occasionally make a grudging reference to other contemporary critics of the primacy of sight, such as Paul Ricoeur, Michel Foucault and Jean-Joseph Goux,[2] he never acknowledges how widespread his own attitude now is, especially in France.

As I have argued elsewhere with special attention to the case of Foucault (1986), there has been a remarkably pervasive and increasingly vocal hostility to visual primacy in France ever since the time of Bergson. Whether in the philosophy of a Sartre or a Lyotard, the film criticism of a Metz or a Baudry, the feminism of an Irigaray or a Kofman, the theology of a Levinas or a Jabès, the literary criticism of a

---

1. See, for example, Susan A. Handelman (1982: 90). It has been argued, however, by W. J. T. Mitchell (1984: 521) that the *Imago Dei* is better understood as a "likeness" than a "picture," that is, as a spiritual similarity.
2. Ellul's animosity toward Goux is particularly striking. He dislikes the psychoanalytic dimension of Goux's *Les Iconoclastes* (1978), as well as his contention that Christianity has an affinity for imagistic representation. Foucault's analysis of the panopticon is mentioned approvingly but criticized for not stressing the evils of technology sufficiently. Ricoeur is treated more kindly.

Bataille or a Blanchot, the literature of a Robbe-Grillet or a Bonnefoy, one can find a deep-seated distrust of the privileging of sight. It is even evident in the last place one might imagine, the visual arts themselves, if the explicitly "anti-retinal" (Duchamp 1977: 65) art of Duchamp is any indication. Perhaps because of the long-standing domination of Cartesian philosophy and the no less powerful role played by spectacle and surveillance in the maintenance of centralized political power in France,[3] the reaction against ocularcentrism has taken a particularly strong turn there.

But it is evident elsewhere. German thinkers like Wagner, Nietzsche and Heidegger must be accounted important voices in the chorus of iconoclasts. There can be few more influential contributions to the critique of ocularcentrism than Heidegger's widely discussed essay on "The Age of the World Picture" (1977). Through the writings of such contemporary philosophers as Richard Rorty, this hostility to visual primacy has also spread to the English-speaking world (1979). As a result, the ground has been prepared for the reception of hermeneutics, for if we pose the good hermeneutical question, "to what question is hermeneutics the answer?,"[4] a plausible candidate would be: on what sense can we rely, if vision is no longer the noblest of the senses? No less an authority than Hans-Georg Gadamer has answered: "the primacy of hearing is the basis of the hermeneutical phenomenon" (1975: 420).[5] In other words, our increasing interest in the truths of interpretation rather than the methods of observation bespeaks a renewed respect for the ear over the eye as the organ of greatest value.

If Ellul's argument is therefore far less unusual than he implies, it is nonetheless useful to dwell on it as an exaggerated expression of many of the charges made against vision. Although as we will see momentarily, *The Humiliation of the Word* does not exhaust the list of those complaints, it does provide a remarkably extensive compendium of them. Visual images, Ellul tells us, echoing Bergson without acknowledgment, are instantaneous snapshots of external reality without any duration. The visual world is pointillist, producing an external presence without any meaningful continuity between past and future. The visual image produces an object outside the self solely there for our manipulation. "Sight," he asserts, "is the organ of efficiency"

3. For an analysis of the importance of spectacle in maintaining political power, see Jean-Marie Apostolidès (1981).
4. For a discussion of this theme, see Odo Marquard (1984). Marquard offers several useful answers (hermeneutics is a response to human finitude, to human derivativeness, to human transitoriness, to the civil war over the absolute text and to the need to break codes) but he does not investigate the crisis of ocularcentrism as another source.
5. Gadamer credits Aristotle with this insight.

(1985: 11). Images can give us nothing but external appearances and behavior, never inward meaning. Claiming to represent the truth, vision actually operates on the level of deceptive artifice. What is seen, moreover, can produce unease and disquietude but never genuine mystery. "Sight," Ellul charges, "introduces us to an unbearable shock. Reality when seen inspires horror. Terror is always visual" (Ibid.: 12).

Vision is also problematic, he continues, because its synchronic gaze produces an instantaneous totality, which forecloses the open-ended search for truth through language with its successive temporality. If we accept the evidence of our senses, most notably sight, we are lost, for "evidence is absolute evil. We must accept nothing based on evidence, contrary to Descartes' recommendation (Ibid.: 97). Vision and the fall are thus coterminous for Ellul. The contemporary version of our fallen condition is exemplified, he claims, in our worship of "Money, State and Technique—the new spiritual trinity that manifests itself in quite *visible* idols, belonging exclusively to the *visible* sphere" (Ibid.: 95).

Other examples of Ellul's critique of ocularcentrism can be adduced but by now its overdetermined status should be obvious. So too should some of its problematic implications. It is worth dwelling on them for a moment before passing on to what I think are some of the deeper sources of the anti-visual discourse that has prepared the way for the popularity of hermeneutics today. To begin with the last charge, claiming that money or technique are inherently visible idols is remarkably anachronistic, for if anything it is their growing immateriality in the age of computers and data banks that should be stressed instead (Théofilakis 1985). Indeed, as Goux has noted, it was the decision to go off the gold standard earlier this century that robbed money of whatever actual visible referent it might have in the world, making it more abstract and empty than ever (1978: 101ff.). Similarly, if Foucault's argument about the Panopticon is correct, we might say the same thing about the state. For surveillance is based on the invisibility of the all-seeing eye that normalizes and disciplines through the power of its assumed gaze. Here it is the experience of being seen (or believing that one is looked at) rather than the images one sees that maintain the power of the political order. This modern version of the old superstition of the evil eye,[6] whose roots are perhaps in the belief in an omniscient God, means that sight may indeed be complicitous with power but not in the way Ellul contends.

Ellul's contention about the inherently synchronic, pointillist, anti-historical implications of vision, made of course by many before him

---

6. For a recent discussion of its significance, see Tobin Siebers (1983). For a study of apotropaic reactions to the evil eye, see Albert M. Potts (1982).

(Jonas 1966)[7], is no less problematical. For vision is not reducible merely to the Medusan gaze freezing everything on which it fixates into death-like stillness. Kinesis is by no means foreign to ocular experience. The antithesis of the gaze is the fleeting and ephemeral glance, darting restlessly from one image to another (Bryson 1983: 87ff.). Although it may well be true that the Western cultural tradition often privileged the violent act of seizing one moment in the visual process and eternalizing it, the alternative potential in vision has never been entirely suppressed. Indeed, as we have known since the work of the French scientist Javal in 1878, the eye is always in constant flux, moving in a series of little jumps or flicks from one short-lived fixation to another (Vitz 1984: 122ff.). These saccadic eye movements, as they are called from the French *par saccades,* suggest that the notion of a frozen gaze is not a biological constant but merely one potential visual practice among others. Based implicitly on a questionable fiction of the disembodied eye gazing from afar, it fails to register what philosophers like Merleau-Ponty and others have stressed instead: the incarnated reality of vision in the corporeal and social context out of which it emerges (Merleau-Ponty 1968).

Also speaking against the static, ahistorical implications of vision attributed to it by Ellul is the counter-evidence he himself supplies by citing the Epistle of Saint John mentioned earlier concerning the "lust of the eyes." A frequent source of hostility to vision has, of course, been the anxiety unleashed by what Augustine called "ocular desire"[8] in the more ascetic, anti-hedonist critics of idolatry. What they have recognized is that desire is a source of restless dissatisfaction, preventing humans from contentment with their lot. As such, it provides a stimulus to living in an imagined future or perhaps returning to a lamented past. That is, it has a deeply temporalizing function. However we may conceptualize the multiple sources of desire—ontologically, psychologically, socially, mimetically or whatever—the recognition that vision plays a key role in generating and sustaining it means that sight, *contra* Ellul, must be understood as far more than an ahistorical valorization of presence. In fact, the current society of the spectacle is based on the stimulation of visual desire without true fulfillment in ways that suggest the complicity of sight and absence. In more positive terms, we might say that the metaphor of far-sightedness, which we use to indicate a capacity to plan for the future, also suggests a potentially temporal dimension of vision forgotten by those who emphasize only the gaze of Medusa.

7. He appends, however, a short discussion of "Sight and Movement," which complicates his argument somewhat.
8. Augustine develops the connection in chapter 35 of his *Confessions.*

Ellul's hostility to vision, like that of many others in the anti-visual discourse, rests, as we have seen, on a concomitant encomium to hearing. Whereas images are like dead objects before us, hearing, they claim, engenders an intersubjective dialogue. Whereas sight encourages the hubris of a subject who can direct his gaze wherever he chooses, hearing entails a healthy receptivity to outside influences, in particular to the voice of God, which cannot be blocked by shutting the ears as we can close our eyes. Hearing calls for a response to clarify the mystery of the interlocutor. As such, it has an ethical import absent from the subject-object manipulation fostered by vision.[9] True religion, Ellul concludes borrowing a dichotomy of Ricoeur's, is therefore derived from proclamation rather than manifestation (Ricoeur 1974).

Here too questions about these characterizations of the essential nature of our senses might be asked. As Hans Blumenberg has suggested, the modern reevaluation of intellectual curiosity as more than merely an idle vice was due in large measure to our liberation from "blind obedience" to voices from the past (Blumenberg 1983: Part III). Only when men and women were allowed the freedom to see for themselves could the modern project of emancipation from illegitimate authority begin. Only with the explicit valorization of our upright posture with its favoring of the far-seeing eyes over senses like smell or touch could human dignity be assured.[10]

Ellul, to be sure, is certainly no friend of the modern project and thus would not find Blumenberg's defense of it compelling. But even if we turn to his argument about the superior ethical implications of hearing over sight, complications arise. For, as a host of commentators have noted, there is also a potential for mutuality and intersubjectivity in visual interaction, however much it may also lead on occasion objectifying the other (Keller and Gronrowski 1983; Weinstein and Weinstein 1984: 349–362). The reciprocal glance of lovers, contrary to the description of the reifying "look" in the anti-visual discourse of critics like Sartre (1956: 310ff), need not always produce a sado-masochistic interplay of power. There is a strong potential for the opposite out-

9. Another French critic of visual primacy who has made a similar point is the Jewish phenomenologist Emmanuel Levinas. For an excellent discussion of his attitude toward the senses, see Edith Wyschograd (1980). Levinas goes beyond the privileging of hearing over sight to emphasize the importance of the caress.
10. Freud (1961: 46–47), of course, had speculated that civilization itself had begun with the abandonment of our crawling on all fours and adoption of an erect posture. On the link between the upright posture and dignity, see Ernst Bloch (1986). A much earlier connection was drawn by Herder, who was criticized for neglecting the transcendental source of rationality by Kant. For a suggestive, psychoanalytically informed treatment of their dispute, see Mark Poster (1974).

come in the exchange of visual tenderness, a potential well captured in the dual meaning of the word "regard."

In short, despite Ellul's rigid dichotomy, the implications of privileging one sense over another are not so straightforward. Rather than essentializing sight, hearing or any other sense, it is far more fruitful to tease out their multiple, even contradictory potentials and recognize that different cultures at different moments have stressed some over others. At present, if the recent popularity of hermeneutics is any indication,[11] we may well be entering a new period of distrusting vision, an era reminiscent of the other great iconoclastic moments in Western culture. Before we allow the pendulum to swing too far in the new anti-visual direction, however, it may well be worth pondering the contradictory implications of the humiliation of the eyes. Some of these have been touched on in our discussion of Ellul's extreme version of ocularphobia. In the remainder of this essay, I will focus on three others, which have particular resonance in the development of hermeneutics.

The first concerns the ancient distinction between two models of light, known as *lux* and *lumen*, a distinction ultimately abandoned because of its problematic implications. The second refers to the tradition of what can be called specularity, associated with Hellenic and idealist theories of mimesis. The third touches on what a recent writer has termed "baroque vision" or *la folie du voir* (the madness of vision).[12] In each case, a crisis in certain assumptions about vision has helped turn attention to other senses and to language. The rise of hermeneutics has been aided by this shift. But in each case, a kind of revenge has also been enacted against the over-privileging of the non-visual, so that sight has reemerged within the hermeneutic realm itself. To borrow a phrase of the literary critic Mary Ann Caws, we can now discern a return of "the eye in the text" (1981).

As Vasco Ronchi and others have pointed out (1957; Lindberg 1976), ancient theories of light, revived by medieval writers like Robert Grosseteste and modern ones like Descartes, distinguished between

---

11. If we employ an elastic concept of hermeneutics, this generalization is especially true. Susan Handelman (1982), for example, has claimed that much contemporary post-structuralist thought can be understood as a secular instantiation of the "heretic hermeneutics" she sees in the Rabbinic tradition. Although more interested in texts than dialogic interactions, this tradition is equally suspicious of the primacy of vision.

12. The origin of this term is Merleau-Ponty (1968: 25). It is the subject of an illuminating essay by Michel de Certeau (1982: 89–99). De Certeau is the figure to whom Christine Buci-Glucksmann dedicates *La folie du voir: De l'esthétique baroque* (1986).

visible *lux* and invisible *lumen*. The former normally meant the phenomenon of light experienced by the human eye, light, that is, with
color and shadow. The latter signified the physical movement of light
waves or corpuscles through transparent bodies that occurred whether
perceived or not. Here the science of optics was developed to study the
laws by which such movement necessarily took place. In the hands of a
religious thinker like Grosseteste, *lux* was understood as the profane,
natural illumination in the eyes of mere mortals, whereas *lumen* was the
primal light produced by divine radiation. In the hands of more secular thinkers like Descartes, *lux* was conceived as both the movement
or action in the luminous body and the experience of colored illumination in the eye of the beholder, while *lumen* was the corpuscular
movement through the transparent medium (Daniel 1976: 323–344).
Lumen for Descartes was the proper subject of those geometric laws of
catoptrics and dioptrics, reflection and refraction, which he claimed
could be studied deductively because they corresponded to the natural
geometry of the mind.

However the dichotomy was construed—and its confusions finally
led to its replacement by one word *luce* meaning light per se—it generally entailed some sort of hierarchical relationship between *lux* and
lumen. Echoes of the old Platonic distinction between eternal forms or
ideas and their imperfect resemblances in the world of human perception can be heard in the privileging of divine radiation or natural
optics in the mind of the viewer over mere perception. In religious
terms, the dichotomy was sometimes expressed as a distinction between a higher mirror of the soul reflecting *lumen* and a lower mirror
of the mind showing only *lux,* the latter allowing man to see only
through a glass (by way of a mirror) darkly (Goldberg 1985: 112ff).
In more secular terms, it suggested the dichotomy between rational
speculation with the mind's eye and the empirical observation of the
actual two human eyes. There was even an aesthetic version of the
contrast in the visual arts with painters like Poussin and Lebrun ex-
pounding a Cartesian denigration of color in favor of distinct and
clear form, while others like Rubens favored the restoration of color
and shadow over pure form (Bryson 1981: 60ff).

One of the most powerful sources of ocularcentrism in the West, it
might be conjectured, was precisely this conception of the dual nature
of light. For if one of its models was discredited, it was always possible
to fall back on the other as a ground of certainty. Thus, for example,
the Platonic denigration of the senses could draw on the power of
internal vision with "the third eye," as it were, as a way to the truth.
Here *lumen* was understood as superior to *lux*. Concomitantly, the em-
piricist critique of deductive reason and innate ideas could invoke the
validity of scientifically controlled observation of *lux* with the actual

eyes as the ground of secure knowledge. In both cases, the monologic vision of a subject contemplating an external object and reflecting on its reality was paramount, although there were more residues of a participatory involvement between subject and object in Platonism than in empiricism.[13]

The crisis of ocularcentrism comes when it is no longer acceptable to oscillate between these two models or to assume a necessary hierarchy between them. In religious terms, the shift involves an abandonment of the metaphysics of divine radiation. Ellul expresses this turn in his interpretation of the famous prologue to the Gospel of John, where it is written, "In the Beginning was the Word. The Word was the light of the world." He reads this passage to mean that light is merely an effect of God's word. "Nowhere is it said that God *is* the light, and even less that the light is God" (Ellul 1985: 233). Nor is it correct, he continues, to rely on the direct observation of Jesus as an historical figure, because that reduces him to a mere image of reality not an expression of truth. Only in the book of Revelation, Ellul concedes, is there an indication of the ultimate reconciliation of word and image but, until the apocalypse comes, it is necessary to ward off the deceptive lures of sight.

For more secular critics of the priority of *lux* over *lumen* or vice versa, one source of skepticism has been the very attempt to posit a hierarchy, making one notion of light essential and primary and the other apparent and secondary. For such commentators as Maurice Merleau-Ponty, it is rather their irreducible interpenetration in a chiasmic interaction that characterizes light and our experience of it (1968).[14] If such an undecidability exists in relation to illumination, then the power of the visual model, in either its speculative or its empirical guise, must be questioned as the ground of epistemological certainty. The implication is that visual perception is a problematic tool in the search for meaning or truth. Language, it is also argued, is always already intertwined with perception of whatever kind, which then opens the door for a new appreciation of its importance. One result is the increased interest in hermeneutic interpretation, which can—but by no means must—seek truth in a recollected word, rather than a visual form.[15]

13. For a subtle discussion of the differences between Greek *theoria* and modern, post-Cartesian science, see Gadamer (1975: 412ff).
14. For a psychoanalytic use of Merleau-Ponty's argument, see Jacques Lacan (1978: 67ff). Neither of them explicitly draws on the *lux/lumen* distinction, but it would be easy to interpret it in their terms.
15. It is, of course, Ricoeur (1978: 28ff) who posits the distinction between a hermeneutics of recollected meaning and a hermeneutics of suspicion. Ellul would clearly be in the former camp; the heretic hermeneuticians discussed by Handelman would belong to the latter.

A second spur to the new focus on hermeneutics emerged from the crisis in mimetic representation occasioned by the collapse of what might be called specularity as a model of knowledge. By specularity, I mean the operation of reflection in a mirror reproducing the observing subject. Rodolphe Gasché describes its importance in his recent study, *The Tain of the Mirror*, in the following terms:

> reflection signifies the process that takes place between a figure or object and its image on a polished surface. As a consequence of this optic metaphoricity, reflection, when designating the mode and operation by which the mind has knowledge of itself and its operations, becomes analogous to the process whereby physical light is thrown back on a reflecting surface. From the beginning, self-consciousness as constituted by self-reflection has been conceptualized in terms of this optic operation. . . . reflection is the structure and the process of an operation that, in addition to designating the action of a mirror reproducing an object, implies that mirror's mirroring itself, by which process the mirror is made to see itself. (1986: 16–17)

The source of this specular notion of reflection has been traced back to the Greeks by commentators like Thorlieff Boman and Susan Handelman, who pit it against the Hebraic critique of vision (Boman 1954; Handelman 1982). Speculation, they note, is, along with contemplation, the Latin translation of the Greek *theoria;* it is rooted in the word "specio," to look or behold. In more modern philosophy, the primary example of specularity can be found in the Idealist philosophers of identity, most obviously Hegel. Here the ultimate dialectical unity of Subject and Object is rooted in the *speculum* of the Absolute Spirit. As Gadamer has noted, "the mirror image is essentially connected, through the medium of the observer, with the proper vision of the thing. It has no being of its own, it is like an 'appearance' that is not itself and yet causes the proper vision to appear as a mirror image. It is like a duplication that is still only one thing" (1975: 423). Thus, in specular thought, vision is understood not in terms of an eye seeing an object exterior to itself but rather of the eye seeing itself in an infinite reflection. Speculation is closely identified with, although need not be considered perfectly equivalent to, dialectical thought, for it both acknowledges the difference between subject and image and sublates it into a grand unity, an identity of identity and non-identity.

The problematic implications of specularity have been no less evident to critics of ocularcentrism than those of the *lux/lumen* hierarchy. On one level, it evokes all of the dangers of narcissism, with its solipsistic outcome. Excessive self-absorption in personal terms has always seemed problematic, even if recent psychologists like Heinz Kohut have made a case for at least one form of a beneficent narcissism

(1966: 243–276).[16] Overly frequent mirror-gazing, medieval moralists warned, led to the deadly sin of Superbia or pride, which was a perversion of the prudential injunction to know oneself (Goldberg 1985: 122). On a more philosophical level, absolute reflection suggested the danger of assuming the metaphysical unity and homogeneity of the universe. Gasché, from his Derridean vantage point, is especially sensitive to this potential, defending as an antidote the irreducible otherness that escapes specular identity:

> The alterity that splits reflection from itself and thus makes it able to fold itself into itself—to reflect itself—is also what makes it, for structural reasons, incapable of closing upon itself. The very possibility of reflexivity is also the subversion of its own source. . . . the generalization of reflexivity becomes at the same time the end of reflection and speculation. It opens itself to the thought of an alterity, a difference that remains unaccounted for by the polar opposition of source and reflection, principle and what is derived from it, the one and the Other.   (1986: 102)

Other recent theorists outside the deconstructionist camp have also been critical of identity theory; Adorno's negative dialectics is an obvious example. So it will come as no surprise to learn that advocates of hermeneutics have recognized the dangers of specularity. Thus, Paul Ricoeur has defended the idea of metaphor as a non-pictorial resemblance that preserves difference, even as it suggests similarity (1978: 7). Gadamer has also noted that "the arguments of reflective philosophy cannot ultimately conceal the fact that there is some truth in the critique of speculative thought based on the standpoint of finite human consciousness" (1975: 308). Although, as we will soon see, there may well be a moment of specularity in certain variants of hermeneutics, the undermining of specular, idealist identity theory must be accounted one of the stimulants to its recent popularity.

A final instance of the crisis of ocularcentrism concerns what might be called the heterodox tradition of baroque vision. Here the recent work of the French philosopher Christine Buci-Glucksmann, *La raison baroque* of 1984 and *La folie du voir* of 1986, has been instrumental in illuminating its implications. Illuminate, to be sure, may not be the right word, for baroque vision entails a fascination for obscurity, shadow and the oscillation of form and formlessness. The notion of *la folie du voir* (the madness of vision) Buci-Glucksmann takes from Merleau-Ponty to signify the imbrication of viewer and viewed in a non-sublatable dialectic of imperfect specularity (1986: 70ff). Here the mirror that reflects is anamorphosistic, either concave or convex,

16. For a creative use of this argument with reference to the theme of vision, see Kathleen Woodward (1986).

manifesting only distortion or disorientation.[17] It produces a schizoid fracture between the eye and the look, which resists recuperation into a perfect reciprocity.

Baroque vision is also deeply anti-platonic, hostile to the ordered regularities of geometrical optics. As such, it opposes both Cartesian philosophy and perspective in painting. The space it inhabits is more haptic or tactile than purely visual, more plural than unified. It presents a bewildering surplus of images, an overloading of the visual apparatus. Resistant to any panoptic God's eye view, any *survol global* (Ibid.: 84),[18] baroque vision is the triumph of color over line, of opaque surface over penetrated depth. It strives for the representation of the unrepresentable and, necessarily failing to achieve it, resonates a deep melancholy, evident in the baroque fascination with the intertwining of death and desire explored by Walter Benjamin (1977).

Buci-Glucksmann, writing from a tacitly post-modernist perspective, is a celebrant of baroque vision, which she lyrically extols as a stimulant to ecstasy. But if we bracket her positive evaluation of its implications, it is possible to discern yet another source of hostility toward ocularcentrism. For the visual experience she describes can easily engender anxiety, uncertainty and dyspepsia in less ecstatic souls. One can easily imagine the response of an Ellul to her self-consciously pagan paean to visual madness. If the eye is so deceptive and the visual scene so replete with dazzling flashes of brilliance casting light only on opaque, impenetrable surfaces, recourse to another sense for security may appear an obvious antidote to its dizzying effects.

Hermeneutics, then, can be said to have flourished in the wake of an over-determined crisis of visual primacy fed by three stimuli in particular: 1) a loss of faith in the objectivist epistemology that searches for a geometrical *lumen* beneath the surface of experienced *lux* (or that claims scientific observation of *lux* alone can be the source of sense certainty); 2) a suspicion of the narcissistic and solipsistic lures of specularity and the identitarian philosophies to which it gives rise; 3) an anxiety produced by the temptations of baroque vision with its theatricalized interplay of disorienting illusions. As a result of these and other influences too numerous to mention, we have increasingly come in the twentieth century to distrust perception in general and vision in particular as the ground of knowledge, often turning instead to language in all its various guises as an alternative. Although, therefore, Ellul may be correct on one level to say we live in a culture

17. The French fascination for anamorphosis was stimulated in part by Jürgen Baltrušaitis (1984). The first edition appeared in 1955 and one can find references to it in Lyotard, Lacan and others interested in visual themes.
18. The term conjures up Merleau-Ponty's critique of "high-altitude thinking."

dominated by images rather than words, on another, he is mistaken. For one might just as easily speak of the humiliation of the eye as of the word in our increasingly iconoclastic discursive climate.[19]

If the rise of hermeneutics to its current place of honor can be traced, at least in part to this denigration of vision, it would, however, be erroneous to conclude that the age-old battle between sight and sound has been definitively resolved in favor of the latter. As W. J. T. Mitchell has recently observed,

> The history of culture is in part the story of a protracted struggle for dominance between pictorial and linguistic signs, each claiming for itself certain proprietary rights on a "nature" to which only it has access. . . . Among the most interesting and complex versions of this struggle is what might be called the relationship of subversion, in which language or imagery looks into its own heart and finds lurking there its opposite number.   (1984: 529)

Hermeneutics is in no way exempt from this pattern, as the eye reasserts itself in the text and the gaze or glance interrupts the voice.

This reassertion is evident even in the vocabulary employed by the major hermeneutic theorists. Thus, for example, for all of Heidegger's hostility to the technological world picture and his frequent use of aural metaphors,[20] he nonetheless supports an alternative notion of circumspect vision called *Umsicht* as a way to describe *Dasein*'s situatedness in the world.[21] And despite his celebrated emphasis on language as the "house of Being," he uses such visual metaphors as a *Lichtung* (clearing) to indicate the way in which Being manifests itself, rather than is merely proclaimed.

As for Gadamer, his emphasis on the historical fusion of horizons shows how indebted he remains to the intertwining of sight and sound. "The horizon," he acknowledges, "is the range of vision that includes everything that can be seen from a particular vantage point. . . . A person who has no horizon is a man who does not see far enough and hence means not to be limited to what is nearest, but to be able to see beyond it (1975: 269). Key hermeneutic concepts like *Bildung* (cultivation), Gadamer recognizes, derive in part from the ancient, mystical tradition of the imitation of God's image. *Bild,* he notes, means both *Nachbild* or copy and *Vorbild* or model (1975: 12).

In addition to these obvious visual residues in the terminology of hermeneutics, which might be attributed more to the pervasiveness

---

19. Goux (1978) makes a strong case for the pervasive hostility to images in modern art, economics, religion and psychoanalysis.

20. For a discussion of Heidegger's use of aural metaphors, see John D. Caputo (1985: 255).

21. For an interesting comparison of Heidegger's use of *Umsicht* with Wittgenstein's notion of *Übersicht*, see Nicholas F. Gier (1981: 80ff).

of ocular metaphors in Western languages than to any deep-seated affinity between vision and interpretation, there are more fundamental ways in which the word and the image are intertwined in certain variants of contemporary hermeneutics. If, for example, we take the critical hermeneutics developed by Jürgen Habermas in his fraternal debate with Gadamer (Jay 1982), the continuing importance of what might be called the objectifying, distantiating implications of the *lumen/lux* tradition might be discerned. For in his analysis of the interplay between explanation and understanding in critical social theory, Habermas defends the necessity of some monologic, subject-object method in making sense of the ways in which contemporary society acts as if it were a "second nature."[22] That is, because we live in a society without the immediacy, transparency and communicative rationality of perfect intersubjectivity, the tools of explanatory distantiation typical of natural science cannot be given up in exchange for a method wholly dependent on empathetic understanding. If society operates at least in part like a reified second nature, then it is wrong to wish this reality away in the name of a hermeneutic community always already in place. Indeed, without the tension between explanation and interpretation—sight and hearing, if you will—there can be no genuine critique of the mixed quality of our society. Each is a necessary check to the totalizing pretensions of the other.

As for specularity in hermeneutics, Gadamer himself admits that it remains an inevitable impulse in language. After a long consideration of Hegel's conflation of speculation and dialectics, which he condemns for its indebtedness to the Greek philosophy of logos, he nonetheless acknowledges that

> language itself, however, has something speculative about it in quite a different sense—not only in that sense intended by Hegel of the instinctive pre-formation of the reflexive relationship of logic—but, rather, as the realization of the meaning, as the event of speech, of communication, of understanding. Such a realization is speculative, in that the finite possibilities of the word are oriented towards the sense intended, as towards the infinite. . . . Even in the most everyday speech there appears an element of speculative reflection, namely the intangibility of that which is still purest reproduction of meaning. (1975: 426)

If I understand Gadamer correctly, his communicative rather than logocentric notion of specularity emphasizes the always, already linguistic quality of thought, which prevents a gap between an idea in

22. Habermas's most sustained discussion of the need to use both interpretative and explanatory models can be found in *Zur Logik der Sozialwissenschaften* (1967). The term "second nature" is, of course, Hegel's and is revived in the Hegelian Marxist tradition begun by Lukács.

the mind and its verbal expression. "To be expressed in language," he notes, "does not mean that a second being is acquired. The way in which a thing presents itself is, rather, part of its own being. Thus everything that is language has a speculative unity: it contains a distinction between its being and the way in which it presents itself, but this is a distinction that is really not a distinction at all" (Ibid.: 482).

In addition to the speculative dimension of language as the realization of meaning in the mirrored reproduction of word and idea, at least as a teleological impulse, there is another, more productive dimension, which Kathleen Wright highlights in her subtle discussion of the speculative structure of language in Gadamer. "That one and the same text can be different and mean more," she notes, "is because language in the interpretative conversation, like the mirror image, reflects back into the text and brings more of its meaning and truth into being" (1986: 211). In other words, in a true dialogue, the mirroring effect of question and answer, or give and take, produces a richer and more developed truth than was there before. Contrary to the model of the divine word spoken to the passive listener defended by Ellul,[23] Gadamer's more specular notion of language allows for a less authoritarian, less past-oriented hermeneutics, which recognizes the moment of what he calls application as an essential dimension of the production of truth. Here the non-logocentric, non-Hegelian specularity he finds in language is a source of its strength, not its weakness.

If we combine this claim for a modified specular moment in hermeneutics with the Habermasian argument developed above, an argument stressing the usefulness of at least some objectifying visual distantiation in explanation, the following conclusion can be drawn. Within linguistic interaction, there may be an implicit teleology towards specular hermeneutic consensus in which transparent intersubjective communication is achieved but, in our current world of distorted and impeded communicative exchange, it is necessary to assume, in an "as if" manner, the possibility of a monological, objectifying gaze in order to examine the blockages. Systematic social obstacles to the realization of linguistic specularity in Gadamer's sense of the term can only be observed from an assumed position of exteriority, even if their removal may well entail action produced by intersubjective consensus and the fusion of horizons. Although it may be impossible ever to achieve such a perfectly objective, synoptic perspective and leave behind our embeddedness in the flesh of the world, the strategy of seeking it may be necessary to realize more adequately

---

23. To be fair to Ellul, he does talk of dialogue, but it would be difficult to call it symmetrical.

the condition of nonlogocentric specularity Gadamer, perhaps too quickly, posits of language as such.

If, however, combining these two perspectives leaves us with this essentially Habermasian conclusion, turning instead to the implications of our third ocular model, that of baroque vision in Buci-Glucksmann's sense, will suggest how difficult its achievement may be. For although she too is interested in the eye in the text, her attitude toward its proper place is very different from those of the more optimistic hermeneuticians. Her exploration of baroque culture focuses on its visual aspect but also includes an arresting discussion of its linguistic dimension, which she identifies with its interest in rhetoric. "Baroque rhetoric," she writes, "inverts, overturns, the traditional schemas and hierarchies between image and concept. The figure no longer 'represents' the concept because the 'concept'—*le concetto*—is itself only a knot of words and images, a figured expression" (1986: 134).[24] This knot, she insists, always resists unravelling to reveal a transparent meaning. It operates instead chiasmically to defeat any specular sublation or mirroring of differences. Like Gasché, she recognizes the materiality of the mirror, its "tain" or silver backing, which pure specularity always forgets.

Explicitly taking issue with Merleau-Ponty's optimistic hermeneutic belief in the saturation of the world with meaning, Buci-Glucksmann understands the implications of baroque rhetoric to be the maintenance of opacity and superficiality. Defying the search for hidden meanings and deep structures, the rhetoric of the baroque is like its visual madness: anamorphosistic, undecidable and resistant to any plenitude. Allegory rather than symbolism is its essential mode because, as Benjamin knew well, allegory expresses the impossibility of a perfect unity between image and concept. The specular moment in language emphasized by Gadamer is thus called into question by the allegorical rhetoric and visual theatricality of the baroque. What is left instead, Buci-Glucksmann concludes, are "palimpsests of the unseeable (*irregardable*)" (Ibid.: 197).

Her celebration of this heterodox tradition of baroque vision and rhetoric culminates in its extension into the modern era, beginning with Baudelaire, where it competes with the alternative visual modernisms of Cartesian subject-object perspectivalism and Hegelian logocentric specularity. It might be more accurate to identify it with the post-modern or at least the post-structuralist movement out of which

24. For another consideration of the interpenetration of words and images in language, which comes to similar conclusions, see Jean-François Lyotard (1971). In a very different way, the importance of the visual in rhetoric is suggested by Frances A. Yates (1966) in her classic study.

Buci-Glucksmann clearly emerges. However we construe it, this third model of the eye in the text provides ample evidence that the crisis of ocularcentrism is by no means resolved, even in our seemingly icono-clastic era of hermeneutic suspicion of the primacy of the image. Ellul to the contrary notwithstanding, the age-old battle between the eye and the ear is far from being decided one way or the other. And per-haps more important, it would be unwise to wish, as Ellul seems to do, for a clear-cut victory of either side. For it is in the remarkably fluid and complex interaction of the two that one of the great motors of human culture can be discerned. Humbling the image is no antidote to humiliating the word. It is far healthier to nurture in both what is best called a mutual regard.

References

Apostolidès, Jean-Marie
   1981 *Le roi-machine: Spectacle et politique au temps de Louis XIV* (Paris: Minuit).
Baltrušaitis, Jürgen
   1984 *Anamorphoses: Les perspectives dépravées* (Paris: Flammarion).
Benjamin, Walter
   1977 *Origin of German Tragic Drama*, translated by John Osborne, introduction by George Steiner (London: NLB).
Bloch, Ernst
   1986 *Natural Law and Human Dignity*, translated by Dennis J. Schmidt (Cambridge, MA: MIT Press).
Blumenberg, Hans
   1983 *The Legitimacy of the Modern Age*, Pt. 3, translated by Robert M. Wallace (Cambridge, MA: MIT Press), 227–453.
Boman, Thorlieff
   1954 *Hebrew Thought Compared with Greek* (Philadelphia: Westminster Press).
Bryson, Norman
   1981 *Word and Image: French Painting of the Ancien Régime* (Cambridge: Cambridge University Press).
   1983 *Vision and Painting: The Logic of the Gaze* (New Haven: Yale University Press).
Buci-Glucksmann, Christine
   1984 *La raison baroque: De Baudelaire à Benjamin* (Paris: Galilée).
   1986 *La folie du voir: De l'esthétique baroque* (Paris: Galilée).
Caputo, John D.
   1985 "The Thought of Being and the Conversation of Mankind: The Case of Heidegger and Rorty," in *Hermeneutics and Praxis*, edited by Robert Hollinger (Notre Dame, IN: University of Notre Dame), 248–271.
Caws, Mary Ann
   1981 *The Eye in the Text: Essays on Perception, Mannerist to Modern* (Princeton: Princeton University Press).
Daniel, Stephen H.
   1976 "The Nature of Light in Descartes' Physics," *The Philosophical Forum* 7: 323–344.
De Certeau, Michel
   1982 "La folie de la vision," *Esprit* 66 (June): 89–99.

Debord, Guy
1977 *Society of the Spectacle* (Detroit: Black & Red).
Duchamp, Marcel
1977 *Ingénieur du temps perdu: Entretiens avec Pierre Cabanne* (Paris: P. Belfond).
Ellul, Jacques
1985 *The Humiliation of the Word*, translated by Joyce Main Hanks (Grand Rapids, MI: Eerdmans).
Freud, Sigmund
1961 *Civilization and Its Discontents*, translated by James Strachey (New York: W. W. Norton).
Gadamer, Hans-Georg
1975 *Truth and Method* (New York: The Seabury Press).
Gasché, Rodolphe
1986 *The Tain of the Mirror: Derrida and the Philosophy of Reflection* (Cambridge, MA: Harvard University Press).
Gier, Nicholas F.
1981 *Wittgenstein and Phenomenology: A Comparative Study of the Later Wittgenstein, Husserl, Heidegger, and Merleau-Ponty* (Albany: SUNY Press).
Goldberg, Benjamin
1985 *The Mirror and Man* (Charlottesville: University Press of Virginia).
Goux, Jean-Joseph
1978 *Les Iconoclastes* (Paris: Seuil).
Habermas, Jürgen
1967 *Zur Logik der Sozialwissenschaften, Philosophische Rundschau*, Supp. 5 (February).
Handelman, Susan A.
1982 *The Slayers of Moses: The Emergence of Rabbinic Interpretation in Modern Literary Theory* (Albany: State University of New York Press).
Heidegger, Martin
1977 "The Age of the World Picture," in *The Question Concerning Technology and Other Essays*, translated with introduction by William Lovitt (New York: Garland), 115–154.
Jay, Martin
1982 "Should Intellectual History Take a Linguistic Turn? Reflections on the Habermas-Gadamer Debate," in *Modern European Intellectual History: Reappraisals and New Perspectives*, edited by Dominick LaCapra and Steven L. Kaplan (Ithaca: Cornell University Press), 86–110.
1986 "In the Empire of the Gaze: Foucault and the Denigration of Vision in Twentieth-Century French Thought," in *Foucault: A Critical Reader*, edited by David Couzens Hoy (London: Basil Blackwell), 175–204.
Jonas, Hans
1966 "The Nobility of Sight: A Study in the Phenomenology of the Senses," in *The Phenomenon of Life: Toward a Philosophical Biology* (New York: Harper & Row), 135–152.
Keller, Evelyn Fox and Christine Grontowski
1983 "The Mind's Eye," in *Discovering Reality: Feminist Perspectives on Epistemology, Metaphysics, Methodology and Philosophy of Science*, edited by Sandra Harding and Merrill B. Hintikka (Boston: D. Reidel).
Kohut, Heinz
1966 "Forms and Transformations of Narcissism," *Journal of the American Psychoanalytic Association* 14: 243–276.

Lacan, Jacques
   1978 *The Four Fundamental Concepts of Psycho-analysis*, edited by Jacques-Alain Miller, translated by Alan Sheridan (New York: W. W. Norton).
Lindberg, David C.
   1976 *Theories of Vision from Al-Kindi to Kepler* (Chicago: University of Chicago Press).
Lyotard, Jean-François
   1971 *Discours, Figure* (Paris: Klincksieck).
Marquard, Odo
   1984 "The Question, To What Question is Hermeneutics the Answer?" in *Contemporary German Philosophy*, Vol. 4, edited by Darrel E. Christensen, et al. (University Park: Pennsylvania State University Press), 9–31.
Merleau-Ponty, Maurice
   1968 *The Visible and the Invisible*, edited by Claude Lefort, translated by Alphonso Lingis (Evanston, IL: Northwestern University Press).
Mitchell, W. J. T.
   1984 "What Is an Image?," *New Literary History* 15(3): 503–537.
Poster, Mark
   1974 "Kant's Crooked Stick," *The Psychoanalytic Review* 61(3): 475–480.
Potts, Albert M.
   1982 *The World's Eye* (Lexington: University Press of Kentucky).
Ricoeur, Paul
   1970 *Freud and Philosophy: An Essay on Interpretation*, translated by Denis Savage (New Haven: Yale University Press).
   1974 "Manifestation et proclamation," in *Le Sacré*, edited by Enrico Castelli (Paris: Aubler).
   1978 *The Rule of Metaphor: Multidisciplinary Studies of the Creation of Meaning in Language*, translated by Robert Czerny, with Kathleen McLaughlin and John Costello (Toronto: University of Toronto).
Ronchi, Vasco
   1957 *Optics: The Science of Vision*, translated by Edward Rosen (New York: New York University Press).
Rorty, Richard
   1979 *Philosophy and the Mirror of Nature* (Princeton: Princeton University Press).
Sartre, Jean-Paul
   1956 *Being and Nothingness: An Essay on Phenomenological Ontology*, translated with introduction by Hazel E. Barnes (New York: Philosophical Library).
Siebers, Tobin
   1983 *The Mirror of Medusa* (Berkeley: University of California Press).
Théofilakis, Élie, ed.
   1985 *Modernes et après? Les Immatèriaux* (Paris: Autrement).
Vitz, Paul C. and Arnold B. Glimcher
   1984 *Modern Art and Modern Science: The Parallel Analysis of Vision* (New York: Praeger).
Weinstein, Deena and Michael Weinstein
   1984 "On the Visual Constitution of Society: The Contributions of Georg Simmel and Jean-Paul Sartre," *History of European Ideas* 5: 349–362.
Woodward, Kathleen
   1986 "The Look and the Gaze: Narcissism, Aggression and Aging," Working Paper #7 of the Center for Twentieth Century Studies (Fall).
Wright, Kathleen
   1986 "Gadamer: The Speculative Structure of Language," in *Hermeneutics and*

Modern Philosophy, edited by Brice R. Wachterhauser (Albany: State University of New York Press), 193–218.

Wyschograd, Edith
    1980 "Doing Before Hearing: On the Primacy of Touch," in *Textes pour Emmanuel Levinas*, edited by François Laruelle (Paris: J.-M. Place), 179–203.

Yates, Frances A.
    1966 *The Art of Memory* (Chicago: University of Chicago Press).

Interpretation, Rhetoric, Ideology

The Ideology of the Aesthetic

Terry Eagleton

The concept of interpretation, as we know it today, perhaps dates back no further than the nineteenth century. This, in my view, is not going back far enough, in any discussion of the relations of criticism and power. For before "interpretation" in its modern hermeneutical sense was brought to birth, a whole apparatus of power in the field of culture was already firmly in place and had been for about a century. This was not an apparatus which determined the power-effects of particular readings but one which determined the political meaning and function of "culture" as such. Its name was and is aesthetics; and part of my argument in this paper will be that it is effectively synonymous with a shift in the very concept of power, which we can characterize as a transition to the notion of hegemony. "Interpretation" might seem a broader, more generous concept than the aesthetic, traversing as it does the border between "artistic" and other texts; but it will also be part of my argument that the "aesthetic," at least in its original formulations, has little enough to do with art. It denotes instead a whole program of social, psychical and political reconstruction on the part of the early European bourgeoisie; and it is to an examination of some of the elements of that program I now want to turn.

Aesthetics is born as a discourse of the body. The vital distinction the term signifies for its inventor, Alexander Baumgarten, is not between art and life but between the material and the immaterial: between things and thoughts, sensations and ideas, what is bound up with our creaturely life of perception as opposed to what belongs to the mind.

It is as though philosophy suddenly wakes up to the fact that there is a dense, swarming territory beyond its own mental enclave, threatening to fall utterly outside its sway. That territory is nothing less than the whole of our sensate life—the business of affections and aversions, of how the world strikes the body on its sensory surfaces, of what takes root in the guts and the gaze and all that arises from our most banal, biological insertion into the world. The aesthetic is thus the first stirrings of a primitive, incipient materialism, politically quite indispensable: for how can everything that belongs to a society's somatic, sensational life—"experience," in a word—be allowed to fall outside the circuit of its reason? Must the life of the body be given up on, as the sheer unthinkable other of thought or are its mysterious ways somehow mappable by intellection in what would then prove a wholly novel science, that of sensibility itself? Doesn't Enlightenment rationality need some kind of supplement—some concrete logic at its disposal which would chart from the inside the very structures of breathing, sentient life?

For Baumgarten, aesthetic cognition mediates between the generalities of reason and the particulars of sense; the aesthetic partakes in the perfection of reason but in a "confused" mode. Aesthetics is thus the "sister" of logic, a kind of inferior feminine analogue of reason, at the level of material life. As a kind of concrete thought or sensuous analogue of the concept, it partakes at once of the rational and the real, suspended between the two in the manner of the Lévi-Straussian myth. Only by such a concrete logic will the ruling class be able to understand its own history; for history, like the body, is a matter of sensuous particulars, in no sense merely derivable from rational principles.

Dominion over all inferior powers, Baumgarten writes, belongs to reason; but such dominion, he warns, must never degenerate into simple tyranny. The aesthetic, in other words, marks an historic shift from what we might now, in Gramscian terms, call coercion to hegemony, ruling and informing our sensuous life from within while allowing it to thrive in all its relative autonomy. Within the dense welter of that life, with all its alarmingly amorphous flux, certain objects stand out in a kind of ideality akin to rational perfection and this is the beautiful. The major aesthetician of the twentieth century might thus be said to be the later Edmund Husserl, whose phenomenology will seek to disclose the formal, rational structures of the *Lebenswelt* in what he calls a new "universal science of subjectivity." (It was not, however, new in the least.)

Schiller's project in the *Aesthetic Education of Man* is similarly to soften up Kant's imperious tyranny of reason in the direction of social hegemony. For if reason is simply at war with Nature and the flesh, how is it ever to take root in the body of lived experience? How is theory to become ideology? Reason will only secure its sway in consensual rather than coercive terms: it must collude with the senses it subdues rather than ride roughshod over them. In a movement of deconstruction, the aesthetic breaks the imperious dominion of the sense-drive not by some external dictate but from within, as a fifth columnist working with the grain of what it combats. Humanity, Schiller remarks, must "take the war against Matter into the very territory of Matter itself." It is easier, in other words, for reason to repress sensuous Nature if it has already been busy eroding and subliming it from the inside and this is the task of the aesthetic. Schiller is shrewd enough to see that Kant's stark imperatives are by no means the best way of subjugating a recalcitrant material world; his Duty, like some paranoid absolutist monarch, puts too little trust in the masses' generous instincts for conformity to it. What is needed instead is what Schiller calls the "aesthetic modulation of the psyche," which is to say a full-blooded project of fundamental ideological reconstruction.

This program consists in the installation of what the eighteenth century calls "manners," which provides the crucial hinge between ethics and aesthetics, virtue and beauty. Manners means that meticulous disciplining of the body which converts morality to style, aestheticizing virtue and so deconstructing the opposition between the proper and the pleasurable. In these regulated forms of civilized conduct, a pervasive aestheticizing of social practices gets under way: moral-ideological imperatives no longer impose themselves with the leaden weight of some Kantian Ought but infiltrate the very textures of lived experience as tact and know-how, intuitive good sense or inbred decorum. Ethical ideology loses its unpleasantly coercive force and reappears as a principle of spontaneous consensus. The subject itself is accordingly aestheticized: like the work of art, the subject introjects the Law which governs it as the very principle of its free identity and so, in Althusserian phrase, comes to work "all by itself," without need of political constraint. That "lawfulness without a law" which Kant will identify in the aesthetic is first of all a question of the social *Lebenswelt*, which seems to work with all the rigorous encodement of a rational law but where such law is never quite abstractable from the sensuously particular conduct which instantiates it. The bourgeoisie has won certain historic victories within the political state; but the problem with such conflicts is that, in rendering the Law perceptible as a discourse, they threaten to denaturalize it. Once the Law is objectified by political struggle, it becomes itself the subject of contestation. Legal, political and economic transformations must therefore be translated into new kinds of spontaneous social practice, which in a kind of creative repression or amnesia can afford to forget the very laws they obey.

Structures of power must become structures of feeling and the name for this mediation from property to propriety is the aesthetic. If politics and aesthetics are deeply at one, it is because pleasurable conduct is the true index of successful social hegemony, self-delight the very mark of social submission. What matters in aesthetics is not art but this whole project of reconstructing the human subject from the inside, informing its subtlest affections and bodily responses with this law which is not a law. The moment when moral actions can be classified chiefly as "agreeable" and "disagreeable" marks a certain mature point of evolution in the history of a ruling class. Once the dust and heat of its struggles for power have subsided, moral questions which were then necessarily cast in stridently absolutist terms may now as it were crystallize spontaneously into that political unconscious we call the aesthetic. Once new ethical habits have been installed, the sheer quick feel or impression of an object will be enough for sure judgment, shortcircuiting discursive labor and thus mystifying the laws which regulate it. If the aesthetic is every bit as coercive as the most barbaric law—for there is a right and wrong to taste quite as absolute as the death sentence—this is not, by any means, the way it feels. "It has been the misfortune . . . of this age," writes Burke in *The French Revolution*, "that everything is to be discussed, as if the constitution of our country was to be always a subject rather of altercation, than enjoyment" (188). The true lawfulness without law is the English Constitution, at once ineluctable and unformalizable. And if one wanted to give a name to the single most important nineteenth-century instrument of the kind of hegemony in question, one which never ceases to grasp universal reason in concretely particular style, uniting within its own depth an economy of abstract form with the effect of spontaneous experience, one might do worse than propose the realist novel.

If beauty is a consensual power, then the sublime—that which crushes us into admiring submission—is coercive. The distinction between the beautiful and the sublime is in part one between woman and man and partly that between what Louis Althusser has called the ideological and repressive state apparatuses. The problem for Burke is how these two are to be reconciled; for the authority we respect we do not·love and the one we love we do not respect. Only love—consent, collusion—will win us to the Law and this will erode the Law to nothing. A Law which engages, hegemonically, our intimate affections will have the laxness of the mother; one, on the other hand, which inspires in us filial fear will tend to alienate such affection and spur us to oedipal resentment. Casting around desperately for a reconciling image, Burke feebly offers us the grandfather, authoritative yet feebly feminized by age. Authority lives in a kind of ceaseless self-undoing, as coercion and consent reinforce yet undermine one another in a cat-

and-mouse game. An ennervated feminine beauty must be regularly stiffened by a masculine sublime whose terrors must then be instantly defused, in an endless rhythm of erection and detumescence. The Law is male but hegemony is a woman and the aesthetic would be their felicitous marriage. For Burke, the revolutionaries who seek to "strip all the decent drapery of life" from political power, de-aestheticize it, are in danger of exposing the phallus of this transvestite law, which decks itself out as a woman. Power will thus cease to be aestheticized and what will grapple us to it will be less our affections than the gallows. The revolutionaries are protestant extremists who would believe, insanely, that men and women could look on this terrible law and still live, who would strip from it every decent mediation and consoling illusion, break every representational icon and extirp every pious practice, thus leaving the wretched citizen naked and vulnerable before the full sadistic blast of authority.

The problem with the bourgeoisie, as Charles Taylor has well argued, is that their obsession with freedom is incompatible with feeling at home in the world. Bourgeois ideology thus continually violates one of the central functions of ideology in general, which is to make the subject feel that the world is not an altogether inhospitable place. When bourgeois science contemplates the world, what it knows is an impersonal realm of causes and processes quite independent of the subject and so quite indifferent to value. But the fact that we can know the world at all, however grim the news which this cognition has to deliver, must surely entail some primordial harmony between ourselves and it. For there to be knowledge in the first place, however gloomy, our faculties must be somehow marvellously, unpredictably adjusted to material reality; and for Kant it is the contemplation of this pure form of our cognition, of its very enabling conditions, which is the aesthetic. The aesthetic is simply the state in which common knowledge, in the very act of reaching out to its object, suddenly arrests and rounds upon itself, forgetting its referent for a magical moment and attending instead, in a wondering flash of self-estrangement, to the miraculously convenient way in which its inmost structure seems somehow geared to the comprehension of the real. The aesthetic is simply cognition viewed in a different light, caught in the act, so that, in this little crisis or revelatory breakdown of our cognitive routines, not *what* we know but *that* we know becomes the deepest, most delightful mystery. The aesthetic, as the moment of letting the world go and clinging instead to the formal act of knowing it, promises to re-unite those poles of subject and object, value and fact, reason and nature, which bourgeois social practice has riven apart; and this is to say that for Kant the aesthetic is nothing less than, in a precise Lacanian sense, the Imaginary. The Kantian subject of taste, who misperceives as a quality of the aesthetic representation what is in fact a delightful coordination of its own powers and who projects onto a blind, mechanical universe a figure of idealized unity, is in effect the infantile narcissist of the Lacanian mirror phase. If human subjects are to feel themselves sufficiently centered and *heimlich* in the Kantian world of pure reason to act as moral agents, there must be somewhere in reality some image of that ethical purposiveness which, in the Kantian realm of practical reason, falls outside of representation altogether and so is not available as a sensuous, which is to say an ideological, force. That image is the aesthetic, in which a mutual mirroring of ego and world is allowed to occur—in which, uniquely, the world is for once given *for* the subject. This, for a bourgeois practice which continually rips humanity from Nature, thus rendering the subject sickeningly contingent at the very acme of its powers, is an essential ideological register. That it should not, for Kant, domesticate and naturalize the subject *too* much, thus fatally slackening its dynamic enterprise, is one of the countervailing functions of the sublime (as are the sublime's *disciplinary* tasks of chastening and humbling this otherwise too inertly complacent subject).

Since the Imaginary of the aesthetic is a matter of universal rather than individual subjectivity, the aesthetic provides a resolution to the tormenting question: where can one locate community in bourgeois society? The problem is that, of the two traditional answers—the state or civil society—neither is adequate. The dilemma of bourgeois civil society is that its very atomizing individualism and competitiveness threatens to destroy the ideological solidarity necessary for its political reproduction. There is, in other words, no longer any obvious way of moving from social practices to culture or, as the philosophers would say, from facts to values. If you derived your values from the marketplace, you would end up with all the worst kinds of values; the *non*-derivability of values from facts in bourgeois society is thus a necessary structural feature of it. Values are indeed related to social practice but precisely by their contradictory dislocation from it; it is materially necessary that ideological values should be related to social facts in such a way as to appear non-derivable from them. At the same time, of course, such a hiatus between practices and values is clearly ideologically disabling. You might thus turn to the state as the locus of ideal unity, as many nineteenth-century thinkers did; but the problem here is that the state is ultimately a coercive power. Solidarity thus needs a third realm and discovers it in the universal subjectivity of the aesthetic. An intimately interpersonal *Gemeinschaft* is mapped onto a brutally egoistic, appetitive *Gesellschaft*. The aesthetic will secure the consensual hegemony which neither the coercive state nor a fragmented civil society can achieve. Paradoxically, it is in the most apparently frail, private and intangible of our feelings that we blend most harmoniously with one another—at once an astonishingly optimistic and bitterly pessimistic doctrine. On the one hand: "How marvellous that consensual intersubjectivity can be found installed in the very inwardness of the subject!" On the other hand: "How sickeningly precarious human unity must be, if one can finally root it in nothing more resilient than the vagaries of aesthetic judgment!"

Aesthetic propositions for Kant appear to be constative descriptions of what is the case but conceal beneath this surface grammar their essentially performative nature as emotive utterances. In this sense, one might claim, they are the very paradigm of ideological enunciations. Like the Kantian aesthetic utterance, the ideological proposition conceals an essentially emotive (subject-oriented) content within an apparently referential form, characterizing the "lived relation" of a speaker to the world in appearing to characterize the world. At the same time, however, such judgments, like Kantian taste, are in no sense merely "subjective." The rhetorical move which here converts an utterance from the emotive to the referential is a sign of the fact that certain attitudes are at once "merely subjective" and somehow ineluctable. In this sense, Kantian aesthetics move us a little way towards a materialist conception of ideology. Given the nature of our faculties, Kant thinks, it is necessary that certain subjective judgments elicit the universal consent of others and this is the aesthetic. Given certain material conditions, it is necessary that certain subjective responses be invested with all the force of universally valid propositions and this is the ideological. In both the aesthetic and the ideological, subjective and universal coalesce: a viewpoint is at once mine and an utterly subjectless truth, at once constitutive of the very depths of the individual subject and yet a universal law, though a law so self-evidently inscribed in the material phenomena themselves as to be quite untheorizable. In ideology and the aesthetic we stay with the thing itself, preserved in all its concrete materiality rather than dissolved into its abstract conditions; yet this very materiality has all the compelling logic of a universal rational law, appearing as it does like a kind of incarnate maxim. The ideologico-aesthetic is that indeterminate region in which abstractions seemed flushed with irreducible specificity and accidental particulars raised to pseudo-cognitive status. Ideology constantly promises to go beyond the particular to some debatable proposition but that proposition continually eludes formalization and disappears back into the things themselves. What is from one viewpoint an absolute rightness is from another viewpoint just something I happen to feel; but that "happen" is *essential*. Aesthetic pleasure cannot be *compelled*; and yet somehow it is, for all that. The ethico-aesthetic subject—the subject of bourgeois hegemony—is the one who, in Kant's phrase, gives the law to itself and who thus lives its necessity as freedom. The pleasures of the aesthetic are in this sense masochistic: as with bourgeois ideology, the delight that matters is our free complicity with what subjects us, so that we can "work all by ourselves."

The problem with such freedom, however, at least for Kant, is that it is entirely noumenal. It cannot be *represented* and is thus at root anti-aesthetic. This is a dilemma which dogs Hegel too. Scornful of aesthetic intuitionism as any kind of metaphysical grounding of bourgeois society, Hegel's theoretical program signifies an heroic eleventh-hour attempt to redeem that society for theoretical reason. But any such project of rational totalization will be forced into a convoluted discursivity which threatens to limit its *ideological* effectiveness. The Hegelian system, as Kierkegaard complained more than once, simply cannot be *lived;* and Hegel is alarmingly cavalier about the necessities of aesthetic representation, in a protestant iconclastic manner close to Kant's own. Hegel gravely underestimates the ideological force of sensuous representation. The bourgeoisie are thus caught in a cleft stick between a theoretical self-grounding too discursive for representation and thus ideologically crippled from the outset and an ideologically seductive aestheticization of reason (Schelling, Fichte) which spurns all rigorous conceptual totalization and leaves the bourgeois social order theoretically disarmed.

Hegel does, however, score some notable advances. For one thing, he spots idealist feebleness of Kant's aesthetic *Gemeinschaft* and cranks the whole argument down to the institutional level of civil society. Like Gramsci after him, he thus shifts the whole concept of culture away from its aesthetic to its everyday or anthropological sense, rooting his ideal totality in the unpromising institutions of civil society itself and so like Gramsci effecting a vital transition from *ideology* to *hegemony*. Unlike Kant, Hegel does not commit the naive error of seeking to root spiritual community in anything as hollow and slippery as disinterestedness; on the contrary, the particularism of private property, the family, abstract right and so on will become the very basis of social totality, once they have dialectically transcended their partiality into the unity of the state. The problem with this solution, on the other hand, is that it is merely unbelievable: there is no way the bourgeoisie can anchor ideological harmony in civil society, even if Hegel is right that this is what is *needed*. If political unity is to be derived from the divisions of civil society, an intricately dialectical form of rationality will be necessary, a good deal less blankly portentous than Schellingian intuitionism; yet by the same token this rationality will slip through the net of sensuous representation and leave itself ideologically disarmed. Indeed the very form of Hegel's work, of cognition itself, is in a way anti-representational. It is as though the Kantian text is still struggling to handle in "realist" or representational style that utterly unrepresentable "thing" which will finally be encircled only by a full-blooded break to philosophical modernism—to the kind of theoretical work which, like the symbolist poem, generates itself entirely out of its own substance, has its tail in its own mouth, projects its referent out of its own formal devices and escapes in its absolute self-groundedness the slightest taint of external determination. In all this, Hegel is at one with Schelling; but unlike Schelling he refuses the supreme concretization of this mode of thought in the work of art itself, which is at least a little more ideologically persuasive than slogans such as "the rational is the real."

What Hegel does marvellously succeed at, however, is in reconciling the conflict between the bourgeoisie's drive for freedom and its desire for an expressive unity with the world—for, in a word, the Imaginary. The dilemma of the bourgeois subject is that its freedom and autonomy, of its very essence, put it tragically at odds with Nature and so cut from beneath its feet any ground by which it might be validated in its being. The more full-bloodedly the subject realizes its free essence, the more alienated and contingent it accordingly becomes. Hegel solves this problem at a stroke by projecting subjectivity into the object itself: why fear to unite with a world which is itself free subjectivity? If Hegel assigns the aesthetic a lowly status, it is in part because, in uniting subject and object in this way, he has already secretly aestheticized the whole of reality.

If German rationalism, with Baumgarten, needed an aesthetic supplement to eke itself out, one might claim that British empiricism was all along too aesthetic for its own good. *Its* problem was not how to descend from the heady heights of reason to inform and encompass the sensuous but how to drag itself free of the clammy embrace of the sensuously immediate to rise to something a little more conceptually dignified. How is a thought so thoroughly sensationalized to break the hold of the body over it, disentangle itself from the dense thicket of perception and launch itself out into theoretical reflection? The answer of the British "moral sense" theorists was that there was really no need. The "moral sense" is that spontaneous, well-nigh somatic impulse within us which links us in the very textures of our sensibility to some providential social whole. If that social whole is now frustratingly opaque to totalizing theory, we can find its trace on the body itself and its spontaneous affections and aversions. In one sense, this is a clear confession of ideological defeat: incapable of extrapolating its desired harmony from the anarchy of the marketplace, the bourgeoisie are forced to root it instead in the stubborn self-evidence of the gut. In another sense, it provides a powerful *ideological* riposte to an arid Enlightenment rationality; if a social order *needs* rational justification, then the Fall has already happened. The aesthetic for a

Shaftesbury or Hutcheson is no more than a name for the political unconscious: it is simply the way social harmony registers itself ineluctably on our senses. The beautiful is just political order lived on the body, the way it strikes the eye and stirs the heart. But to assimilate moral judgment to spontaneous feeling in this way is to risk aestheticizing it, thus opening the floodgates to an ethical relativism which is ideologically dangerous. The "moral sense" theorists see shrewdly that the rationalists wantonly elide the whole medium of senses and sentiments—call it the aesthetic–through which abstract ethical imperatives can alone take political flesh in human lives. But virtue, so their rationalist opponents claim, is thereby reduced to a matter of taste and ethical ideology accordingly subverted. The bourgeoisie, once again, is divided between a rationally grounded ethics which proves ideologically ineffectual and an ideologically forceful theory which rests itself on nothing more respectable than the gut. In seeking to anchor one's political power more deeply in the subject—the project of aesthetics or political hegemony—you risk ending up undermining it.

There is a greater risk still, however. The aesthetic begins as a supplement to reason; but we have learned from Derrida that it is in the manner of such lowly supplements to supplant what they are meant to subserve. What if it were the case that not only morality but cognition itself, were somehow "aesthetic"? That sensation and intuition, far from figuring as reason's antithesis, were in truth its very basis? The name for this subversive claim in Britain is David Hume, who, not content with reducing morality to a species of sentiment, threatens to collapse knowledge to fictional hypothesis, belief to intensified feeling, the continuity of the subject to a fiction, causality to an imaginative construct and history to a kind of infinite intertextuality. For good measure, he also argues that private property—the very basis of the bourgeois order—rests simply on our imaginative habits and that political order—the state—arises from the *weakness* of our imagination.

We seem, then, to have traced a kind of circle. Reason, having spun off the subaltern discourse of aesthetics, now finds itself threatened with being swallowed up by it. The rational and the sensuous, far from obediently reproducing one another's inmost structure à la Baumgarten, have ended up in Hume wholly at odds. What, after all, to paraphrase Nietzsche, if experience were a woman? What if it were that slippery, tantalizing, elusive thing which plays fast and loose with the concept, the eternally labile which is gone as soon as grasped? At once intimate and unreliable, precious and precarious, indubitable and indeterminate, the very realm the aesthetic addresses itself to would seem to have all the duplicity of the eternal female. If this is the case, then the only possibility would seem to be to go back to where you started and think everything through again, this time from the basis of the body. It is exactly this which the two greatest aestheticians, Marx and Freud, will try to do: Marx with the laboring body, Freud with the desiring one. To think everything through again in terms of the body: this, surely, will have to be the logical next stage of the aesthetic and the one which carries its earliest proto-materialist impulses to their logical conclusions.

There is more than this, however, to be rescued from this otherwise somewhat discreditable current of bourgeois thought, which far from being centrally about art is in effect about how best to subdue the people. (It is not for nothing that Kant refers at one point to the senses as the "rabble.") Aesthetics are not only incipiently materialist; they also provide, at the very heart of the Enlightenment, the most powerful available critique of bourgeois possessive individualism and appetitive egoism. Before we have even begun to reason, there is, for the British "moral sense" theorists, that nameless faculty within us which makes us feel the sufferings of others as keenly as a wound, spurs us to luxuriate in another's joy with no thought of self-advantage, pricks us to detest cruelty and oppression like a hideous deformity. The body has its reasons, of which the mind knows little or nothing. Speaking from the Gaelic margins, from Scotland and Ireland, these men denounce bourgeois utility and speak up bravely for sympathy and compassion. Disinterestedness, against which modern radicals have learned to react with Pavlovian precision, means indifference in the first place not to the interests of others but to one's own. To judge aesthetically, for Kant or Hume, means to bracket one's own sectarian interests and possessive desires in the name of a common general humanity, a radical decentering of the subject. The aesthetic may be the language of political hegemony and an imaginary consolation for a bourgeoisie bereft of a home but it is also, in however idealist a vein, the discourse of utopian critique of the bourgeois social order.

What happens, in the early development of the bourgeoisie, is that its own secularizing material activities bring into increasing question the very metaphysical values it urgently needs to validate its own political order. The birth of the aesthetic is in part a consequence of this contradiction. If value is now increasingly difficult to derive from a metaphysical foundation, from the way the world is or from the way it might feasibly become, then it can only be derived in the end from itself. Value, as with Kant, is what is radically autotelic, bearing its own conditions of possibility, like the Almighty Himself, within itself. Alasdair MacIntyre has well shown in his *Short History of Ethics* how this idealist self-referentiality of moral discourse is a result of that great historical transition in which moral rights and responsibilities, in the growing anomie of bourgeois society, can no longer be derived from one's actual social role and practice. The only alternatives are then to see value as self-grounded—for which the model is the aesthetic—or to ground them in feelings—for which the model is also the aesthetic. But if this signals a certain ideological crisis from which we have never recovered, it also releases an opportunity. The aesthetic is at once eloquent testimony to the enigmatic origins of morality in a society which everywhere violates it and a generous utopian glimpse of an alternative to this sorry condition. For what the aesthetic imitates in its very glorious futility, in its pointless self-referentiality, in all its full-blooded formalism, is nothing less than human existence itself, which needs no rationale beyond its own self-delight, which is an end in itself and which will stoop to no external determination. For the Marx of the *18th Brumaire,* the true sublime is that infinite, inexhaustible heterogeneity of use-value—of sensuous, non-functional delight in concrete particularity—which will follow from the dismantling of abstract rational exchange. When Marx complained that he wished to be free of the "economic crap" of *Capital* to get down to his big book on literature, he did not realize that an aesthetician was what he had been, precisely, all along.

References

Baumgarten, Alexander
  1961 *Aesthetica* (Hildesheim: Georg Olms).
Burke, Edmund
  1969 *Reflections on the Revolution in France*, edited by Conor Cruise O'Brien (Harmondsworth: Penguin).
Kant, Immanuel
  1952 *The Critique of Judgement*, translated by James Creed Meredith (Oxford: Clarendon Press).
MacIntyre, Alasdair
  1966 *A Short History of Ethics* (New York: Macmillan).
Marx, Karl
  1939 *The Eighteenth Brumaire of Louis Bonaparte*, translated by Eden and Cedar Paul (London: George Allen & Unwin).
Schiller, Friedrich von
  1965 *On the Aesthetic Education of Man: In a Series of Letters*, translated by Reginald Snell (New York: Frederick Ungar).

The Promised Body: Reflections on Canon in an Afro-American Context

Houston Baker

Marx wrote somewhere that literary scholars make their own canon. But, he said, they do not make it just as they please, but rather under circumstances directly encountered, given, and transmitted from the past.[1] This dictum seems unexceptionable, stressing as it does a particular kind of historical determinacy. Yet, what it does not clarify is the ideological orientation Marx was gesturing toward. The "past" is always a selected phenomenon, arranged for class usage. The past conditioning canons—their discussion, implementation, pedagogy, or other uses—is always an ideologically conditioned *version* of events and occurrences gone by.

In recent United States literary study, Marx's insight—like other considerations of history—has been pointedly ignored in pursuit of *theory*. Rather than looking to either the immediate or distant past of the United States to arrive at useful observations on such matters as the founding rhetoric and representational practices of, say, Colonial America or questions of canons and canonicity in the New World, United States literary scholars have bent their best attention toward theory. In their discussions, theory has been both a covering term

---

1. I am indebted to Alan Wald's "Hegemony and Literary Tradition in America" (1981) for the reflections on Marx. Wald's own observations on canons are energetic and valuable.

for literary study in general and, I believe, a disguise of sorts. It has allowed scholars to avoid a self-conscious perspective on their specific historical situation in the United States and the active implications and imperatives of such a situation.

The stance taken by United States scholars has, more often than not, been that implied by Isaac D'Israeli in his 1791 essay "Literary Fashions" (Fowler 1979: 97–119): "prose and verse have been regulated by the same caprice that cuts our coats and cocks our hats." Whirled around by the whirligig of theoretical taste (Fowler 1979: 97–119), United States literary scholars have recently been concerned only with next fall's fashionable theoretical line rather than with history. It would be fair to say, I think, that "theory" has implied—especially in its poststructuralist manifestations—an ideological and sometimes willed blindness to any version of the past that suggests *real* events, *actual* human bodies or a responsibility to such phenomena on the part of literary scholars themselves.

In this essay I look specifically at the embodied and actual past of the United States, summoning for sight and hearing rhetorics that imply a promised canonical body described neither by the term "dismantling" (as in taking apart existing canons) nor "replacement" (as in a liberal substitution of *Invisible Man* for *Henderson the Rain King*). To set such a uniquely American historical and scholarly scene, I suggest immediately that the most impressive sound in the domain of United States canon formation during recent decades was that of tens of thousands of Civil Rights marchers singing "We shall not, we shall not be moved / Just like a tree that's planted by the waters / We shall not be moved."

The song is a metonym for historical and radical African American energies that exploded like TNT on the American scene. It is a name for the resonant topsy-turvydom that marked every walk of American life in recent decades. A dramatic social initiative was seized and overseen by Black Americans during the 1960s and 1970s and preeminent in this initiative were questions of canons and canon formation—questions, that is, of binding contractual cultural texts, the production and reproduction of culture, and cultural axiology.

And when Black Power and the Black Arts Movement in combination with the Black Aesthetic found their way (under the aegis of Black Studies) onto the stage of the American academy, the black initiative became a reality for every student, woman, or man—every secretary, security guard, resident advisor, professor, or administrator.[2] If the Black Power epoch was tragically short-lived (I believe the window of opportunity opened for no more than a decade—from the 1968

2. For an account of the effects of the Black Power movement on the American academy, see Professor Nathan I. Huggins (1985).

assassination of Martin Luther King, Jr.), it nonetheless dramatically altered long-standing modes of literary creative and literary critical understanding. It seems appropriate, therefore, in any discussion of canons, to emphasize a United States situation. To do so we might look first at that New World interaction of actual black and white bodies and historical conjunctions that wrote themselves in unique ways during the eighteenth century.

II

In the eighteenth century, in British Mainland North America and in England itself, a peculiar writing of *nature* and *culture* occurred. The query posed by St. Jean de Crevecoeur, an American farmer, "What then is the American, this new man?" was answered in "natural" terms by British colonists. What constituted an American, for the colonists, as for Bernard Malamud and Robert Redford, was what they called a *natural*.[3] The American in their view was a blessed human being endowed by Nature and Nature's God with inalienable rights. It was only necessary for the colonists to rise and look around them to arrive at this response. For if they had absorbed from Locke a doctrine of the Freeborn Englishman as a spiritual inscription of the natural, they found incarnation of the spirit in the endless forests, swelling waterways, and sweeping tracts of fertile land surrounding them.[4] Born free and situated on fruited plains, Crevecoeur's new man regarded any tyrannical attempt to constrain him as a moment of crisis. We hear George Washington, for example, declaring: "The crisis is arrived when we must assert our rights, or submit to every imposition that can be heaped upon us, till custom and use shall make us tame and abject slaves, as the blacks we rule over with such arbitrary sway" (Jordan 1969: 292).

Similarly, Thomas Jefferson, drafting the Declaration of Independence, saw an impending crisis in terms of bondage and freedom. In words quickly expunged from the final draft of the Declaration, Jefferson asserted:

> He [King George] has waged cruel war against human nature itself, violating its most sacred rights of life and liberty in the persons of a distant people who never offended him, captivating and carrying them into slavery in another hemisphere, or to incur miserable death in their transportation thither. This piratical warfare, the opprobrium of INFIDEL powers, is the warfare of the CHRISTIAN king of GREAT BRITAIN.   (Baym 1985: 613–614)

---

3. My references to Malamud and Redford suggest the former's novel *The Natural* and the leading role that the latter performed in the film of that novel.
4. For a treatment of this American "incarnation," one can consult Myra Jehlen (1986).

In *White Over Black*, Winthrop Jordan notes that a "stout semantic link" binds the revolutionary struggle of natural man to the "Negro's condition" (1969: 292). The Negro's condition, of course, was *slavery*. Slavery is the semantic sign that marks dimensions of the *unnatural* standing in direct contradiction to claims of an American natural. The best definition, however, of Washington's and Jefferson's rhetorical postures is "revolutionary irony."

For the Founding Fathers, as their words reveal, summoned their own "unnatural" practice of *slavery* as a trope for revolutionary arguments for freedom. Words of freedom are tropologically energized, that is, by deeds of slavery. The defining warrant of natural freedom's necessity is, thus, *slavery*.

Washington, Jefferson, Madison and others had only to return from Philadelphia to places like Mount Vernon and Monticello to find a binary opposition and empowering warrant for their semantics of natural freedom. They could look at the whole laboring bodies of their African male slaves and go to bed with the whole bodies of their African women slaves as confirmations of slavery's "arbitrary" and awful sway. There is then—standard American histories to the contrary notwithstanding—no "gap" between the words and the deeds of the Founding Fathers. The Afro-American historian John Hope Franklin insists that the preeminent concerns noted in the Founders' own words were concerns having to do with their slaves. Franklin suggests that if they had spent half as much time on affairs of State as on embedding affairs of slave management, the United States would be a more desirable place in which to live in the late twentieth century.[5]

What has been patriotically written as a "gap" is, in reality, the very body of the African. And like the Founding Fathers who drafted it, the Constitution of the United States metaphorizes this body or takes it in merely tropological terms.

In the language of the Constitution, the African body is fragmented into fifths, modeled into an object of trade, and subjected to immobile enslavement. The Afro-American legal scholar Derrick Bell notes that as many as "ten constitutional provisions" like the continuation of the slave trade, the fugitive slave provisions, and the three-fifths clause are designed to protect "property in slaves" (1985: 7).

With respect to the African body, then, the Constitution is a gothic romance. It writes an "unnatural" African as a liberated zone where

---

5. Franklin's remarks were delivered during his acceptance speech of the Clarence Holte Prize in 1987. He was responding to criticisms of his own biographical candor in his portrayal of the less positive aspects of his subject in his biography *George Washington Williams*. He urged a similar candor on biographers of white founding fathers.

natural man's revolutionary imagination proposes dreams of order. The space of the African body, let us say, is the creative dreamwork of American democracy.

Let us look now at an "unnatural" story.

III

We turn to African and African American expressive cultural production of the eighteenth century and find in a selected group of narratives rich possibilities of Africans writing their own corpuses into English. Such possibilities are immediately manifested in the first chapter of *The Life of Olaudah Equiano or Gustavus Vassa. The African. Written by Himself* (1789) (Bontemps 1969). Speaking of the *mark* of grandeur conferred on elders or chiefs of his native African tribal group, Equiano first notes that both his father and brother had received the designation. He then writes:

> This mark is conferred on the person entitled to it, by cutting the skin across at the top of the forehead, and drawing it down to the eyebrows; and while it is in this situation applying a warm hand, and rubbing it until it shrinks up into a thick *weal* across the lower part of the forehead. Most of the senators and judges were thus marked. . . and I also was *destined* to receive it by my parents.   (Bontemps 1969: 5)

Kidnapped by African slavers and transported in a terrible middle passage to the New World, Equiano's destiny shifts. Slavery forecloses the possibility of his body's becoming marked or inscribed in traditional Ebo discourse. And when he seeks first to comprehend the markings of a new cultural discourse, he is at a loss, speaking no English and unable to make books "talk" to him as they seem to do for his master. (Ibid.: 39). Gradually, however, he transforms himself from a mere body of exchange—a victim of a metaphorizing chatteldom— into an embodiment of cultural exchange.

After several years among the English, Equiano reports:

> I could now speak English tolerably well, and I perfectly understood everything that was said. I not only felt quite easy with these new countrymen, but relished their society and manners. I no longer looked upon them as spirits, but as men superior to us; and therefore I had the stronger desire to resemble them, to imbibe their spirit, and imitate their manners. (Ibid.: 48)

Indeed, he does both. Sold to the West Indies, he enters a financial arrangement with his master to purchase his freedom. Taking up the role of mercantilist trader, he earns sixty pounds sterling, purchases his freedom and returns to England. Finally, he takes up abolitionist labors before marrying an English woman of Soham in Cambridge- shire. His narrative is, in effect, an account of a marking anew of the

African body. The middle chapters of the work describe—in fascinating detail—how he entered West Indian bartering with alacrity, learned navigation and became an invaluable asset to his master. The body's chief function, in addition to displaying an uncanny resilience and adaptive flexibility, however, is to serve as an I/eye witness to the treachery and barbarity of West Indian slavery.

The catalogue of cruelties in Equiano's *Narrative* is a stunning indictment of the *weals* and other marks inflicted on African bodies by the unnatural and enslaving practices of men who are debased in a "West India climate." Equiano, though, avoids such abuse by always keeping his English and African wits about him. In the midst of barbarity, he plies a mercantilist trade and resolves to make his way back to England as a free and freely self-improved man. Under critical scrutiny, the narrative reveals a writing of the African body in ways unnatural to white American male founders. The body becomes a transformative space where commodification rather than being torturously sanctioned is converted, as I have suggested, to revolutionary black commerce in words.

By writing and controlling the versions of self (what James Olney calls "metaphors of self" [1972]) that constitute his autobiography, Equiano converts terror (the initial kidnapping and transport of the middle passage) into suave, learned, committed abolitionism. It is no surprise that his first act on being manumitted mirrors his new linguistic skills. He buys a suit of new clothes. He then throws a party at which the "sable females" reward him with attention. Further, we come to understand after reading his self-told accomplishments why his body is elegantly clothed as that of a genteel Britisher in the portrait that forms the frontispiece for the first edition of his *Narrative*.

There are a number of embedded documents in the concluding chapters of the work, representing representations of the narrator's abolitionist labors. These documents are, finally, signs that confer upon the African a noble status and make him true to his original Ebo name of *Olaudah,* which means both "loud voiced" and "favored one." Appropriately, for an autobiography, it is the hand of the African himself that kneads, warms, rubs and produces these *marked* documents as contributions to the common weal.

I believe we can justifiably claim that Equiano's embodiment of self brings into the master language, English, a remarkable complication of perspective. Certainly, the look of both "natural" and "man" are sharply qualified by the peculiar resonances that the *Narrative* introduces with its opening portrait—a picture that finds its marking text in the work's various chapters.

A Narrative of the Most Remarkable Particulars in the Life of James Albert Ukawsaw Gronniosaw An African Prince (1770), however, suggests a writing of the African body very different from Equiano's (1972). Favored like Olaudah with royal ancestry, Gronniosaw is sold into slavery and brought to New York by a Dutch gentleman. He, too, attempts but fails to make books "talk" to him. Unlike Equiano, however, Gronniosaw's subsequent attempts prove abortive. When he receives a letter in English about his wife's ill health, he says: "As I could not read English, I was obliged to apply to some person to read the letter I had received relative to my wife" (1972: 21). In fact, the African's account is not written by himself but is told to a "young lady of the town of Leonminster." Hence, the manner of his entry into the discourse of natural man is by the pen of a white, presumably British, woman. Some tonal variations between the text that bears his name and Equiano's account, whose title includes "written by himself," result from the "as told to" status of the earlier spokesman's autobiography. Nonetheless, it is quite apparent that Gronniosaw was able to maintain an observable purpose for *the life as told* and to control the signal image of the body African that emerges from the "most remarkable particulars" of his life.

The principal image of Gronniosaw's text is one of Christian, spiritual man reliant on God's Providence and British philanthropy for everything—including bed and board. Rather than a victim of hapless mischance, the mendicant Gronniosaw becomes an emblem of the figure who marks his entry into what he calls "New England." His Dutch master's minister prays for him in a language he does not understand, and his mistress gives him John Bunyan's *The Holy War* to read. The confusion of the African's text, it seems to me, is abundantly apparent at just this missionary moment.

For, as we know from Gronniosaw's own later record in the narrative, he never learned to read English. How, then, could he possibly have read Bunyan and then progressed to Baxter's "Call to the Unconverted"? It seems to me that "design" or poetry rather than truth, or fidelity to actual events, is very much at the helm of this conversion sequence.

Ironically, it is rather the pre-conversion and post-Bunyan phases of the sequence that carry the primary spiritual significations of the African's text. For Gronniosaw, like his successor Equiano to a lesser degree, first effects the posture of Caliban on his entry into the discourse of New England. He learns to curse:

> the servants used to curse and swear surprisingly, which I learned faster than anything; indeed, it was almost the first English I could speak. If any of them affronted me, I was sure to call upon God to damn them immediately; but I was broken off it all at once, occasioned by the correction of an old black servant that lived in the family.   (1972: 8)

As with Shakespeare's Caliban, Gronniosaw could have said, "You taught me language / And the profit'on it is I have learned to curse."

But there is more to the African's story than its redaction of a curse, for what the old servant tells Gronniosaw is that a "wicked man" (Ibid.: 9) called the devil will punish him in hell if he continues to swear. Terrified by this prospect and only half-instructed, Gronniosaw chastizes his mistress for cursing, telling her "there is a black man called the devil, that lives in hell, and he will put you in the fire and burn you, and I shall be very sad" (Ibid.). Discovering that old "Ned" has instructed the African, the boy's enraged mistress does not have him whipped but rather his aged instructor, who is then banished from the kitchen.

The irony of the scenes of swearing seems to reside in misperception. Gronniosaw has an inversive code of communication—i.e., cursing—under control. But he is persuaded to relinquish it by a seasoned servant whose knowledge of, presumably, both language and Christianity leads him to convey to the boy the message that the devil is black, wicked, and averse to a countercode of cursing.

Surely, though, the African servants in the kitchen were doing more than swearing. Perhaps they were speaking, as well, a vernacular of their own? When Gronniosaw relates old Ned's seemingly assimilationist wisdom to the mistress, she realizes the actual accusation of the servant not simply as a rebuke but also as an articulate and forceful rebuke. She understands, also, that the aged servant is a potentially disruptive influence on the enslaved labor of her kitchen. For why, indeed, should slaves know more English than a curse and how to obey her commands?

But the misperception of significance in the scenes of swearing is Gronniosaw's translation of Old Ned's "wicked" into "black." A more perfect command of dominions of English beyond mere swearing reveals to the African boy that wickedness and deviltry themselves are implicitly written by the master discourse as black and African. Is it surprising, then, that Gronniosaw rejects both Bunyan and Baxter as models for his life and body?

Of Bunyan he writes: "I thought him too much like myself to be upright, as his experience seemed to answer with my own" (Ibid.: 11). "This," he says speaking of Baxter's "Call," "was no relief to me either." It is, in fact, outside the book, language and assimilation that Gronniosaw achieves a blessed status for embodiment.

The African fasts and prays for three days in the woods, whereupon he receives a sign. With this sign, his narrative becomes a true conversion account. After the words "Behold the Lamb of God" come to him, he goes once more to the woods where he does, indeed, become enlightened by "a dart [of light] from heaven" (Ibid.: 13). He thus achieves mystical communion with a God and Father whom he has always suspected as existing above the cosmologies of his native

African tribal beliefs. After this communion, he accepts his station as ordained, saying, "I blessed God for my poverty, and that I had not worldly riches or grandeur to draw my heart from him" (Ibid.).

On the one hand, the African's conversion sequence reads like a traditional testimonial. But if we consider that it is focused on both language and misperception (a type of misprision), I believe we can see the story as a writing of the African body *outside* a standard language or, better, inscribing an additional dialect and dialectic transformatively into that standard.

For a mendicant mystic such as Gronniosaw, only a single commerce matters—nonlinguistic communion with the very face of God. He gives up the golden chains that have ornamented his African body when he is first sold into slavery. Similarly, it seems to me, he gives up the dress and ornament of the Dutch or English fashions in which he is clothed by his master. His life is reduced, in fact, to a precarious social beggary where not even his bed can be called his own and in which he, his wife and children are reduced at one point to a miserably sparse diet in the dead of English winter. Surely the African body is here beyond norms of the commercial worlds of either Africa or New England.

> Though the grandson of a king, I have wanted bread, and should have been glad of the hardest crust that I ever saw. I, who at home was surrounded and guarded by slaves, and clothed with gold, have been inhumanly threatened with death, and have frequently wanted clothing to defend me from the inclemency of the weather; yet I never murmured, nor was I ever discontented. I am willing, and even desirous to be counted as nothing, a stranger in the world, and a pilgrim here; for "I know that my Redeemer liveth." (Ibid.: 19)

In sum, Gronniosaw is the spiritual version of the African body. Scantily clad, this body signifies grace abounding to the meanest of men. Such an embodiment provides a contrapuntal text for Equiano's display of handsome dress, successful mercantilism, and civic accomplishment.

Yet, Gronniosaw's spirituality does not rob him of a desirable public role. It qualifies him, in fact, to take on the mantle of the prophet. Like Jonah, he enters the cities of the wicked. Ironically, those cities in his account—in contrast to Equiano's portrayals of a civil and civilizing Old England—are the towns of the United Kingdom.

Having, he states, entertained a notion that living in England would be equivalent to dwelling in a land of charitable Christians—an image inferred from the bookish examples of Whitfield, Bunyan, and Baxter —Gronniosaw finds after his first encounters with the English that he has been dreadfully mistaken. The English are defrauding swearers short on charity. "I soon perceived," says the African, "that I had got among bad people" (Ibid.: 17). How different is this assessment from Equiano's proud boasts of England's fortunes and his own attainment of English virtues!

Gronniosaw presents a bleak, fraudulent, meager landscape. This can never be his permanent home. He, thus, longs for a habitation "over Jordan." His impoverished and enfeebled African body rich in grace becomes, finally, an embodied testament against the enslaving and uncharitable landscapes of England and America.

The African body as a marked sign of spiritual man is, ultimately, in Gronniosaw's narrative, the figuration of "A Prince." It foreshadows The Prince of Peace—the Christian Messiah. The fact that we—as readers—are compelled to see this body (in its "as told to" inscription) situated outside *written* language means that we must find ways alternative to a strictly literary critical attention for perceiving it. We must, in fact, do as Gronniosaw himself does—move beyond bookish discourse to the enlightening face itself—in this case, that of the African.

IV

In the United States, the first face encountered appears in the *Narrative of the Uncommon Sufferings and Surprising Deliverance of Briton Hammon* (1972). This narrative shares the episodic character of Equiano's account, tracing a thirteen-year peregrination that carries Hammon through Indian captivity, Spanish imprisonment, West Indian bondage, naval battles and, finally, a surprising reunion with his master on a return voyage to Boston. The determinacy of a world arrangement that leaves the African abandoned and bereft of means of redress is qualified by the fact that he survives his voyage and, in the words of a famous American epilogue, can alone "tell thee" the tale. His very telling suggests a resilience and articulation that move the body decisively beyond fictions of chattel status and a three-fifths fragmentation.

But it is the 1794 narrative of two Africans from Philadelphia that most aptly figures forth in the United States the lineaments of a body foreshadowed in England by the combined accounts of Gronniosaw and Equiano. *A Narrative of the Black People During the Late Awful Calamity in Philadelphia in the Year 1793 and a Refutation of Some Censures* was written by Absalom Jones and Richard Allen (1972). It is an account of the heroic service rendered by Africans to white citizens of Philadelphia during an epidemic of yellow fever. What emerges from the account are proliferating images of self-sacrificing Africans juxtaposed with images of avaricious, drunken, and fraudulent whites who charge exorbitant fees to nurse those dying of yellow fever and then render them little service. Case after case, anecdote after anecdote reveal the perseverance of the Africans and their magnanimity.

Yet, Allen and Jones's narrative is not wholly spiritual. It was occasioned in the first instance by charges that the Africans not only shirked their spiritual duties but also profited materially from the city's calamity.

Here, Jones and Allen become commercial men par excellence, outdoing even Equiano's mercantilism in setting forth their account of expenditures and revenues, beds disposed of and property handled. In all, their narrative reveals the African body as a financially reliable and spiritually gifted public servant.

As an autobiographical account, the self that emerges most clearly from Jones and Allen's work is one of African civic leadership. The body is, finally, the body politic. Included in *A Narrative of the Black People* are documents similar to the embedded ones in Equiano's work. Among them is a letter from the Mayor of Philadelphia commending the services of the Africans followed by hortatory addresses from the African writers themselves to Africans of Philadelphia and their white friends.

Surely, the bodies of Jones and Allen were those of African Founders. For in the same year of the "late awful calamity," the roof was raised over the "African Episcopal Church of St. Thomas," which stands today as a landmark of the African body. It marks that body as a spiritual, financially astute and public spirited self.

V

One might use a very economical shorthand at this point and suggest a homology. Jones and Allen replace Washington and Jefferson under the sign "Founder," in the same way that Mother Bethel Church of Philadephia refigures Mount Vernon and Monticello as "Home." In such a shorthand, the *natural* is refigured; the African body becomes natural ground and grounding for the American body politic. As a first instance remaindered fiction of *unnaturalness,* the African body returns, through African narrative embodiment, to disrupt a systematic complacency of traditional American historical and literary historical discourse.

That is, the marked or inscribed African body is a trace, a figure in the weave, that always haunts a European system of the *natural.* Refusing general American definitions of nature, the eternally returning body African claims that all inscriptions of nature or the natural that mark it as "unnatural" are cultural tricks with mirrors.

The *virtual* African image in natural man's mirroring discourse, thus, does not forestall an *actual* embodied African voice. When the African ceases placing his ear futilely to the European's books in strict emulation of white voices and attends, like Gronniosaw, to the spicy vernacular of the kitchen, an entire culture rearranges itself.

Similarly, if those who consider themselves American naturals attend seriously to African embodiments such as those of Equiano, Gronniosaw, Hammon, Jones and Allen, a rearrangement of canonical questions becomes de rigueur.

VI

Transactions of black and white bodies in the United States—historical dynamics, that is, of the European slave trade and its British and United States expressive consequences—provide a frame for canonical discussions. Such a frame removes a protective and consoling theoretical safety from matters of canonicity and does not allow academic discussants to pretend that the American academy is moving progressively and humanely ahead simply because it has made some sort of inquiry into the matter of canons. However, before attempting an unacademic definition of "canon" in harmony with my foregoing remarks, it is, perhaps, advisable to clarify the sign "body" as I have meant it in those remarks.

Speaking of the female body in her engaging collection of essays *The Female Body in Western Culture* (1986) Susan Rubin Suleiman says:

> The cultural significance of the female body is not only (not even first and foremost) that of a flesh-and-blood entity, but that of a *symbolic construct*. Everything we know about the body—certainly as regards the past, and even, it could be argued, as regards the present—exists for us in some form of discourse; and discourse, whether verbal or visual, fictive or historical or speculative, is never unmediated, never free of interpretation, never innocent. (1986: 2)

Implicit in Suleiman's observation is a cautious anti-essentialism. Rather than a firm testing ground for experience, the *body* is written as a site accessible only through the mediating agency of discourse. The traditional philosophical question arises: Where does the body end and the symbolizing mind begin? Surely one of the most sensitive sightings of this question for us today is biomedical ethics: Does a severely malfunctioning "body" signal human death or not?

While such philosophical conundrums are of interest and, indeed, crucial for our consideration, we might now introduce lines from Frederick Douglass's *My Bondage and My Freedom* (1968) as a way beyond a too strict or too cautious, anti-essentialism.

> The cowskin is a kind of whip seldom seen in the northern states. It is made entirely of untanned, but dried, ox hide, and is about as hard as a piece of well-seasoned live oak. It is made of various sizes, but the usual length is about three feet. The part held in the hand is nearly an inch in thickness; and, from the extreme end of the butt or handle, the cowskin tapers its whole length to a point. This makes it quite elastic and springy. A blow with it, on the hardest back, will gash the flesh, and make the blood start. . . . The temptation to use it is ever strong; and an overseer can, if disposed,

always have cause for using it. With him, it is literally a word and a blow, and, in most cases, the blow comes first.   (1968: 103)

Though theologians from the beginning of the slave trade to Emancipation debated the question of the African's possession of a "soul" and, hence, raised the mind/body problem in racialistic terms, the essentiality of the African body was scarcely ever in question. That body was, first and foremost, essential for the commercial venture that was New World colonization and plantation agriculture. That body was, in a second and imprinting instance, the dark slate on which the cowskin whip of southern inventiveness wrote its brutal legacy. And, we recall, southerners such as Washington and Jefferson played preeminent roles in inscribing the African body in both fragmenting and brutalizing ways as an essential instance of "American" independence. The "word" and the "blow"—the symbolically discursive and the essentially brutalizing—are coextensive in the writing of New World economies.

Douglass, who was as astute a reader and interpreter of both words and blows—discourse and essential brutality—as any nineteenth-century American intellectual, refigures the entire problematic of the African body as ground or slate. In a letter to his former master appended to *My Bondage and My Freedom*, he writes:

> "You well know that I wear stripes on my back, inflicted by your direction; and that you, while we were brothers in the same church, caused this right hand, with which I am now penning this letter, to be closely tied to my left, and my person dragged, at the pistol's mouth, fifteen miles, from the Bay Side to Easton, to be sold like a beast in the market, for the alleged crime of intending to escape from your possession."   (Ibid.: 426)

The record of an *essential* brutality is written by the master on the slave's back. But with hands now unfettered, the slave is penning *the letter*—establishing a new primacy in the unconscious, refiguring the master discourse inscribed on his back. He employs and deploys the master's discursive instrument for this task. He appropriates the entire symbolic *and* essentialist system to his own ends of revulsion and revolt.

Questions of the body as a foundational, testing ground—i.e., "Did the experience of an essential *body* really happen?"—do not arise. "You well know that I wear stripes on my back. . . ."

In legal terms, we might call the essentialist experience "battery."[6] We are then in the domain of touch, the tactile, and, as jurists say, "hurt is presumed." This is the dimension of Shylock who queries his Christian adversaries about pinching and other tortures of the flesh as proof of essential humanity. The symbolic, semiotic, or theoretical

6. I am indebted to Professor John T. Baker of the Indiana University Law School for the insights concerning battery and assault.

domain might, under certain readings, be reduced to a type of "assault." That is, the mere wagging of a finger in an opponent's face, shouting obscenities or threats can be assault. What is presumed here is "intention to hurt."

But the perceptual—what Luce Irigaray calls the *scopic*—has interesting turns in southern justice.[7] Douglass and other slave narrators as well as hundreds of African-American vernacular accounts tell us that a black person's merely "looking" with "impudence" on a white body was considered a punishable assault equivalent to battery and translated itself into actual corporeal (tactile/essentialist) lashes with the cowskin. In the American South of the first two decades of the twentieth century, a black man's "gaze" upon the white female body was scarcely a colonizing gesture. Rather, it was a look subject to interpretation as rape and could produce not an objectifying mastery but a tactile lynching.

What I am suggesting is that while we want to preserve ourselves duly sophisticated in the employment of the sign *body*, we do not want to ignore a mnemonics of brutalizing cowskin on African bodies. Just as Douglass realizes that his hand—once free—must re-pen the scarifications of his body, so a present-day critic or theorist must realize that it is not simply a "symbolic construct" at stake in matters of American canonicity but rather an essential embodiment.

One cannot merely turn one's eyes toward or away from the body African or adopt its *representation*—whether by self or others—for a spring-term syllabus. The tactile, essentialist, historical dimensions of that body—its incarnation as it were—are too integrally involved in even the most judicious writing of *discursive* to enable such a casual and consoling regard.

Which brings me to the "unacademic" definition of *canon* I promised. The writing of the term *canon* I have in mind is one that marks the celebration of the mass. In that ceremony, "canon" defines the

---

7. In *This Sex Which Is Not One*, Irigaray writes:

Woman takes pleasure more from touching than from looking, and her entry into a dominant scopic economy signifies, again, her consignment to passivity: she is to be the beautiful object of contemplation. While her body finds itself thus eroticized, and called to a double movement of exhibition and of chaste retreat in order to stimulate the drives of the 'subject,' her sexual organ represents *the horror of nothing to see*. A defect in this systematics of representation and desire. A 'hole' in its scoptophilic lens. It is already evident in Greek statuary that this nothing-to-see has to be excluded, rejected, from such a scene of representation. Women's genitals are simply absent, masked, sewn back up inside their 'crack'. (1985: 26)

The emphasis on "hole," "crack" and "nothing-to-see" in the *imaginary* described surely parallels the *gap* proposed between word and deed by traditional historians of America's founding. The Cornell edition of Irigaray's text was translated by Catherine Porter. The original text appeared in 1977 as *Ce sexe qui n'en est pas un*.

great eucharistic prayer. At the core of this prayer are words said over the bread and wine: "This is my body which will be given up for you ... This is the cup of my blood, the blood of the new and everlasting covenant."

What is central in this ceremony—as for my own discussion—is not only the idea of sacrifice but also the materialization and engorgement of the body as a promise. I want to suggest that the African body's emergence out of a supposed "gap" is, in fact, the canonical announcement of a promised body.

VII

In *The Ethics of Reading* (1987), J. Hillis Miller discusses what he describes as necessary fictions that create social orders.[8] Miller refers specifically to Kant's categorical imperative in which one acts "as if" (and here, for Miller, the "fiction" resides) one's act establishes a universal legislation.

> Such an act creates the social order. It establishes the code of law which makes a people a community, not just a lawless conglomeration in which each man's hand is against his neighbor. This inaugural act, moreover, has an implicit teleology. It creates history. It is the prolepsis of a story not only with a beginning but with a middle and an end. Like all founding legislation or drawing up of a social contract it makes a promise: if you follow this law you will be happy and prosperous; if you do not, disaster will follow. (1987: 29)

Miller's account seems, at first blush, unexceptionable. But closer reflection such as he himself, as an astute deconstructionist, would require allows us to see that any fictive act of founding—any metaphysics of inauguration—tells its story at the radical expense of other possible accounts. A host of particulars disappear with the parasitic inscription of a "standard story."

The great glory of human ingenuity, of course, is the ability, as Miller so clearly demonstrates in his own appropriative readings of a variety of ethical readers, to see promises and promising territories other than the founding ones in any inaugural story. Hence, we have the stunningly humanizing amendments to our own Constitution of the United States. We have, as well, the emergence from the Constitution—out of its supposed natural gaps and fissures—the canonical appearance—as consecration and promise—of an African body carrying an alternative story of founding.

The constitutive "as if" of natural white Founding Fathers in the United States left the African body fragmented and enslaved. But

8. I want to thank my graduate assistant Pat Redmond for suggesting Miller's work to me as a helpful source for the present discussion.

the whole and promised body—discovered in the types of narratives constituted by Equiano, Jones and Allen, and hundreds of others—reveal the fathers' act as but an interested fiction, in no ways universal.

The African body emergent from the type of ethical reading Miller recommends—reading that does not attempt to take the text itself as exemplary but strives rather to review or revise the very principle (the Law itself) written by the text—does bespeak a new promise for canons and canon-formation in the United States. It proclaims, I think, the possibility of writing an American story and an American history and literary history in newly canonical ways that involve both sacrifice and community. It covenants a world where not only reading but also pedagogy will be fully ethical insofar as it seeks not to preserve the prerogatives and politesse of a traditional few but to ensure the functional literacy of the world's many.

What occurs, with the appearance of the African body as canonical promise, as I stated earlier, is neither a dismantling nor a replacement. What occurs is rather an *emergence* through suppressing forms and exclusive rhetorics of that which is, in the truest possible sense, "emergent": *Viz.* "demanding immediate action."

Ushered into the academy by emergent calls for revisionary action during the 1960s and 1970s, the promised African body is—even as one reads these lines—threatened today by all manner of violence and exclusion on campuses of American colleges and universities. There is nothing mystical about cross burnings at the South Carolina Citadel and bodily injury suffered by Afro-American students at the University of Massachusetts in Amherst.[9]

Afro-American students enrolled in substantial numbers are, it seems to me, the best promise the American academy has ever known. The demanded canonical action today, therefore—that which most effectively writes a new promise of a truly different academic and social order—is one in which a traditional canonization of polite theoretical and ideologically racist and sexist discourse gives way to pedagogical, historical, and personal attention to the fate of the African body on campuses where we work.

That such a body is capable of a brilliant moral entry into more traditional ranges of our literary concerns is fully signified, of course, by the awarding of the 1987 Nobel Prize for Literature to the Nigerian writer Wole Soyinka. Significantly, Mr. Soyinka's acceptance speech urged immediate attention to the still incarcerated and suppressed bodies of South Africans. The promised body—one that canonically

9. The events mentioned have formed part of a round of reports and stories in leading newspapers of the United States such as the *New York Times* and the *Washington Post* as well as periodicals such as *Newsweek* in recent weeks (January–June 1987).

inscribes a new covenant for the world—Mr. Soyinka seemed to indicate, is that of Nelson Mandela.

Here again and finally in the African Nobel Laureate's dedication of his acceptance speech to the imprisoned South African political leader we move usefully beyond anything approaching self-congratulatory and consolingly fashionable theoretical reflections on a promised body or canon.

References

Baym, Nina, et al, ed.
  1985 *The Norton Anthology of American Literature*, 2nd. ed. (New York: W.W. Norton).
Bell, Derrick
  1985 "The Civil Rights Chronicles," *Harvard Law Review* 99 (1): 4–83.
Bontemps, Arna, ed.
  1969 *Great Slave Narratives* (Boston: The Beacon Press).
Douglass, Frederick
  1968 [1855] *My Bondage and My Freedom* (New York: Arno Press).
Fowler, Alistair
  1979 "Genre and the Literary Canon," *New Literary History* 11 (Autumn): 97–119.
Gronniosaw, James Albert Ukawsaw
  1972 [1770] *A Narrative of the Most Remarkable Particulars in the Life of James Albert Ukawsaw Gronniosaw An African Prince* (Nendeln, Ger.: Kraus Reprint).
Hammon, Briton
  1972 [1760] *Narrative of the Uncommon Sufferings and Surprising Deliverance of Briton Hammon* (Nendeln, Ger.: Kraus Reprint).
Huggins, Nathan I.
  1985 *Afro-American Studies* (New York: Ford Foundation).
Irigaray, Luce
  1985 [1977] *This Sex Which Is Not One*, trans. Catherine Porter (Ithaca: Cornell University Press).
Jehlen, Myra
  1986 *American Incarnation* (Cambridge, MA: Harvard University Press).
Jones, Absalom and Richard Allen
  1972 [1794] *A Narrative of the Black People During the Late Awful Calamity in Philadelphia in the Year 1793 and a Refutation of Some Censures* (Nendeln, Ger.: Kraus Reprint).
Jordan, Winthrop
  1969 *White over Black: American Attitudes Toward the Negro 1550–1812* (Baltimore: Penguin).
Miller, J. Hillis
  1987 *The Ethics of Reading* (New York: Columbia University Press).
Olney, James
  1972 *Metaphors of Self* (Princeton: Princeton University Press).
Suleiman, Susan Rubin
  1986 *The Female Body in Western Culture* (Cambridge, MA: Harvard University Press).
Wald, Alan
  1981 "Hegemony and Literary Tradition in America," *Humanities in Society* 4: 419–430.

History and Literary History:
The Case of Mass Culture

Richard Ohmann

I intend a straightforward exposition, although my subject is messy enough. I will offer readings of two simple texts; one is an ad for Quaker Oats and the other a story I will soon outline. Both appeared in the same issue of a popular American magazine in 1895. I argue that a reader cannot adequately understand either without grasping its relation to the other and to the ensemble of historical forces that brought them together.

As for the story, I hope not to distort it much in compression; it is only about 3000 words long. It is called "On the Way North" and was written by Juliet Wilbor Tompkins. I quote the two opening sentences to give you a feeling for its tone:

> The train strolled along as only a Southern train can, stopping to pick flowers and admire views and take an unnecessary number of drinks. Why should you hurry when you have barely a dozen people in your three cars, and the down train will keep you waiting anywhere from half an hour to half a day at the switch?

The third sentence introduces the hero, a "young man from the North," impatient with the train's progress; and the fourth gives us his name and his way of thinking about himself: "Gardiner Forrest —of New York City, thank goodness!" Having entered his mind, we stay there through the next paragraph and find his thoughts occupied with an unnamed "she," the "nicest, jolliest girl in the world," whom he ardently wishes on the pokey train with him, and free of the watchful scrutiny of her chaperone aunt.

Incident rapidly ensues. A conductor enters the nearly empty car, seeking the help of a "negro nurse" there, for a lady who has fainted in the forward car. The nurse deposits a white baby she is caring for next to Forrest, to his dismay and rushes off. A dialogue follows, of which this exchange is typical: "The baby leaned towards him and said distinctly, 'Papa!' 'Good heavens!' ejaculated Forrest. 'Do you want to start a scandal? I'm not your papa. You have made a mistake.'" The infant threatens to cry and Forrest takes it onto his lap, not noticing that the train has made a stop "and that a tall girl, evidently of the North, was staring at him in utter amazement from the door of the car." *We* are scarcely amazed to discover that this is the "she" of Forrest's longings. Her name is Amy Baramore, and she indeed proves to be a jolly girl who banters with Forrest and talks baby talk to the baby: "I didn't know how dear they were," she says.

They devise a scheme for its entertainment. Forrest will tell a story in "straight ahead English," and Miss Baramore will translate into baby talk. The story serves as a veiled communication between the two adults. It is about a poor boy—obviously young Forrest himself—who lives next to a rich girl (obviously Miss Baramore) and is too ashamed of his "shabby back yard" and "disgracefully unpatched" trousers to do more than gaze at her over the fence. Amy's "translation" makes it clear that she liked him in spite of his "poor patches." A delicious bond of intimacy has begun to grow between the two. "Her lips twitched a little, then their eyes met, and they both laughed."

At this point the conductor brings news that the nurse is still needed in the forward car and that the train will be on a switch for quite a while, so they may alight if they wish. They choose to sit on the rear platform of the empty car at the rear of the train where they exchange more tender information: in sum, each had been romantically interested in the other for a few days when they were both in St. Augustine, but he had left early because he wrongly thought that a certain very rich Mr. Douglas had the inside track to her affections. We and Forrest now learn that Amy, unlike her watchful Aunt Emma, rates character above wealth in potential husbands.

Before Forrest can digest this welcome news, adventure interrupts the idyll. The train has gone on, leaving the empty car on the isolated siding. How to get the baby back to its presumably distraught nurse? They reject the idea of walking to the next station (too slow) and Forrest proposes a bold strategy: release the brakes and roll several miles to the valley town. Amy barely hesitates; all her concern is for the "baby in her lap," and they begin to coast. Suddenly the grade becomes much steeper: "Forrest's heart leaped as he looked first at the descent before him and then at Amy beside him, for there was real danger." He races to the rear brake, she bravely holds the front one, and they ride out the peril. Returning, "he flung his arm around her to steady her. Their eyes met, and it was all said without words." As they reach safety, Forrest "stooped and kissed her," saying, "You're dead game, Amy."

The denouement is quick. They declare their engagement, coyly using the baby as an intermediary. Amy reveals that the rich Mr. Douglas had proposed to her and that she had declined; that she had felt an attraction to Forrest that was confirmed when she saw how "dear" he was with the baby. One more false fright and they are at the station. The train is delayed there by "the daily hot box." The nurse and the conductor never even noticed that the rear car was missing. The ferocious Aunt Emma is there, "inspecting Forrest through her lorgnon" and tut-tutting, but without power now to harm the betrothed couple. Baby has the last word: Amy notes that "But for him it might never have happened" and wonders what they might give him. " 'Dindin!' suggested the little Napoleon."

The story is slight and conventional. It demands little interpretation and hardly calls criticism into play. Nonetheless, I will offer a few critical comments of a traditional sort to establish points of reference to which I will return later in the discussion.

The plot moves Gardiner Forrest and Amy Baramore from unspoken longing, to veiled declarations of interest in one another, to a wordless embrace, to an understanding then briefly realized in fuller verbal intimacy. The Aristotelian "action" (or motive) of the story is, roughly, "To give words to the heart's desire and fulfill it in marriage." That can happen only after Forrest shows himself to be amateurishly tender with the baby as well as resourceful in a crisis, and after Amy shows herself to be "dead game" in the face of physical danger. Character, so revealed and enacted, manifests their rightness for each other. I would also mark how the couple are stranded in an asocial space, almost a wilderness—"blue outlines of the hills, rising above the thick tangle of woods in which they stood"—and how, passing the test of character there, they return deservedly to the social world and to the socially defined relation of betrothal. I would tie the story to the structure of literature through Northrop Frye's scheme, remarking that we have here in nearly perfect miniature the mythos of comedy, complete with tyrannical old order, blocking characters, even the green world and the city. And I might situate the story in American literary history by setting its breezy dialogue and relaxed, accepting narrative voice against the formality of a genteel narrative voice, now falling into disuse. More might be said, but probably few would sense the need for even this much.

The Quaker Oats ad (Figure 1) requires still less interpretation. Its verbal rhetoric is direct enough, with the appeal to a reader's pru-

108

Quaker Wisdom

"Don't cry herrings until they are in the net "—nor imagine you have the best breakfast cereal until you have Quaker Oats—Sweet and wholesome.

Quaker Oats

Sold only in 2-lb. Packages.

Figure 1. *Munsey's Magazine*, October 1895.

dence, taste and sagacity. Where its text exhorts, its image offers; yet the pitch is much the same in text and image, for the Quaker figure projects seriousness, reliability and robust health, even without the aid of his scroll and its message of purity, making a semantic link with "wholesome" in the text. One might wonder about the connection between herrings and cereal, or indeed about that between Quakers and oats. These lacunae suggest either incoherence in the message or a reader-viewer who will know how to supply the needed tissue of meaning, a reader initiated into this discourse. The ad itself cannot tell us which of these hypotheses is correct, though historical hindsight will surely incline us toward the latter.

But how are we to fill in the much wider gap between the Quaker Oats ad and "On the Way North"? How do they belong in the same bundle of signs, *Munsey's Magazine* of October 1895? Is there *any* connection beyond that of physical proximity? I mean to problematize what may seem unproblematic. In spite of the ubiquity of such odd conjunctions now, there is nothing inevitable about them. Indeed, they were nowhere to be found 150 years before this issue of *Munsey's* appeared; they were unusual before the Civil War; and they were uncommon even in the early 1880s.

There are no breakfasts in the story or even any commodities. There is no love or danger in the cereal ad. The story makes no sales appeal. The ad may be read as implying a sort of narrative (if you go to the store and buy Quaker Oats, you will be satisfied) but, apart from the happy ending, this plot has nothing in common with that of "On the Way North." The only connection I can easily spot is in the register and tone of the two voices that address us in ad and story. Both are casual, familiar, a bit coy.

To bring these two cultural productions closer, we will have to look for a different kind of connection than structural similarity. I believe we can locate such a connection only in a broad social process "outside" the magazine, where meaning emerges from historical change. I will now briskly indicate the kind of change I think most pertinent, before returning to the ad and the story. I refer *my* story of historical change, first, to production.

Let me characterize the middle decades of the American nineteenth century as the epoch of competitive capitalism or entrepreneurial capitalism. As industrial production approached and then surpassed the magnitude of farm production, the men who organized it followed straightforward procedures. Find the capital needed, build the factory, stock it with machines, buy the raw materials, hire workers, produce the goods, convey them to jobbers and wholesalers for distribution, realize profits (if any), and—more often than not—reinvest those profits in further productive capacity. Firms were small by later standards. Price competition was intense.

The invisible hand worked busily. Production became more and more efficient, and total product grew. By the end of the century the process had accelerated to an extraordinary rate. Between 1865 and 1900, roughly speaking, the value of manufactured goods increased seven fold, the number of factories quadrupled, the number of industrial workers tripled, and industrial capital increased fourfold. As the figures suggest, production changed utterly, bringing a host of other changes, like the great movement from country to city.

The brilliant success of the system also generated dangers and failures. The boom-and-bust cycle intensified: there were three major depressions between 1870 and 1900. As companies fought for markets, naturally many of them lost out in the competition. Bankruptcies were endemic; individual businessmen felt—and were—able to do little to alleviate chaos and risk. Pools, gentlemen's agreements, price-fixing arrangements of every legal and illegal kind, failed to stabilize the environment of capital accumulation. And toward the end of the century, after reaching its highest level in American history, the rate of profit began to fall. Capitalism was triumphant; capitalism was in profound crisis.

What gave it new life and created our world was a new kind of social formation sometimes called advanced capitalism or late capitalism, but for which I use the marxist term, monopoly capitalism. Its characteristic unit is the giant, vertically integrated corporation, a form that emerged with great rapidity in the 1890s. Such a corporation brought the entire economic process within its compass, from raw materials through production through marketing. Rather than simply producing the goods and hoping they would sell, it tried to coordinate making with selling and to guarantee that what the machines turned out would find buyers, thus eliminating a main source of uncertainty and risk. Let me make this more concrete through the homely example of Quaker Oats, one of the early innovators.

Through the 1860s and 1870s, producers of oats perfected machines for milling and "cutting" the grain. In 1882 Henry P. Crowell, one of the leaders, built a mill that took it through a continuous process from grading and cleaning to packaging, all under one roof. By then, production of rolled oats was twice the demand and makers faced the usual choice: cut prices until some lost out in the competition, or leave the machines idle much of the time and lose the advantage of low marginal cost accruing from a large capital investment. Crowell hit on a third possibility: increase demand. Oats were virtually unknown as a breakfast food, and Crowell set out to promote that use of the cereal, simultaneously changing the form of distribution. Oats had always been shipped in bulk: barrels a grocer would dip into for individual customers. One of Crowell's competitors had begun selling the product in individual sacks. Crowell took a further step and put oats into two-pound cartons like the one the Quaker is holding in the ad. (A machine for producing such cartons had been perfected in the 1870s.) He also put the Quaker on the package and registered him as a *trademark,* the first for a cereal.

I will return to that part of the story, but first a word about the corporate aftermath. In 1888, Crowell and his six leading competitors merged their operations into the American Cereal Company, one of the first large, vertically integrated corporations. It established offices around the U.S. and abroad, where its people scheduled the flow of packaged oats to jobbers, taking much more direct control of distribution than formerly. At the other end of the process, it employed fieldmen to purchase oats from farmers, and buyers on the Chicago commodity exchange. It developed the multi-level table of organization characteristic of the modern corporation, to organize and monitor this complex of making and selling.

From its position of dominance, the company now looked almost directly into the American home. There, if it actually had had corporate eyes, it would have seen a very different configuration of spaces and practices than was common fifty years earlier. I will characterize it with brutal simplification by saying that it was now an urban or suburban home rather than a farmhouse; that it was more a place for recuperation from work, for child-rearing, and for much-simplified tasks of cooking, sewing, etc., than the center of an elaborate and nearly self-sufficient home production; that the men of the house went out to sell their labor power in the market, while home was the domain of the women; and that the women, too, went out into the market, not to sell labor power but to buy the commodities which were increasingly the basis of survival. These homes were, then, *ready* for Crowell's idea. He did not so much create a need (the common charge against advertising) as show housewives how a generalized and very real historical need—itself created by the new factory production that Quaker Oats instanced—might be narrowed and met through purchase and use of a particular kind of commodity.

To effect the necessary connection between home and corporation, Crowell placed his package in local stores and its image in a thousand places where it could register upon the eye and emotions of the housewife. In short, he turned to advertising: on billboards, in streetcars, in newspapers, on calendars, on fences, on blotters, in cookbooks and so on. In 1890 he undertook a coordinated national *campaign.* The old military word now assumed a new commercial meaning: an assault on the consciousness of the *consumer* (another new sense for an older word). And Crowell turned to a new kind of institution to plan and execute his campaign: an advertising *agency*. Specifically, sometime before 1894 he engaged the Paul E. Derrick agency, which opened an office in London that year to spread the Quaker Oats image and message abroad. In 1894, Derrick also took the Quaker image off the box, enlarged and varied it, and put it in magazine ads like the one displayed here. Meanwhile, as almost every mind in the country absorbed and retained the image and the idea of purchase, the four-color package carried recipes to instruct the housewife in creative and caring *use* of the new product. The new bond between corporation and home was secure (Marquette 1967; also Chandler 1977: 294; Pope 1983: 54–55; Presbrey 1929: 107–406; Schudson 1984: 64–66).

Before taking a fresh look at the ad and story which were my point of departure, I must turn to one more part of this historical transformation. How did the Derrick agency hit on magazines as a medium, and on *Munsey's* in particular, which had begun publishing only four years earlier? Until the late 1880s, general monthly magazines were a rather sleepy genre; none had a circulation of more than 250,000 or so and, with their cover prices of 25¢ or 35¢, they were too expensive for a much broader audience, as well as too genteel in content. With a few exceptions (*Century, Cosmopolitan*), they carried little or no advertising. This began to change around 1890. Publishers of general monthlies, perhaps taking a hint from more commercial women's magazines (notably the *Ladies' Home Journal*) and the so-called "story papers," reconsidered their prejudice against advertising and sought to enlarge their circulations. The big break came in 1893. In the midst of that year's financial panic, S. S. McClure came out with his new magazine, at an unprecedented cover price of 15¢. *Cosmopolitan* quickly dropped *its* price to 12½¢. And in October, Frank Munsey, with a great deal of publicity, lowered his single issue price from 25¢ to 10¢—a figure that soon became standard but not before *Munsey's* had taken a quick lead in the competition.

Munsey's gamble and his one-man war against the American News Company's distribution monopoly instantly paid off. The circulation of his dying magazine went from 20,000 to 60,000 in two months, passed 200,000 in six, and was close to 600,000 in two years, when the issue I am discussing appeared (Peterson 1956: 7–9). Munsey had "invented" the general mass circulation magazine, with luck, desperation, and genius, and in tandem with his competitors. They and he created a cultural industry of quite new dimensions which was not just a matter of size. They had reached a wider and *different* audience, not previously included in this form of culture. Most important, they had hit on a business formula new to national media: sell the magazine for less than its cost of production, build a huge circulation and make your profit on advertising revenues. In other words, they were no longer dealers in their physical product and became dealers in groups of *consumers*. What they came to sell, like radio and television later on, was *us*—or more precisely, our attention. This appears to be a development of world-historical importance: the invention of the mind industry or, more commonly, of mass culture.

So *Munsey's Magazine* was a perfect vehicle for the Quaker Oats ad in 1895. The 600,000 imprints of the ad passed in front of still more pairs of eyes, all over the country. It was in the company of many hundred other ads, most of them, like the ones on the accompanying page, for inexpensive items of housekeeping or personal care. The October 1895 issue carried 78 pages of ads, with its 128 pages of editorial matter. (Soon the former would outweigh the latter.) The contents of the magazine drew readers into the milieu of the ads with a mix of light fiction, articles, celebrity gossip, art and theater news, sports, semi-clad women, and dozens of photoengravings of artwork and famous people. This mix was as forward looking as the commodities in the ads.

We are now in a position to think again about relations of the Quaker Oats ad to Tompkins's story. Most obviously, the ad *paid for* the story and probably for a good deal more. At Frank Munsey's famous rate of a dollar per page per thousand of circulation, he would have received $600 for the ad space, and I doubt that Miss Tompkins got more than $50 for her story. Reciprocally, "On the Way North" helped bring the reader's attention into proximity with the image of the wise Quaker. Furthermore, this silent interaction of ad and story was part of a complex, new, and intensifying historical process, with many agents not discernable on the page or even deducible from it.

In the context of this history, we can read the ad more "thickly." For just a few examples:

1. The Quaker is *already* known to the viewer; his image reinforces many previous impressions and barely requires interpretation. This is a discourse of repetition.
2. His relation to oatmeal is arbitrary and conventional; signifier and signified hang together almost as with a common noun of the language.
3. Yet the signifier retains its own aura of meaning: solidity, respectability, thrift, honesty, etc., and all this slides over as a secondary aura for the product.
4. Both that aura and the explicit message—"pure," "wholesome," —make historical sense in mediating a new relationship of individual, corporation, and name-brand product. People were only now learning to depend on commodities produced at a distance by strangers. *Trust* was necessary but had to be funded over time.

114

Figure 2. *Munsey's Magazine*, October 1895.

5. One means toward that end was linking the new product to old and familiar things: the Quaker himself; and the proverb with its wisdom from time out of mind and from an oral tradition in sharp contradiction to the industrial and commercial relations that actually surround the ad. Thus herrings and breakfast cereal turn out to have a most intimate and dialectical connection, a simultaneity and exchange of old and new.

6. The *new* figures here as the product itself, in its mentioned and novel use as a breakfast food; as the manufactured package (in silent opposition to the unbranded barrel of oats): and in the legend at the bottom of the page, now understandable as insistent praise for a new way of buying things.

7. Modernity also expresses itself through two *absences:* nowhere do we find the name or address of the corporation (cf. the other three, more old-fashioned ads in Figure 2) or of the ad agency. The voice that invokes and constitutes "you" comes from no identifiable source; it materializes out of the opaque space of monopoly capital.

8. Yet it speaks to you in an amiable, familiar, personal though authoritative voice. An imaginary social relation effaces the real ones that populate the historical stage, just beyond the ad. The ad in a way refers to that stage and cannot be understood apart from it; yet it mutes, distorts, or denies most of its connections to the historical process.

These principles of reference and meaning structure a micro-language, that of modern advertising. As I have said, ads like this were a recent historical innovation. But already by 1895 the ad man addresses the reader as a knowing participant in the discourse: able to assume the strange role of "you"; able to become the consumer to whom the Quaker offers his product; able to decipher the relation of image to text and of both to product; savvy in the oppositions of old and new that organize the ad's appeal. That tacit knowledge was necessary in 1895 for quick interpretation of the ad. Presumably, most readers had it: they had acquired a new kind of literacy. I conjecture that they were also learning to collaborate in a kind of tacit *ignorance*— of the social relations being effaced by advertising: relations of labor and making, of corporation and consumer, of ad agency and cultural production. The "magic system," as Raymond Williams calls it, was in place (1980: 170–95).

I will now turn again to "On the Way North" (in a more conjectural way because fiction is more mediated persuasion than advertising) and will posit some ways of re-reading the literary features I mentioned earlier. Later, I will dwell a bit more on their ensemble.

Against the historical emergence of monopoly capital, I read what I called the Aristotelian motive of the story—to give words to the heart's desire and to fulfill it in marriage—as validating the personal, internal self, by confirming its feelings through the preverbal understanding of another person, then by making those feelings at home in the social medium of language and finally by projecting them toward a marriage that will keep the private self intact even while giving it institutional embodiment. Nothing new about that, of course: much the same could be said of a Jane Austen novel. But the utopian impulse grows more urgent and its fictional realization less grounded, in a context of impersonal corporations, bureaucracies and great cities. Perhaps that explains why the test that proves affection and equal worth occurs in a natural setting away from other people, certainly away from economic life, yet in an archetypal product of the industrial system, the railroad car, cut loose from the control of its inept corporate master and tamed by individual courage and cunning. (That the dual test of worth moves toward obliterating the differences between the sexes—*he* holds the baby; *she* joins in a bold adventure—seems to contest the separation of spheres and of gender roles and to affirm the ideal of the "new woman" which was ascendent in the nineties.)

I see the offhand, colloquial style of the story as much akin to the voice of the Quaker Oats ad, eradicating the distance that print interposes and proclaiming a kind of generalized neighborliness and affability which weighs in against the thoroughly corporate transaction in which the reader is engaged.

I could spell out and defend each of these rather gnomically stated interpretive claims but instead, I want to spend a few paragraphs on the comic plot, which gives shape to Tompkins's story. It is of course unabashedly traditional, hardly a feature out of place. (That's one reason the story can be told so brusquely: we all know it already.)

Yet this rendering of the myth also strains *against* tradition, by highlighting and historically referencing that part of the mythos that identifies the marriage or feast at the end with a freer social order. Aunt Emma is not just Holdfast, *the* tyrant; she figures a particular nineteenth-century generation seen as checking the evolution of the new woman—a girl "you liked to travel with," who can handle herself outside the home and away from chaperonage, being a good sport and making alliances on her own. The shadowy Mr. Douglas, the other blocking character, is not just a seemingly advantaged rival in love; he represents a retrograde upper class, out of touch with *work*. (Forrest was in St. Augustine on "business"; Douglas was there to play on his yacht; to Amy he represents a brougham and a maid, not a person active in the world.) Forrest—a "rising young lawyer, who hasn't risen yet"—is obviously putting a lot of distance between himself and that dingy back yard, by strenuous effort and a technical rationality that comes forward right at the beginning of the story, when the impatient young man reads "his paper down to the last 'Wanted,' and calculate[s] in the margin" how much money the railroad is losing on the nearly empty car. This technical rationality, of course, is what later conquers the runaway car and wins Amy's kiss.

Forrest is the socially mobile individual, whose power and ambition have affinities with and a clear place in the new corporate order. And, one more point, Tompkins aligns him with the North (where his marriage and future will take place) and its commercial center, and makes the South stand for a backwater that has never learned corporate efficiency. A "lazy, slipshod, good for nothing country," he calls it, when he discovers that the train has left the car on the siding.

In short, the marriage of Forrest and Amy may be read as harmoniously conjoining the age-old myth of comedy and the new epoch of monopoly capital, much as the ad links a new market relation to folk wisdom and a seventeenth-century Quaker. I might add that if Amy Baramore really does have to forgo the services of a maid for this love match (and who can doubt that such deprivation will soon end?), she will herself run a modern household, efficiently preparing modern breakfasts with wholesome Quaker Oats. The story glances forward toward an urban nuclear family. Neither partner has visible parents, and Aunt Emma will surely not be there to transmit generational skills and technique in kitchen or sewing room. *That* role has been deeded over to the outside expert and the neighborly voice of the ad man.

That is how I would jointly read these two productions of the mind industry, under the sign of progress. But there is another stage in the argument. To reference the narratives and icons of mass culture to epochal change is necessary but not sufficient. I have so far left *conflict* out of my picture, as if change were an uncontested linear process in which all participated equally. Speaking of the crises that businessmen faced toward the end of the century, I left out the deepening antagonism between capital and labor. The emergent industrial system was not kind to its workers. All-but-total class warfare erupted in 1877, 1885, 1892 and 1894, in close synchrony with the cycle of depressions, because capitalists generally responded to bad times with wage cuts and layoffs. Thus, in addition to the other pressures on competitive capitalism, there was the persistent threat of rebellion from below.

Eventually, the productive power of the system would help to ease that conflict, partly as a result of the very flow of cheap, name-brand commodities to consumer markets of which I spoke earlier. Even in the late 1890s, many workers could buy Quaker Oats and Wool Soap, though few could yet afford the more expensive household goods.

But the opposition of capital and labor relaxed somewhat in the new social order at least as much for another reason. A new class was rapidly growing *between* capital and labor, distinct from the old petty bourgeoisie. It included the middle managers who proliferated in the new integrated corporations, upper-level office workers, professors in the fast-growing universities, service professionals who helped moderate the worst consequences of inequality and urban decay, government bureaucrats, doctors, lawyers, engineers, and so on. By the 1890s, most of these groups were busy forming organizations, setting professional or business standards, regulating admission to their ranks: in short, becoming a self conscious stratum of society. Barbara and John Ehrenreich dubbed it the Professional-Managerial Class (PMC) and argued that, toward the end of the century, it came to occupy a complex position in partial antagonism to and partial alliance with both the ruling class and the working class. It associated itself with science, technique, efficiency and the rational analysis and management of society (Ehrenreich 1979: 12–27; Weibe 1967: 111–32).

I argue that the primary audience of the mass circulation magazines was just this class, along with those who had reasonable or unreasonable hopes of joining it. I cannot prove that; reader surveys and market research by publishers and advertising agencies were still in their infancy in the nineties. But certainly some of the publishers *thought* they were reaching a moderately well off group of educated and semi-educated, urban and suburban, upwardly mobile people and they pressed such claims on potential advertisers.

Certainly the contents of the magazines imply such a readership, as I suggest by taking a final interpretive pass at "On the Way North." Not only is Gardiner Forrest oriented toward the dynamic and progressive future, but he is moving into it as a young professional, a lawyer. He comes from humble origins and is entering the business world, evidently with some university education in his background. He is sharply differentiated from Mr. Douglas ("Croesus, Jr., and his yacht") by having to work for a living, from Aunt Emma by the haughtiness and conservatism of her manners and by her class-bound views on matrimony, and from Amy herself by the contrast in their childhood backyards and present circumstances. Clearly the comic resolution of the story spreads its utopian good will not only over modernity and the free bourgeois self, but over the future of Forrest's class as well. It does so through an unequivocal triumph of this class hero's values and capabilities over those of the upper class. Forrest takes "the jolliest girl in the world" away from her socially natural mate and his inherited money. Amy herself, free spirit and new woman, defects from her class in favor of a husband who can both handle a child and stop a railroad car: the domestic and heroic virtues seem a manifestation of the same abilities that enable him to rise through law and business. And Aunt Emma shrinks into powerlessness.

In short, a third reading of the comic plot, this time foregrounding the dynamics of class, suggests that the aura of its benign fulfillment confers ideological blessings not only on a vague doctrine of progress and a new economic order, but more specifically on the project and prospects of an emergent class. "They lived happily ever after," the unwritten final sentence in every story of this kind, refers to more than the fortunate couple; it applies also to the future of the lawyers, businessmen, planners, and mediators for whom Gardiner Forrest stands and whose values bask in the glow of requited love.

Let me briefly annotate the other literary features of "On the Way North," against this third interpretive grid. Evidently the "motive" of the story gains much of its appeal from the fact that when desire breaks into speech, the words overcome a silence imposed partly by class exclusions on the one side (Aunt Emma would condemn any relation more intimate than "casual acquaintance" between Gardiner and Amy), and by class timidity on the other (he "wouldn't stand much of a chance"). That the forbidden words issue first in the oblique mode of baby talk and with reference to a childhood misunderstanding, signifies that this particular class boundary is an artifact of the adult social world and its unfair distinctions, which the forthcoming marriage will nullify.

The test of character occurs in a space and a situation where such distinctions have no power and where timeless virtues like boldness and ingenuity take precedence. That Forrest should turn out to possess those traits, along with class-specific ones like pragmatism and technical rationality, aligns the latter with the hero myth and so *naturalizes* them. (I would note in passing that the hero's name, while impeccably Anglo-Saxon and indeed highbrow, blatantly asserts his affinity with the natural; while the heroine's first name, invoking the classless feminine role of beloved, negates her uncompromisingly aristocratic surname.)

The narrative voice of the story also naturalizes the outlook of the PMC. It is a knowing, confident voice that takes its values as unproblematic and uncontested. Thus the narrator and the reader strike an amused alliance with Northern, technical superiority, in a clause like "the daily hot box had not been omitted." Mock heroic prose ("The two eyed each other in silence a few minutes, each measuring his man") glides effortlessly into genuine heroic ("Forrest's heart leaped," "there was real danger," "a sharp whistle . . . made his heart contract with a fear that was not for himself"), with no self-consciousness of how the first tone might imply criticism of the cliches in the second. Nor is there any felt contradiction between the narrator's tacit praise for Amy's masculine "calm directness" of speech and her coy conspiracy in Amy's feminine *in*directness, as she bends over "the sleeping baby, who would have seen something if he had been awake." The narration effortlessly draws upon a variety of registers and codes, as a social group might do which felt itself liberated by culture and privilege from any one class rhetoric. (The same kind of stylistic mobility is present, though less comfortably managed, in the voice of the ads in Figures 1 and 2: "nor imagine . . ." v. "Sweet and wholesome"; "FOR STYLE AND FIT" v. "Correct the figure to the latest fashionable contour"; "Woolens will not shrink if Wool Soap is used in the laundry" v. "*Buy a bar at your dealers.*") The voice proclaims its freedom from traditional manner or conventional restraint.

In general, read as taking part in a discourse of class, the story manages to announce on behalf of the PMC its own recognition as darling of history, yet also to annul any thought of irreconcilable conflict. True, Forrest defeats Aunt Emma and Mr. Douglas, but that Amy should marry him shows the class rivalry to be bridgeable; that she should *love* him discloses that PMC charms can win over progressive members of the upper class.

It would be convenient for my argument if Gardiner Forrest had managed along the way North to stave off a rebellion of railroad workers and earn their gratitude and respect. Failing such aid to the critic from Tompkins, I must be satisfied that the ineffectual workers ("one of the wheels, at which men were still tinkering") blend in harmlessly with the backward, pastoral scene and that the conductor—a labor aristocrat—is suitably inept and properly amiable toward Forrest. Forrest's managerial talents hold center stage; were *he* to run the railroad, defective brakes would not stay long unrepaired, and there would be no daily hot boxes. But mainly, the working class is an absence here, offering no obstacle in fact or imagination to the PMC thrust. Even racial conflict is nullified by the complacence of the nurse, who, with "only a slight negro accent," is clearly on the way toward integration—quite an augury of social peace. In the early days of Jim Crow and just one year after the Pullman strike, this happy PMC dream pushes racism and class warfare beyond the field of vision.[1]

I claim that this way of reading "On the Way North" does not look *behind* or *through* the text to "background" conditions but reconstructs

---

1. Juliet Wilbor Tompkins was a recent graduate of Vassar College. I don't know if she came from wealth, but she headed straight for the kind of PMC career to which college education was increasingly adapted. In 1897 she became an associate editor at *Munsey's*. Frank Munsey himself was a farmer's son; in 1895, age 41, he had several entrepreneurial failures behind him and was just beginning his rise to great wealth. His work as editor, publisher and writer put him squarely in a PMC context at this time. His prescriptions for fiction stressed the dynamic: "stories, not dialect sketches, not washed out studies of effete human nature, not weak tales of sickly sentimentality, not 'pretty' writing" (Britt 1935: 98). This was a repudiation of upper class culture as presented by the elite monthlies.

meanings that were "there" in the text for properly schooled contemporaries. Like the Quaker Oats ad, the story called tacit knowledge of old and new into play and also of class-based values and ideas. An interpretive strategy not grounded in such knowledge and in such habits of decoding would have given the reader an experience of the story almost drained of tension, affect, and satisfaction. Surely there were such readers in 1895; just as surely, readers literate in the codes of popular fiction were in the majority, or Frank Munsey's formulas would not have won a mass audience for his magazine. The story resembles the ad, too, in that its code demands some areas of what I called tacit ignorance. For any reader who puzzled about the relations between Mr. Douglas's old wealth and Gardiner Forrest's "business," or who understood the railroad as indexing the Great Upheaval and the Pullman Strike, or who read North-South coordinates as evocations of slavery and civil war, Tompkins's idyll would collapse into incoherence or into reprehensible silliness.

Even so, mine is a rather heavy reading of a light story. If anyone were to enter that as an objection, I would reply, first, that the formulas of mass culture work as smoothly as they do, in part because they incorporate dense historical understandings and reduce them to comfortable ideology. They offer possibilities of meaning that seem untroubled and uncontested. That is generally the case because cultural producers like Munsey must deliver to advertisers not simply the attention of many readers but attention of a certain quality. Readers must feel broadly content with their place in the world, so that the flow of their anxieties may be channeled into smaller concerns like the need for a healthy breakfast or for a laundry soap that won't shrink clothes—worries that may be allayed by purchasing commodities.

For mass culture at its inception was a discourse inseparable from the circulation of commodities. It was also a discourse carried on especially among members of the PMC and aspirants to it, a sharing of commercial messages and cultural practices that helped define the class, while bathing it in self-congratulation. There is no way adequately to read the popular literature of this period without building that historical process into its understanding.

In closing, I want to situate the kind of literary history I have tried to mobilize here by acknowledging two ways in which it is old fashioned. First, I have privileged a version of what really happened in history and used it to explain and interpret the texts at hand. Some recent theorists would object that my story of capitalist crisis and transformation can itself be no more than a distillation of other texts, and that it and they have no epistemological priority over texts like "On the Way North." For such thinkers, history dissolves into a parity of infinitely many structures, with no center except language and at that a language severed from its capacity for reference or action. This is a history without causes or agents; to the extent that it admits of change at all, it attributes change to something like the random collision of molecules. I have no philosophical reply to what Perry Anderson nicely calls this "megalomania of the signifier" (1984: 46, 48), nor do I think there is one. Rather, a person who wants to do causal history must take Jonathan Culler's advice and ignore deconstruction—not kick the stone in useless refutation like Dr. Johnson, but adopt the double consciousness of Hume when he repaired from his skeptical labors to dinner and backgammon (Culler 1982: 130; Abrams 1986: 132–33). Ignoring deconstruction won't make it go away but neither will ignoring history stop it from happening or perhaps from doing us in, unless we intervene as if it had causes and we might be agents.

Having opted for causes, one must make the more vexed and interesting decision which causes to take as most deeply determinative. In assigning priority to forces and relations of production I have committed myself to a second premise some think old fashioned. I think that commitment right, though I recognize the vulnerability of traditional conceptions of base and superstructure, because there is no way to account adequately for mass culture (or for much else) without seeing that the needs and projects of capital counted more powerfully than those of housewives in reshaping the markets for breakfast food and culture. Still, the needs of housewives set limits to what capitalists could do. I hope that by acknowledging those limits and giving weight to the projects of intermediaries like ad men, magazine publishers, writers and the PMC, I have drawn a sketch of the cultural process complex enough to be exempt from the charge of vulgarity. Henry Crowell and his peers couldn't have built monopoly capital without Paul Derrick, Frank Munsey, Juliet Wilbor Tompkins, and *their* peers, many of whom had little interest in enriching the American Cereal Company. But if their aspirations had not harmonized with his, he could have found other, structurally similar ways to achieve his ends. That proposition doesn't work the other way around. Hegemony is the diffusion of power, not its equalization.

References

Abrams, M. H.
  1986 "Construing and Deconstruing," in *Romanticism and Contemporary Criticism*, edited by Morris Eaves and Michael Fischer (Ithaca: Cornell University Press), 127–182.
Anderson, Perry
  1984 *In the Tracks of Historical Materialism* (Chicago: University of Chicago Press).
Britt, George
  1935 *Forty Years—Forty Millions: The Career of Frank A. Munsey* (New York: Farrar & Rinehart).

Chandler, Alfred D., Jr.
  1977 *The Visible Hand: The Managerial Revolution in American Business* (Cambridge, MA: Harvard University Press).
Culler, Jonathan
  1982 *On Deconstruction: Theory and Criticism After Structuralism* (Ithaca: Cornell University Press).
Ehrenreich, Barbara and John Ehrenreich
  1979 "The Professional-Managerial Class," in *Between Capital and Labor*, edited by Pat Walker (Boston: South End Press), 5–45.
Marquette, Arthur F.
  1967 *Brands, Trademarks and Goodwill: The Story of the Quaker Oats Company* (New York: McGraw-Hill).
Peterson, Theodore
  1956 *Magazines in the Twentieth Century* (Urbana: University of Illinois Press).
Pope, Daniel
  1983 *The Making of Modern Advertising* (New York: Basic Books).
Presbrey, Frank
  1929 *The History and Development of Advertising* (New York: Doubleday, Doran).
Schudson, Michael
  1984 *Advertising, the Uneasy Persuasion: Its Dubious Impact on American Society* (New York: Basic Books).
Wiebe, Robert H.
  1967 *The Search for Order, 1877–1920* (New York: Hill and Wang).
Williams, Raymond
  1980 *Problems in Materialism and Culture* (London: Verso).

Culture and Ideology: From Geertz to Marx

Dominick LaCapra

> *The culture concept to which I adhere has neither multiple referents nor, so far as I can see, any unusual ambiguity; it denotes an historically transmitted pattern of meanings embodied in symbols, a system of inherited conceptions expressed in symbolic forms by means of which men communicate, perpetuate, and develop their knowledge about and attitudes toward life.—* Clifford Geertz, *"Religion as a Cultural System"*

The anthropological concept of culture, of which Clifford Geertz has been both a notable advocate and an influential definer, has played an important role in contemporary historiography and social science. It has focussed attention fruitfully on the problem of meaning and symbols. Especially in Geertz's formulation, it has combatted crude sociological reductionism and engendered a concern for close reading of cultural phenomena construed on the analogy of texts. It has also sensitized researchers to the problem of attempting to understand groups and societies in terms of their entire way of life as mediated in symbols. In contrast to both narrowly causal models of explanation and modes of "thin" description, Geertz's non-reductive emphasis upon the interpretation of symbolic practices has marked a clear advance in the understanding of culture.

In *The Interpretation of Cultures* (1973) (particularly in the essay, "Ideology as Cultural System"), Geertz has applied his general concept of culture to the particular problem of ideology. In line with his more general concept, he criticizes the reductionism of both the Marxist notion of ideology in terms of interest and the functionalist notion in terms of tension-management (or the reduction of "strain"). While not entirely denying the partial applicability of these notions (especially the Parsonian version of functionalism), he insists on the "autonomy" of symbolic processes and finds in it the missing link that redirects attention to the precise workings of ideology:

> The link between the causes of ideology and its effects seems adventitious because the connecting element—the autonomous process of symbolic formulation—is passed over in virtual silence. Both interest theory and strain theory go directly from source analysis to consequence analysis without ever seriously examining ideologies as systems of interacting symbols, as patterns of interworking meanings. (1973: 207)

Geertz, moreover, proposes a "genuinely nonevaluative concept of ideology" (Ibid.: 196) as the proper way to examine its interworking meanings, and he concludes the essay with an opposition between ideology and science, thereby reinforcing his own program for a social-scientific study of ideology as a cultural system. In his expansive idea of ideology as a system of symbolic meaning as well as in his quest for a science that may be both opposed to ideology and posited as the "nonevaluative" way of comprehending it, Geertz formulates views rather typical of recent social-scientific perspectives. For example, one finds analogues of Geertz's approach in figures such as Alvin Gouldner and the early Louis Althusser.

Without denying the many fruitful aspects of Geertz's approach, I would argue that it should be supplemented or emended in at least two significant ways. First, one needs a more differentiated analysis of culture in modern society, for an anthropological model may prove excessively homogenizing with relation to societies which in the modern period have been sources of both emulation and imperialistic imposition in the rest of the world. I shall devote attention to significant features of modern Western societies, although certain problems I discuss also have relevance for contemporary state-socialist societies. Second, there may be good reason to return at least in part to a modified Marxist conception of ideology. Geertz's insistence on the autonomy of symbolic forms may avoid reductionism at the price of regressing to precritical idealism. In any event, it dissolves the problem of ideology into that of symbolic meaning and culture in general, and it gives rise both to a dubious binary opposition between ideology and science and to a social science that lacks a link with critical theory.[1] A more specific concept of ideology may be necessary insofar as one recognizes that

---

1. For an approach to the problem of ideology that in important respects converges with the one taken in this essay, see John B. Thompson (1984). I read Thompson's study only after completing this essay. Although I do not agree with all aspects of its argument, the degree of convergence in perspectives is an encouraging sign of discontent with more firmly established approaches to the problem of ideology in academia.

ideology in a delimited sense does not exhaust all culture and that its relation to given symbolic systems or artifacts remains problematic. In other words, symbolisms or signifying practices may be both relatively autonomous and partially ideological in variable ways, and the concrete tàsk of analysis is to specify the relation between ideological and other than ideological aspects of a complex, ambivalent phenomenon. Indeed one crucial way in which a symbolism or a specific text becomes relatively autonomous is by engaging in a critical relation to the ideologies it conveys. The latter point would apply as much to social science or historiography as to other signifying practices.

In the analysis of modern cultural systems, one needs to distinguish —and to pose the problem of the relations—among a number of aspects or levels: official culture, high or elite culture, mass culture, and popular culture. I have discussed this issue in an earlier work (1985: 73–79), and I would here expand upon and partially revise that discussion. I would begin by noting that each of these aspects or levels is internally differentiated or even divided in ways I shall at times try to indicate. In addition, the relation among levels poses the problem of a hegemonic formation and its social correlates or bearers. For, while there is never a simple one-to-one equation between culture and society, cultural differentiation is related to social differentiation and actual or potential conflict. Indeed this relationship is one reason why there is a place for a specific concept of ideology. It is, I think, initially plausible to argue that in Western countries, mass culture tends to be the dominant force in a hegemonic formation, while in state-socialist countries, official culture, under state and party, tends to be dominant but in ways that must nonetheless confront problems attendant upon mass and even commodified culture (for example, a crucial concern for productivity, the technically rational organization of work, a functional division between work and play, a reliance on public relations and public opinion research, the growing importance of the media especially among the young, the replacement of publics by audiences, and so forth).

Official culture refers to culture actively shaped or at least influenced by the state. Political culture is a broader concept relating to traditions and practices in a polity, for example, the practices of state-worship and deference to superior authority, on the one hand and of constitutional rule, civil liberties, and participation or at least consent of the governed, on the other. Political culture may thus provide resources that either reinforce or limit the scope of official culture—or at times do both insofar as practices and traditions are equivocal or subject to variation over time. It would be simplistic to believe that one may categorically contrast West and East on this dimension of political culture, for one has important differences between countries situated within either bloc (for example, between England and West Germany or Poland and East Germany). The more significant difference comes with the relative role of constitutional guarantees implemented through the courts and effective in the political process. The state in its more official capacity, moreover, may intervene to shape culture in both direct and indirect ways—directly through support for certain programs (endowments on the level of high culture, welfare on more "popular" levels) and indirectly through the priorities it underwrites and the models of success it projects (the importance of national security, military preparedness, and party loyalty or business acumen, for example). State influence may at times be rather subtle, as when a seeming collection agency, such as the Internal Revenue Service, actually comes to affect life styles as its policy on records and documentation confronts citizens with the option of either paying higher taxes or living as if they were bookkeepers. Whether its influence be subtle or not, the massive importance of the state in all modern societies raises the question of its differential impact on cultural processes often treated in abstraction from political ones.

High or elite culture is an equivocal term. It may refer to the artifacts and the general culture (or discursive practices) of elites in the arts and sciences. It may also refer to the culture of other elites—political, military, socioeconomic, bureaucratic, academic, and so forth. In the latter sense, it merges in part with official and political culture. It should be obvious that the degree of integration of various elites and elite cultures is not a foregone conclusion, nor is the relation of elite to hegemonic culture. I would contend that it is misleading simply to conflate hegemonic with elite culture because this conflation occludes the problematic degree to which there may be critical or contestatory tendencies in elite culture itself.

It is often assumed that the stability of a social and political order depends on a workable degree of integration among elites or at least on modes of non-communication and functional specificity that do not undermine the legitimation of the state and the social order. The diversity of historical developments among nations and states in the modern period nonetheless makes generalizations hazardous. For example, the French Revolution created barriers among elites themselves, and the instability of France in the nineteenth century was due in part to the absence of consensus among elites on a legitimate form of government and society. In England, by contrast, there was widespread agreement among elites on the legitimacy of a constitutional monarchy as well as on a capitalistic economy and the degree of democratic participation enabled issues to be open to resolution through a combination of agitation and negotiation. In England one had an "establishment" in a sense that was not in evidence in France.

In Germany, national unification was not achieved until the end of the nineteenth century through political and military means (Bismarck's "blood and iron") and coincided with problems created by rapid and extremely disruptive large-scale industrialization. An older agrarian elite of Junkers retained political and administrative power despite the importance of newer socioeconomic groups. And academics maintained a "mandarin" position that aligned the traditional ideal of *Bildung* with opposition to newer forms of social activity and political participation. I recall these clichés of comparative social history simply to underline the difficulty in generalizing about the nature and role of elites in the modern period.

I would also observe in passing that a crucial problem in the analysis of ideologies in contemporary Western societies is the complex and to some extent differential relation between integration through shared belief or ideology in the older sense and negative integration or dissensus through an absence of widely shared commitments. Negative integration abets the play of divisive or at least functionally specific interests and inhibits the formation of oppositional movements. I would suggest that, in the contemporary context, there is a combination of at least three factors: 1) older ideological formations appealing especially but not exclusively to lower-middle and blue-collar groups, for example, in terms of national security or "our way of life" (including the "born-in-the-USA" syndrome); 2) particular or functionally specific ideologies appealing largely to middle and upper class groups, for example, on the level of professional concerns; 3) the weakness or absence of ideologies that enable oppositional groups to articulate their differences and form effective political alliances. This threefold complex is ignored in the notion of an "end of ideology" and is oversimplified even in Jürgen Habermas's more pertinent and sophisticated idea that in modern societies false consciousness, dependent upon older ideological formations, finds its functional equivalent in "*fragmented* consciousness, which precludes enlightenment about the mechanism of reification" (1981: 522). It is also oversimplified in the notion that fragmented ideologies and dissensus, enabling a hegemonic strategy of divide and rule and disabling effective protest, simply eliminates ideology in the older sense of a consensual or shared system at the level of society as a whole or even significant segments of society.[2]

One generalization that has at least limited validity is that, in the modern period, artistic and intellectual elites—at times scientific elites —have had significantly adversarial relations to features of the domi-

2. This perspective is stressed in Thompson (1984). To some extent, it may be related to the greater degree of disaffection in contemporary Britain in comparison with the United States.

130

nant culture and state policy, however limited the political effect of
such relations may have been. Even noteworthy conservatives, such as
Edmund Burke and Joseph de Maistre, have not simply defended a
status quo but often inveighed against it in defense of older values they
felt were threatened. To some extent, more recent conservatives, such
as William Buckley, have been constrained to follow their example.
It is, however, true that the role of the critical intellectual, of whatever ideological bent, has been more enshrined in Western European
(especially continental) than in American culture, for the pragmatic
tendencies and common-sensical orientation of the latter have affected
the potential of even the questioners of the "system." European trans-
plants, such as affiliates of the so-called Frankfurt school, have recognized this point to their chagrin. In addition, the very antipathy to
the term "high culture" in the United States and the preference for
the "pop" distinction between high brow, middle brow, and low brow
are themselves signs of the different cultural ambience on this side
of the Atlantic. Who, for example, could be considered the American
analogue of Jean-Paul Sartre, politically committed, accomplished in
so many areas one is tempted to invoke the phrase "Renaissance man"
—and someone whose funeral could bring out a spontaneous *cortège*
of fifty thousand people? Elvis Presley or some grade-B movie actor
might elicit popular support of that magnitude, but not an intellectual.
Still, the differences between the United States and Europe in these
respects should not be overdrawn. There have been important critical
currents in the United States having more or less marked connections
with European thought. Recent forms of socialism and feminism are
among the more prominent, with the latter having a greater social and
political resonance than the former. And the regard in which social
elites and the general public have held artistic and intellectual elites
in Europe itself involves the role of what Pierre Bourdieu somewhat
indiscriminately terms symbolic capital. The canonization of classics,
including some of the most adversarial works of modern culture, reinforces the tendency to set up artists or intellectuals as fetishized
sources of prestige and status for privileged social groups.

The socially stabilizing function of canonization has induced recent
critical theorists to embark on a program of "canon-busting" in which
attention is paid to works excluded from canons, particularly works of
oppressed groups such as women, workers, and ethnic minorities. My
own view is that the necessary investigation of non-canonical artifacts
and their sociopolitical contexts should not replace but supplement
a program of noncanonical readings of canonical texts and artifacts.
More precisely, one should attempt to reopen the question of the way
given texts or artifacts included in canons have complex ideological,
critical, and at times possibly transformative implications for their

own contexts and perhaps even for our contexts of reading and interpretation. This type of inquiry is hardly exhaustive of all significant problems or exclusive of other modes of investigation, and it may—indeed should—be undertaken in conjunction with broader sociocultural and historical research. But it has its role to play, especially at the present time. It may still be plausible to see certain departments of literature or art history as subsisting on a neo-Arnoldian ideology that upholds a canon as a feature of both intellectual and sociopolitical standing. But to generalize this into a vision of modern—and particularly American—culture is at present extremely short-sighted and narrowly academic. If anything, high culture of a traditional sort (particularly print-culture) is an endangered species. And the abilities developed in a close study of it may be one crucial source of critical judgment in coming constructively to terms with the forms of mass and commodified culture which have assumed an important if not clearly dominant role in modern life. It is not, I think, accidental that the most cogent critics of a canon, such as Walter Benjamin or, in a different register, Jacques Derrida, have had an intimate acquaintance with their objects of criticism.

Mass culture evokes the image of large numbers of people who do not form face-to-face publics but rather audiences of spectators or more or less organized crowds of participants in events such as rallies and parades. Sociologically, it is related to urbanization, the rise of the middle classes, and the spread of *embourgeoisement* through widening circles of the population. It is also related to the fear of being lost in the crowd and no longer being recognized, as well as to the ambivalent exhilaration that anonymity in an urban environment brings. In these respects, it is a term difficult to extricate from ideological considerations. In a more limited sense, it denotes culture in good part dependent upon mass media for dissemination—what is currently termed "mediated" culture in a specifically modern sense. Particularly in the West, it also denotes commodified culture, that is culture further mediated by the market and converted into a commodity bought and sold in accordance with market criteria. But even in countries where the media are owned and controlled by the state, procedures perfected under commodified conditions, such as public relations and public opinion research, are employed to curry favor with large audiences. Advertising may itself either provide the frame emulated by other mass-appeal programming or be literally replaced by appeals to patriotic sentiment. (In Western non-commercial, educational television, advertising of course finds its functional equivalent in marathon fund-raising drives which may be so tedious and inept as to make one crave commercials employing professional talent.)

The effect of mass and mediated culture is difficult to calculate.

This is particularly true to the extent that it becomes a primary culture, as television assumes the role of a baby-sitter if not a surrogate parent, and people have fewer alternative sources of culture to serve as countervailing forces. Certainly, mass culture today affects all other aspects or levels of culture, and a crucial question is the extent to which it has passed beyond the status of a technology and assimilates or modifies various forms of elite and popular culture to become a culture in its own right. In any case, it should be evident that media such as television and film are not simply neutral technologies but active forces in shaping and transforming culture; the product they create is distinctive. I would simply note one recent feature of religion on TV that is relevant to the question of the extent to which the medium affects the message. There is a remarkable similarity in rhetoric, personality type, and pitch between preachers on televised religious programs (so-called electronic evangelists) and proliferating real-estate hucksters who have managed to convert advertising into full-time programming. This epiphanic convergence may, moreover, be related to the more general resurgence of evangelical capitalism that has marked the Reagan years—a resurgence abetted by the type of media "hype" that has itself helped to create the image of the "great communicator."

Even when the media tend to replicate older distinctions such as that between elite and popular culture, for example, in the case of art films and "popular" films, they do so within a context they help generate —a context that has more than a mimetic relation to other levels of culture. A crucial question here is whether or to what extent the media reduce other cultural forms to the level of raw material for readily consumable and instantly intelligible, "off-the-rack" products that in turn become the models for "spontaneous" emulation in "popular" culture. The "Madonna" look in fashion and even in attitude is one recent serio-parodic example of the ability of the media to transform older models or schemata.

Advertising itself has in certain ways become the most "advanced" sector of the media and particularly of television. Given its importance in a commodity system, it is heavily funded, and the care with which commercials are made often makes ordinary programming seem amateurish by comparison. Ad men were able to assimilate the so-called modernist "tradition of the New" and the cult of formal experimentation by adapting the techniques of the avant-garde to the celebration of the dominant culture. Their success in this venture should give the quietus to any general idea that formal experimentation is invariably contestatory or "subversive" in a sociopolitical sense. The formally aesthetic quality of certain ads is in fact quite remarkable, and it includes the use of self-referential and mildly ironic techniques. Given the nature of recent programming, especially with the movement of soap-operas into later time slots and the blending of soaps and comedies into sudsy sitcoms, certain viewers may actually look forward to well-crafted, vaguely adult commercials and experience a reversal of the standard pattern of expectation punctuating television viewing.

Before leaving the topic of mass culture, I would point out one of its important features, the relation between work and play (a problem I think is radically underemphasized in Habermas's reformulation of critical theory). In modern culture, work tends on one level to be effectively split off or "alienated" from play in that it is defined in terms of instrumental or technical efficiency, while play is confined to a separate sphere of leisure-time activity. The very idea of work as "serious play" or of a different rhythm between labor and enjoyment may seem far-fetched or patently utopian. "Leisure-time" is itself organized on a mass-cultural basis with the individual either in the role of spectator or of an amateur performer who tries to do what professionals do better. (The jogging craze is perhaps paradigmatic here, for it presumably has the utilitarian value of improving one's health and is an activity that may be performed either alone or while trying to have a conversation with a few huffing-and-puffing friends. The element of invidious comparison with professionals is also reduced to a minimum, for distance seems to be the most differential criterion among joggers, thus making it a rather democratic sport if not a ritual.) With commodification, moreover, the opposition between work and play—so important on the level of production—collapses on that of consumption, for leisure time is recycled into a market system and serviced by "culture industries" specializing in the satisfaction of leisure-time needs. It is in this sense that leisure time may be defined as commodified play. I would simply propose without further argumentation that a massive problem in modern society and culture is how to give all jobs a craft component and to articulate them with more "playful" or carnivalesque activities in a different rhythm of social life—a problem denied or occluded both in the rarified Habermassian ideal speech situation based on a restricted notion of serious, rational communication and in the prevalent idea that one needs to increase leisure time on the basis of functionally specific and at times automatic work.

Popular culture is an equivocal and ideologically invested term, hovering between a critical fiction if not a myth ("the world we have lost") and a residual category (everything that is not elite or mass culture). Its clearest reference is to culture generated or at least enacted in face-to-face groups of people who at least know one another. Its privileged bearers for historians have tended to be peasants and workers, but the disappearance of a distinct peasantry and the decline of a recognizable working-class culture have made its social bases more indeterminate.

Today "popular culture" is often used interchangeably with mass and "mediated" culture, but this misleading usage begs the question of the historical and sociological relations between levels of culture. In a more limited sense, "popular culture" is employed with respect to more or less residual traditional forms of various sorts ("superstition," witchcraft, magic, folklore, fairy tales, carnival, and so forth). In a somewhat more general sense, it sanctions the investigation of a laundry list of activities and beliefs: family history, peer group relations, the culture of oppressed and minority groups, grass-roots sports, relations to nature and to animals, and so forth. It may guide inquiry into less savory topics such as the role of invidious stereotypes, prejudices, and forms of scapegoating or intolerance for outsiders. In a professional sense, it may also have the viciously paradoxical function of underwriting claims to disciplinary hegemony of those who study it on the grounds that it constitutes the most basic or significant of social realities.

It would seem essential to give the study of popular culture a better theoretical and methodological grounding. It would also seem pollyanna to believe that this grounding may be fully provided when the phenomenon itself is in such a problematic state in contemporary society. For the uncertainties and hyperboles of the study of popular culture are not unrelated to the condition of popular culture itself in the modern world. One of the tell-tale uses of the term is with reference to the study of the consumption of mass culture that may be produced by elites. Here the point is that on the level of consumption (or "reader-response"), there may be contradictory or at least different tendencies from those manifest in the artifact in isolation or interpreted on its seemingly manifest level. Of course one question is whether the critical or transformative treatment of the artifact by the viewer or reader takes place on the level of the isolated individual and the small circle of family and friends or whether it has a broader resonance that may help convert an audience into a public. In any event, this example serves the purpose of raising the larger question of the interaction among levels of culture and the role of phenomena or artifacts that represent amalgams of different levels. Nationalism, for example, is obviously a phenomenon of modern history that exists on all levels of culture and an adequate analysis of it would have to investigate the interplay of official, elite, mass, and popular cultures.

I have already referred to the assimilative and assimilating capacity of mass culture and the question of the extent to which it tends to be a dominant force in a hegemonic structure. Mass culture has shown an ability both to recycle popular and elite forms and to affect newer products of popular and elite culture in more or less decisive ways. It is, for example, the rare novel that does not get converted into a soap opera when it becomes a TV drama or even a film, and much talent is currently employed in writing scripts directly for the media. The soap-opera form has a tremendous homogenizing effect as it takes incidents more banal than those of daily life and charges them with a level of emotional intensity rarely achieved in daily life. (A crucial device in this respect is the use of eye contact to generate more or less unearned and evanescent recognition scenes.) To the extent that the soap-opera form provides a space for women (its primary audience) to take stock of problems, it is a relatively small space and the desire to empha-size its importance as a force of resistance may in good measure be a symptom of wishful thinking. The principal point is that at best a mild and readily contained level of social and cultural criticism is the price of access to the mass media, and the exception (say, Monty Python) is relatively rare. There is a sense in which viewing habits may reinforce this point, for one's mind may go into neutral when one switches on the TV, and one may well want a program that does not add critical reflection to the ordinary troubles of the day or the stereotyped dis-asters of the news. The increase in customized and privatized modes of viewing, such as cable channels and VCR's, may well have the effect of lessening even the level of awareness of national and local problems necessarily conveyed through regular programming, for they enable the viewer to concentrate exclusively on the genre or genres he or she prefers, that is, to consume more and more of them. In addition, the growth of seemingly sophisticated media criticism can accompany a collapse of critical discrimination insofar as the analyst engages in projective reprocessing of artifacts by providing an intricate semiotic, deconstructive, or dialogical account of *Dynasty* or *Magnum* as if it were *The Brothers Karamazov* or *Moby Dick*.

"Elite culture" at present may to a significant extent mean works that make the kinds of demands on readers which insure relatively small readerships and dependence on assignment in college courses for dissemination. One technique of the older artifact of elite culture was to take endangered popular forms and translate them into its own medium, in part as a protest against the nature of the dominant cul-ture in which these very forms were undergoing eclipse or repression. For Mikhail Bakhtin, the process of carnivalization in literature began in an interaction with social carnival but became relatively autonomous as a literary genre with the decline of carnival in society. Bakhtin indi-cated, in his study of Dostoevsky for example, that literary carnivaliza-tion might retain an insistence and potency even in the modern pe-riod, but he was clear that carnivalization in art or literature remained most vital when it could indeed interact with social and popular cur-rents such as carnival in society. One might add that a tendency in elite culture has been what one might call the hermetic appropriation of the carnivalesque, that is, the insertion of an older popular form into a framework that cuts it off from popular communication and understanding. This phenomenon poses a problem often ignored by those who argue for the political or pedagogical effect of critical tendencies in elite culture (including modes of deconstructive or disseminatory writing). At present much art and literature relies for its knowledge of older popular forms on aesthetic and scholarly traditions, for there is little role for them in many contemporary societies, and the form they take may be highly commercialized (such as carnival in New Orleans). (Here of course certain writers, such as those in South America, may have an advantage to the extent their cultures retain older popular forms.)

Elite culture has increasingly had to come to terms with mass and commodified forms from advertising to television and beyond. Responses have ranged from assimilation to resistance, with black humor and satire as prevalent modes of integration. Yet fascination with technology, even when combined with aversion to its excesses or its mindless use, can engender an acrostic ingenuity that threatens to give rise to a baroque technologism in the construction of intricate plots or mechanical wonders. Whether such a procedure is symptomatic or critical of larger cultural trends may at times seem undecidable. Still, one may point to modern works in which the relation to both older popular forms and newer mass or commodified currents is often handled with critical and aesthetic power (for example, William Gaddis's *The Recognitions*).

The very complexity of culture in the modern period and its relation to social stratification and conflict would indicate the need for a concept of ideology that is not simply conflated with a homogenized idea of a cultural system. Tendencies in recent history might even lead to a partial rehabilitation of the crudest version of "interest theory," for example David Stockman's revelation that even for some of its promulgators Ronald Reagan's policy of "supply-side economics" was little more than media hype devoid of credibility. Indeed there are times when the level of public discourse falls so low that anthropological talk of the wonderful world of meaning and symbols seems like little more than idealistic humbug and the historical interest in past popular cultures amounts to one more nostalgia trip. Public life then approximates a grade-B movie, and the kind of rhetoric and response typical of that genre may have sure-fire efficacy and significant popular appeal in politics.

A relatively specific sense of ideology refers to modes of legitimation and justification in public life. In this sense, ideology spans what Karl Mannheim distinguished as ideology and utopia, in other words, situationally congruent and situationally transcendent modes of legitimation. One may certainly use the term "ideology" in a sense that equates it with ethicopolitical and publicly normative discourse in general. In the Marxist tradition, however—particularly in Marx and Gramsci—ideology is further specified in certain ways, and this specification has at least limited validity for critical analysis.

I would suggest five features of ideology when it is not simply identified as a general "cultural system" or even as a mode of legitimation.

1. Ideology involves mystification, illusionism, or illegitimate masking in the interest of legitimation or justification. It is in this sense the public and sociopolitical analogue of rationalization (whether through secondary revision or more deep-seated unconscious processes) in Freud. I would, however, leave open the question of whether there may be legitimate modalities of masking (for example, in carnival) which have variable interrelations with illegitimate or invidiously deceptive forms. The obvious but extremely difficult task which is both analytic and critical is to distinguish legitimate from illegitimate modes of masking and to prevent the latter from dominating the former.

2. Ideology is illegitimate insofar as it serves the interest of a part of society which is generalized to appear as the good of society as a whole. Ideology is in this sense falsely synecdochic in a given social order. I would also leave open the question of whether there can be egalitarian ideologies that serve a particular interest or whether egalitarianism may be equated with "truth"—as it commonly if implicitly is, especially by students of "popular" culture. My own view is that the relation of equality, reciprocity, and difference represents an extremely knotty problem avoided by the simple equation of egalitarianism with "truth" and the correlation of ideology with the domination or hegemony of a superordinate class. I have already indicated at least two dubious features of populistic egalitarianism: the scapegoating tendency of populism with respect to outsiders and exceptions and the inclination of at least some students of popular culture to appeal vicariously to the experience of the oppressed to justify their own pretensions to disciplinary hegemony.

3. Ideology presents what is historically variable—although perhaps recurrent (not unique)—as if it were universal or eternal. In Marx's typical example of the naturalizing or essentializing nature of ideology, the economic bases of a commodity market may be construed as if they were conditions of economy and society in general. Gift exchange, from this market-oriented ideological perspective, may be interpreted as an aberrant or incomprehensible form of commodity exchange, and all exchange may be

equated with exchange value (in the specific sense of equalization or commensuration with respect to a universal equivalent). I
would note in passing that there is a danger in Louis Althusser's
contention, on the basis of his understanding of psychoanaly-
is via the work of Lacan, that ideology, like the unconscious,
is both trans-historical and centered on the subject. This view
threatens to repeat essentialism in the very definition of ideology,
and it both ignores the historical nature of displacement (or repetition with variation) in unconscious processes and obviates the
possibility of an objectivist or scientistic ideology (toward which
Althusser himself at times veers).

4. Ideology is related to the hegemony of one formation, bloc, or
group over others, and hegemony in this sense cannot be reduced to power for it requires a nexus of power and consent,
in other words, a form of authority at least partially accepted
and internalized by all relevant groups, including the oppressed.
The notion of hegemony casts doubt upon the attempt to analyze
social and cultural processes in terms of a concept of power (or
even of power-knowledge) alone. It also raises the possibility of
self-deception in groups who may believe, to a greater or lesser
extent, that something is in their interest when it may not be—or
at least when it involves losses that outweigh gains (economic or
other). As I intimated earlier, the alternative to the hegemony of
an elite is not total egalitarianism or populism which is typically
attended by intolerance for outsiders and exceptions. I would
suggest that the alternative should be seen in terms of the articulation of differences, including the differences between the
exception and the rule—an alternative that poses the problems
of justice and generosity. Here Marx's formula—from each according to his ability, to each according to his needs—remains a
fruitful beginning point (yet only a beginning point) for reflection.

5. A particularly prevalent if not typical form ideology assumes is
the attempt to see "meaningful" order in chaos. Here ideology
most approximates Freud's notion of secondary revision through
which the distorted procedures of dream-work are straightened
out and made compatible with the demands of an ego in quest of
coherent meaning and identity. In culture and society, the often
incoherent modes of collective life—including the uncontrolled
oscillation between excessively restrictive control, for example
in narrow forms of technical or formal rationality and chaotic
excess or transgression—are covered and assuaged by attempts
to interpret existence as somehow imbued with satisfying meaning. The very quest for meaning and order that misconstrues

its object by infusing it with the overall coherence it lacks may of course be transferred into social science methodology itself. Such methodology deceptively provides methodological or "symbolic" solutions for substantive problems—problems that it does more to conceal than to disclose for critical analysis. And it may be seen as the complement to "positivism" rather than its alternative. The two seemingly opposed methodologies feed on one another and collaborate in diverting attention from the possibility of a more critical apprehension of the actual and desirable interaction between "meaningful" order and challenges to it in society and culture. In this sense, one may ask whether Geertz's entire "hermeneutic" orientation is itself ideological, for he has done much to focus if not fixate attention on the problem of social "meaning," including the way ideology presumably furnishes satisfying "meaning" for the collectivity. He has also tended to replicate the providential task of ideology in his own methodology and style—a fast-paced, eminently "readable" style that threatens to gloss over certain problems in both culture and its own stylized approach to cultural studies.

I would here note a difficulty in my analysis of ideology thus far. I seem to have correlated mystification or dissimulation with deceptive, essentializing, hegemonic modes of "meaningful" order, thereby creating at least by implication the impression that one may correlate "truth" or correctness with division, difference, and heterogeneity. I would, however, resist this implication (which is often associated with "poststructuralism") or attribute to it at best a provisional significance. It is, for example, possible that divisions and differences are introduced into an object of analysis in a distorting and deceptive manner, particularly when one believes that in so doing one is invariably furthering a critical if not subversive movement of theory and praxis. An endlessly "differing" procedure may take thought on increasingly involuted and conceit-laden paths that have at best the most problematic of relations with political and social criticism and may even instill more or less compulsive habits of discourse—what might be called discursive *tics douloureux*—that can be incapacitating in the attempt to confront sociopolitical and institutional issues. In addition, the one-sided stress on difference or disjunction joins the exclusive emphasis on "meaningful" order in diverting attention from the more general problem of the actual and desirable interaction between unity or order and various challenges to it.

This entire line of inquiry suggests a further point. Ideology may be contrasted with critical and possibly transformative—for Marx revolutionary—thought and practice. It need not be construed one-dimensionally as "false consciousness" and placed (as sometimes by Marx himself) in a binary opposition with absolute truth (itself often equated with positive science). I would argue that anything like social or human science arises—both historically and theoretically—in the recurrent yet variable interaction between ideology and critique, and it cannot be given a purely positivistic or value-neutral status (despite Marx's own inclination at times in this direction). Critique discloses what ideology mystifies, and it does so with implications for praxis. But just as ideology itself cannot be fixated in one essential form—be it as essentializing wholeness or "meaningful" order—so critique is recurrently subject to self-mystification and never entirely transcends this possibility in a realm of absolute truth or pure, value-neutral theory and method.

This kind of argument is not without its internal difficulties. It places science and critique within the same larger paradigm of critical theory. And it makes at best a limited and guarded appeal to universal norms which themselves may be seen as ideological naturalizations or fixations of the recurrent process of argument. (In any case, such norms have at best had an abstractly formal rather than a concretely substantive role in thought.) The approach I suggest situates critique in a discursive and argumentative context which itself has no absolute or ultimate grounds—a variable context that cannot even be labelled "pragmatic." This approach perhaps has the minimal value of making explicit what processes of inquiry and argument have always been, and it does not pretend to any transcendental or fully systematic (or "totalized") perspective. Rather it insists on the problematic connection of scientific inquiry and ethicopolitical judgment. This connection, it should be further noted, does not invalidate the idea of accuracy in propositions or the role of testing of hypotheses. In certain ways, it might even be seen as an attempt to situate a conception of science such as that elaborated by Karl Popper in a larger model of critical theory, at least with respect to the so-called human sciences.

I would note in concluding that this is precisely the type of model that is difficult to locate in Geertz's account, for Geertz runs the risks of voiding social science of a critical dimension and of providing deceptive if not ideological definitions of science itself. The terms in which Geertz, in quest of a "genuinely nonevaluative conception of ideology," opposes science and ideology are particularly instructive.

> The differentiae of science and ideology as cultural systems are to be sought in the sorts of symbolic strategy for encompassing situations that they respectively represent. Science names the structure of situations in such a way that the attitude contained toward them is one of disinterestedness. Its style is restrained, spare, resolutely analytic: by shunning the semantic devices that most effectively formulate moral sentiment, it seeks to maximize intel-

lectual clarity. But ideology names the structure of situations in such a way that the attitude toward them is one of commitment. Its style is ornate, vivid, deliberately suggestive: by objectifying moral sentiment through the same devices that science shuns, it seeks to motivate action. . . , The existence of a vital tradition of scientific analysis of social issues is one of the most effective guarantees against ideological extremism, for it provides an incomparably reliable source of positive knowledge for the political imagination to work with and to honor. It is not the only such check. The existence . . . of competing ideologies carried by other powerful groups in the society is at least as important; as is a liberal political system in which the dreams of total power are obvious fantasies; as are stable social conditions in which conventional expectations are not continually frustrated and conventional ideas not radically incompetent. But, committed with a quiet intransigence to a vision of its own, it is perhaps the most indomitable.   (1973: 231–33)

One may well agree with a number of the sentiments Geertz expresses in this passage, notably concerning the importance of relative social stability, groups with roughly equal power, and traditions of liberal politics and scientific investigation. But his account threatens to import a metascientific (or "ideological") conception of science into a seeming definition of science itself, and in so doing it relies on an "ornate, vivid, deliberately suggestive" opposition between science and ideology. Science presumably requires a "disinterested" attitude, a "restrained, spare, resolutely analytic" style, and a disavowal of extremism. One might object that science itself is not defined by questions of attitude, rhetoric, and political stance but by certain procedures of inquiry. What attitude, rhetoric, and politics go with these procedures cannot be derived from a definition of science itself; they at best constitute either empirical generalizations about scientists or ideologically normative prescriptions about the way scientists ought to behave. The fact that they are masked and naturalized in a seemingly neutral, universal definition of science may make Geertz's approach "ideological" in the narrower Marxist sense of the term.

In a footnote, Geertz acknowledges that science and ideology, while "two sorts of activity," may be combined, although "most such attempts to mix genres are . . . distinctly less happy" [than the putative success of Edward Shils in *The Torment of Secrecy*] (Ibid.: 231). But what tends to drop out of Geertz's account is the possibility of an articulation of science and ethicopolitical judgment in a broader conception of critical theory. This possibility is not adequately covered by a passing footnote about the role of so-called mixed genres (later thematized in Geertz as "blurred genres")—a notion parasitic upon an unargued prior analytic definition of pure genres. Also occluded are the problems engendered when the concerns active in the object of study are regenerated in one's account of it—what might be called a transferential relation to the object that cannot be transcended through seemingly anodyne definitions of culture, ideology, and science but must be worked through in a careful, critical, and self-critical way. Indeed the belief that one can avoid or transcend a transferential relation to the object of study tends to foster definitions that are covertly ideological and less subject to critical control than they might otherwise be. What is striking is that Geertz implicitly excludes options between extremism and moderation or neutrality, especially the possibility that certain situations may call for basic criticism that cannot be identified in patently ideological fashion with extremism and irresponsibility. One such situation involves a state of affairs in which just conditions for relative social stability are absent, power is distributed among groups in markedly unequal ways, and traditions of liberal politics and scientific investigation are jeopardized. The only gate Geertz leaves open for criticism is that presumably embodied in science itself in its ability to "force [ideologies] to come to terms with (but not necessarily surrender to) reality" (Ibid.: 232). Yet this notion of criticism receives no further discussion in "Ideology as a Cultural System." Nor is there any recognition that it requires an approach to problems not defined by the simple binary opposition between science and ideology. It is, I would suggest, in developing this approach that both a critical conception of ideology and a viable relation between science and critique may be most cogently elaborated.

References

Geertz, Clifford
  1973 *The Interpretation of Cultures* (New York: Basic Books).
Habermas, Jürgen
  1981 *Theorie des kommunikativen Handelns*, Vol. 2 (Frankfurt: Suhrkamp).
LaCapra, Dominick
  1985 *History & Criticism* (Ithaca: Cornell University Press).
Thompson, John B.
  1984 *Studies in the Theory of Ideology* (Berkeley: University of California Press).

Interpreting Rhetoric

Parodic Play and Prophetic Reason: Two Interpretations of Interpretation

Susan Handelman

That which imparts truth to the known and the power of knowing to the knower is what I would have you term the idea of the good, and this you will deem to be the cause of science, and of truth in so far as the latter becomes the subject of knowledge. . . . The good may be said to be not only the author of knowledge to all things known, but of their being and essence, and yet the good is not essence, but far exceeds essence (epekeina tes ousias) *in dignity and power.   Plato,* The Republic *508e–509b*

The place of the Good above every essence is the most profound teaching, the definitive teaching, not of theology, but of philosophy.   Emmanuel Levinas, Totality and Infinity *(103)*

The breakup of essence is ethics.   Levinas, Otherwise Than Being *(14)*

To laugh at philosophy (at Hegelianism)—such, in effect, is the form of the awakening—henceforth calls for an entire "discipline," an entire "method of meditation" that acknowledges the philosopher's byways, understands his techniques, makes use of his ruses, manipulates his cards, lets him deploy his strategy, appropriates his texts. Then, thanks to this work . . . but quickly, furtively, and unforseeably breaking with it, as betrayal or detachment, drily, laughter bursts out . . . a certain burst of laughter exceeds it and destroys its sense.   Derrida, Writing and Difference *(252–53)*

Modern antihumanism, denying the primacy of human reason, free and for itself is true over and beyond the reason it gives itself. It clears the place for subjectivity positing itself in abnegation, in sacrifice, in a substitution preceding the will. Its inspired intuition is to have abandoned the idea of person, goal, and origin of itself, in which the ego is still a thing because it is still a being. . . . Humanism has to be denounced only because it is not sufficiently human. Levinas, Otherwise Than Being *(127)*

The Alternatives

These epigraphs by Derrida and Levinas represent two different outcomes of the radical critique of philosophy in our era. I will call them here "parodic play" and "prophetic reason" and the contrast between them as alternative models for literary theory is what I wish to examine in this essay.

Needless to say, much deconstructive literary theory over the past decade has modelled itself after the first mode: the "play of the text." Although a kind of ennui has set in as the infatuation with "free play" wanes, many literary critics continue to be inspired by the other facet of deconstruction, its rigorous epistemological critique. The recent interest in Bakhtin, Foucault, and the New Historicism all indicate a desire to move "beyond" deconstruction, while accepting some of its important critiques of representation, meaning, signification. The "Beyond," in these cases, of course, is the return to the social and material matrices of meaning.

"Reason" and "ethics," however, are most often associated with the conservative attacks on deconstruction as nihilistic, self-indulgent, and elitist. Frustrated by these polemics, J. Hillis Miller though, has tried to recoup and articulate "the ethics of reading." Yet most post-structuralist critics, be they Lacanians, semioticians, New Historicists, feminists, or cultural materialists still suspect any call for ethics and reason as a mask for a discredited bourgeois humanism. Not only are God and the author dead but so too, they would say, is the "subject"—especially as some kind of unified, autonomous center. So what are the choices but anarchic dissemination of signs or analysis of the "codes" determining meaning or demystification of oppressive ideologies by revealing their status as constructs.

Here Levinas's critique of Western ontology and philosophy—a critique which preceded and inspired Derrida's—offers what I argue is a compelling alternative.[1] Levinas, too, has worked at the very limits

1. Levinas, in fact, originated the idea of the "trace." See Levinas (1966). Derrida (1976) refers to this essay: "Thus, I relate this concept of *trace* to what is at the

of philosophy, pondered "the end of metaphysics" and above all so-licited the breakup of "totality" by the "Other"—as an "otherwise than being" whose structure turns out to be radically ethical and leads to the infinite and transcendent. Ethics here is not conceived as a deter-minate set of beliefs or practices but the most original "ontological" structure which is the very "relation to the other." Levinas, that is, does not abandon reason but opens it to the command of the Other, in a prophetic and ethical call, that comes prior to and makes possible consciousness, representation, knowing, will. "The essence of reason does not mean securing foundations and powers for man, but calling him into question and inviting him to justice" (1969: 88); "We name this calling into question of my spontaneity by the presence of the other ethics" (Ibid.: 43).

For Levinas, the role of critique itself, of "calling into question," leads neither to self-reflexive undecidability nor to ideology. Critique is indeed the questioning of all foundations as in deconstruction but the calling into question of the same—that is, of a repressive logic of identity—is neither produced by nor results in any free play or arbitrariness of signs. It comes, rather, from the demanding appeal, order, call of the other. In other words, the "call" from the other resounds through the human Other, through whom the "other" of the "other than being" passes: "L'autre c'est L'Autrui."

The other, moreover, is neither hostile nor a scandal nor a plaything but "the first rational teaching, the condition for all teaching" (Ibid.: 203). To welcome the other leads to a knowledge beyond that of the cogito; it means to be conscious of my own injustice. Philosophy as a critical knowing thus begins with conscience (Ibid.: 86). And calling into question, then, is a calling to account for the other as neighbor in personal responsibility.

Levinas' Background

Despite his celebrity and influence in France, Levinas has not been as well known in America, especially in literary circles. In fact, Levinas brought phenomenology to France with his translation of Husserl's *Cartesian Meditations* in 1931 and became one of the first great inter-preters and critics of Heidegger and Husserl beginning with his first book in 1930, *The Theory of Intuition in the Phenomenology of Husserl*. He has continued to produce widely read books and essays up to the

---

center of the latest work of Emmanuel Levinas and his critique of ontology. . ." (1976: 70). In the first of his essays on Levinas, "Violence and Metaphysics," Der-rida writes: ". . . the thought of Emmanuel Levinas can make us tremble. At the heart of the desert, in the growing wasteland, this thought, which fundamentally no longer seeks to be a thought of Being and phenomenality, makes us dream of an inconceivable process of dismantling and dispossession" (1967: 82).

present.[2] As he wryly notes in an interview, "But it was Sartre who guaranteed my place in eternity when stating in his famous obituary essay on Merleau-Ponty that he, Sartre, 'was introduced to phenomenology by Levinas'" (Cohen 1986: 16).

Levinas did not only introduce phenomenology, he radically critiqued it. As Blanchot, a long-time friend, has written: "When Levinas asked if ontology were fundamental . . . [the question] was unexpected and unheard of, because it broke with what seemed to have renewed philosophy [Heidegger], and also because he was the first to have contributed to understanding and transmitting this thought" (Ibid.: 43). Levinas is one of the thinkers who made Derrida and deconstruction possible and Derrida, in turn, has made possible a renewed appreciation of Levinas.

Although my main focus in this essay is the relation between deconstructive parodic play versus Levinasian prophetic reason in light of the present cry for a "beyond deconstruction," I also briefly want to consider this subject in terms of the relations among theology, Judaism, and literary theory. "Briefly" solely for reasons of space; I assume that most readers of this collection are far more familiar with Derrida than Levinas, so I will need to take considerable time here to outline (albeit roughly) some of Levinas's key ideas. I will focus here mostly on his ideas of language; I cannot touch on his many other analyses of topics such as temporality, labor, the feminine, history, eros, the body, eschatology, or his talmudic analyses.

Like Derrida, Levinas is a Jew who came to France from elsewhere —in this case from Russia after the Bolshevik revolution and then again after his studies in the late 1920s in Germany with Husserl and Heidegger. There were profound philosophical reasons for his critique of Heidegger but there were also personal and political ones as well—especially after Heidegger's temporary alliance with Nazism. As a Jew, Levinas himself was a prisoner in a detention camp in Germany during World War II. Although these personal experiences are not overtly mentioned in his philosophical writings, in his Jewish writings he is quite pointed: "It is difficult to forgive Heidegger" (1968: 56).[3]

---

2. The most complete bibliography of Levinas has been compiled by Roger Burggraeve (1986). It lists approximately 400 items by Levinas himself and about 800 more essays and books written about him over the past fifty years. A recent collection in his honor, *Textes pour Emmanuel Levinas* (1982) contains Derrida's second major essay on Levinas, along with contributions by Blanchot, Jabès, Lyotard, Ricoeur and others.

3. In an autobiographical essay, Levinas writes that his biography is "dominated by the presentiment and the memory of the Nazi horror" (1928: 177). And he also states: "No generosity which the German 'es gibt' is said to express showed itself between 1933 and 1945. This must be said! Illumination and sense dawn only with

His attack on what he calls the neutral impersonal realm of the *il y a* ("There is") is a critique of Heidegger's subordination of individual existents to existence or being to anonymous Being.

But Levinas did not view the cry of protest of the personal subject to be the answer—just as he never thought the subjective irrationalism of Kierkegaard could be an effective antidote to Hegel. Existentialism, of course, was superseded in France by structuralism which destroyed the freedom of the personal self as a locus of meaning in favor of impersonal structures and codes. Levinas contested this move but, unlike many others, he did not do so to uphold the personal ego; to him, the ego in its natural state is narcissistic and violent. But he also condemned the "structures" of structuralism as neutral, anonymous, indifferent and oppressive. "Structuralism," he writes, "is the primacy of theoretical reason" (1974: 58).

Levinas instead defined the existent by its relation with the Other, a relation which is not a subject/object relation, as we shall see. The other is disproportionate to all "the power and freedom of the I" and this disproportion between the other and I is precisely "moral consciousness." It is not "an experience of values" but an access to exteriority, to Being as other, and finally beyond ontology to the otherwise than being (1978: 183).

At the same time he was writing his later philosophical masterpieces, Levinas was also acting as the Director of the Ecole Normale Israélite Orientale, a Jewish school which was part of the Alliance Israélite Orientale, an organization dedicated to spreading French and Jewish culture throughout Jewish communities in France and its former Mediterranean empire. He was also writing prolifically on Judaism and Jewish life. In fact, his first collection of philosophical interpretations of the Talmud (the massive compilation of ancient Rabbinic law and commentary) *Quatre lectures talmudiques*, appeared in 1968 in the "Critique" series by Editions de Minuit—the same series in which Derrida published *De la grammatologie, Marges de la philosophie, Positions* and which also includes the key works of the intellectual avant-garde of France: Bataille, Deleuze, André Green, Irigaray, Lyotard, Robbe-Grillet, Marin, Serres.

---

the existing beings' rising up and establishing themselves in this horrible neutrality of the *there is*" (Ibid.: 181).

In *Difficile liberté*, a collection of essays on Judaism, Levinas puts this in other terms and writes that Heidegger "inundates the pagan corners of the western soul" (1963: 256). His fascination with the mystery of place and Being is the "eternal seduction of paganism, beyond all the infantilism of idolatry, long surmounted . . . of the sacred filtering through the world . . . Judaism is perhaps the negation of that. . . . The mystery of things is the source of every cruelty in relation to men" (Ibid.: 257).

What his writing shares with the works in the "critique" series is this question of the "other"—the other of philosophy, the disruption of the logic of identity by the irruption of the heterogenous other in the homogenizing same. As Vincent Descombes argues so well in *Modern French Philosophy* (titled in French *Le Même et L'Autre*), this attempt to absorb and then break free of the philosophy of the "three H's," Hegel, Heidegger, and Husserl and to redefine the relation of same and other is a central aim of all modern French philosophy . . . from phenomenology through post-structuralism.

In one of his most recent and telling interviews, Derrida says that he was fascinated by Levinas because he was "the philosopher working in phenomenology and posing the question of the "other to phenomenology; the Judaic dimension remained at that stage a discrete rather than decisive reference" (Kearney 1984: 107). The relation of "Jew" and "Greek" in Levinas's thought, however, is one of the main preoccupations of Derrida's long, admiring essay on Levinas's first masterwork *Totality and Infinity*. The last paragraph of the essay ponders a split and double identity:

> Are we Jews? Are we Greeks? We live in the difference between the Jew and the Greek, which is perhaps the unity of what is called history. We live in and of the difference, that is, in *hypocrisy*, about which Levinas so profoundly says that it is "not only a base contingent defect of man, but the underlying rending of a world attached to both the philosophers and the prophets" (1969: 24). . . . And what is the legitimacy, what is the meaning of the *copula* in this proposition from perhaps the most Hegelian of modern novelists: "Jewgreek is greekjew. Extremes meet." (1978: 153)[4]

The Greek/Jew conflict/synthesis recapitulates the rabbi/poet conflict Derrida had written of that same year (1964) in an essay on another Jewish immigrant to France, the poet Edmond Jabès. Here the conflict is identified as heteronomy versus autonomy, the poet's freedom versus the rabbi's subjection to the Law. And two years later, this dichotomy became the famous "two interpretations of interpretation" which Derrida defines at the end of the essay "Structure, Sign, and Play": one interpretation nostalgically seeking origin, the other affirming free play. Readers often neglect Derrida's conclusion that the two interpretations, though irreconcilable, are lived simultaneously—

---

4. I do not have space in this essay to discuss Derrida's intricate analyses of Levinas. Moreover, this has already been done superbly by Robert Bernasconi (1985) and (1987). I agree with Bernasconi's conclusion that "The question remains whether Derrida in being deaf to the ethical voice of saying, does not fail to do justice to all the possibilities of language to which Levinas has introduced us and does not therefore ultimately fail in his description of the necessities governing Levinas's language" (1985: 40). Bernasconi does not, however, consider the "Jew/Greek" issue.

and there is no possibility of choosing between them. Similarly, at the end of the Jabès essay, he writes that there will *always* be Rabbis and poets and two interpretations of interpretation.

As to the location of his own thought: "While I consider it essential to think through the copulative synthesis of Greek and Jew, I consider my own thought, paradoxically, as neither Greek nor Jewish. I often feel that the questions I attempt to formulate on the outskirts of the Greek philosophical tradition have as their 'other' the model of the Jew, that is, the Jew-as-other." But his project is to find a "non-site beyond both the Jewish influence of my youth and the Greek philosophical heritage" of his French schooling (Ibid.: 107). One of Derrida's main disagreements with Levinas is Derrida's assertion that the non-site "cannot be defined or situated by means of philosophical language" (Ibid.: 108). Thus, as we know, Derrida turns to those literary writers and poets who press the limits of language—such as Mallarmé and Blanchot or Genet whom he juxtaposes to Hegel in *Glas*. That, too, is why his own writing style becomes increasingly "monstrous," an off-centered mixture of philosophy, literature, seriousness and joking.

Parody and Otherness

Here is one key to the issue of parody which Alan Megill has insightfully described in his recent book *Prophets of Extremity* (1985): "Derrida is a supreme ironist: undoubtedly the most accomplished ironist of our age. He is also a parodist" (Ibid.: 260)—not the apocalyptic prophet of crisis in the high modernist vein but the very underminer of crisis thought (Ibid.: 266). In the works after *Glas*, "comic catharsis once more becomes possible, for Derrida's is a post-ethical, aesthetic laughter that knows the limit of the thought of crisis" (Ibid.: 267) a freer and less strained laughter than Nietzsche's and "less bitter and hysterical" than Foucault's (Ibid.: 266).[5]

Megill makes the important connection between the strategy of the "double science," Derrida's style of repetition and difference in his readings—and parody, which also is a way of doubling another text in a heightened and reflexive way. Parody, though, is by no means

5. I am grateful to David Hoy for this reference. Hoy's analysis in his essay "Foucault: Modern or Postmodern?" forthcoming from Rutgers University Press in a volume on Foucault edited by Jonathan Arac is also very helpful. Here Hoy contrasts the "lightheartedness" of post-modernism and its attraction to parody and pastiche to the more ponderous seriousness of modernism.

Foucault (1977) also specifies the "parodic" as one of the Nietzschean modes to be emulated in opposing a Platonic sense of history. Citing Nietzsche: "Perhaps, we can discover a realm where originality is again possible as parodists of history and buffoons of God" (*Beyond Good and Evil*, 223). This would be the "parodic double" of "monumental history."

anarchic or nihilistic; it has its own "rules" as Margaret Rose shows in *Parody//Meta-Fiction* (1979). Parody is a species of imitation or quotation—indicated in the etymology of the word *parody: para* meaning both "nearness" and "opposition." The crucial point here is that unlike satire, which suppresses the target text, parody, "makes the object of attack part of its own structure" (Ibid.: 35). It is never torn away and free of it but closely attached. Parody is also a kind of meta-language, self-reflexive and self-critical—not mere mockery" but a "refunctioning" of the target text.

Now if the project of finding a non-site for philosophy to appear to itself as other, to interrogate itself, is central for Derrida, parody is a highly appropriate form. Derrida, like Levinas, views the Hegelian dialectic as ultimately a tyranny of the logic of identity, of the same, a self-enclosed and imperial (as in Derrida's pun on Hegel's name as "Eagle" at the beginning of *Glas*) narcissism which mutes other and always returns to itself.

For Derrida, it would not be enough, therefore, to criticize philosophy in its own voice, through its own reason. Nor would it be enough to find a complete opposite—first, because the opposite would still be defined by the same and second, because all discourse takes place in the space philosophical speech has created. But if one could show the *other to be already in the same*, from the beginning fissured, that would be an alterity that could not be reabsorbed. Thus Derrida has to remain extremely close and faithful to the text under analysis as he moves through his readings—and why his is a deeply parodic structure, incorporating the target text in the very structure of his own writing . . . parody as decentered mimesis. And why, too, even when he is less overtly parodic, his own writing is so frustratingly off-centered, indirect, elliptical, dissimulating, digressive.

But the key question is precisely what and who is the "other"? As Robert Bernasconi writes, one of the central differences between Levinas and Derrida is located right at this point. For even though Derrida adopted the notion of the trace from Levinas, "for Derrida the trace is of a text and not of the Other" (1985: 35). Derrida's use of the Levinasian trace to attack Saussure and Heidegger has more to do with Derrida's concern for the philosophy of presence "than to do justice to Levinas' attack on the neutrality of philosophy" (Ibid.: 28). Indeed, post-structuralism, for all its variegated attempts to show the instability of structures—whether linguistic or political—continues to pit one form of anonymous or impersonal force against another.

In a Derridean reading, as Vincent Descombes points out, the vital point is that no synthesis is possible between the two texts, "no fusing into one, for the second is not the opposite of the first, but rather its counterpart, slightly phased" (1980: 150). The double science shows the duplicity of any text and enacts a duplicitous metaphysics. That is, "It is itself as other. Every metaphysics, being double, is its own simulacrum, a slight displacement, a slight play in the reading sufficient to collapse the first into the second, the wisdom of the first into the comedy of the second." Thus one can never quite tell, says Descombes, whether Derridean deconstruction is a tyrannicide or a game (Ibid.: 151). It is obviously both, a tragi-comedy, entitled "The Death of Philosophy."

But Bakhtin has also reminded us in *The Dialogic Imagination* and his book on Rabelais that laughter and parody are among the most ancient forms of linguistic representation and that "there never was a single strictly straightforward genre, no single type of direct discourse —artistic, rhetorical, philosophical, religious, ordinary everyday—that did not have its own parodying and travestying double, its own comic-ironic *contre-partie*" (1981: 53).

In Bakhtin, parody is a "relation to another's word" (Ibid.: 69), again involving the key question of the relation of the same and the other, the ambiguous relation between two intermixed speeches and the contest between them. The relation can be reciprocal, a dialogue, questioning, argument, appropriation, regeneration, illumination, a mix of both reverence and ridicule.

Here again, there is an interesting Jewish undercurrent . . . the pre-eminent philosopher of "dialogue" in our century was, of course, the Jewish thinker Martin Buber. As Joseph Frank reports, Bakhtin preserved his admiration for Buber to the very end of his life and said he thought Buber: "the greatest philosopher of the twentieth century, and perhaps in this philosophically puny century, perhaps the sole philosopher on the scene . . . I am very much indebted to him. In particular for the idea of dialogue. Of course, this is obvious to anyone who reads Buber" (1986: 56 n.2).

The Other as Ethical Relation and Language

Levinas has strongly disagreed with Buber's idea of the other as a *symmetrical* partner (1967: 133–150). For Levinas, the other is not in a reciprocal relation to the same; rather the other calls, appeals, commands from the dimensions of both height and depth; this is what he calls the "Face" in *Totality and Infinity*. The face of the other is the cry of naked destitution demanding response. But the Other is also the elevation of the "Good beyond Being." For our purposes, the essential point about his complex idea of "face" is that it does *not* mean visual perception. It is a figure which tries to describe a different kind of reflection, cognition, and perception than egoistic contemplation in solitude.[6] It indicates a kind of immediate relation where one is captured, compelled, taken in, but not in any kind of irrational delirium; the "nakedness of the face" is an exposure which is the "very possibility of understanding" (1963: 21). This vulnerable nudity of the face becomes itself the primordial appeal/command of "Thou Shalt Not Kill." Later, in *Otherwise Than Being*, Levinas will define subjectivity itself precisely as vulnerability.

The notion of the face, in other words, describes a self-already-in-relation: an other-in-the-same. The welcome of the face is not a Heideggerian "disclosure" or bringing to a light. For the relation between the same and other is not reducible to *knowledge* of other by the same or even revelation of other to same (1969: 28). The face is prior to every question about the "What" of things, the "What is it?" The face refers to the question, "Who is it," the question of the other which for Levinas is already present in any question put, for the question is always *put to* someone. The face is the irreducibly prior and given, a "condition of possibility."

But the face as the "who is it," the *to* whom of the question, is not the realm of representation or cognition but desire—a desire beyond satisfaction or non-satisfaction, which Levinas calls "metaphysical desire." This desire is distinguished from need and as desire for the absolutely *other*, alterity, it can never be satisfied. It is not a desire for an "object" but for the "other"; as such it remains separated, not dissolved into the other. The urge behind the very "calling into question" is itself an aspect of metaphysical desire. As other-in-the same, the face is also the uncontainable excess, the more-in-the-less, or Infinite-in-the-finite. And the relation with the other is the call of the "good beyond being," a positivity.

It is this *separated* relation between same and other, he claims, that institutes language. "The revelation of the face is language" (1978: 185). Language, that is, connects but does not fuse the separated subject and other. Language as conversation with the other retains the separation and difference necessary for the integrity of other as "other." "Truth does not undo distance, does not result in the union of knower and known, does not issue in totality . . . [it is] epiphany at a distance" (1969: 60).

The relation with the other shatters the narcissistic unity of the subject—but this is not accomplished through any "anonymous" function

6. James Ponet (1985) argues that Levinas's sense of the face "is clearly biblically derived," citing the connotations of the term especially in the Jacob stories; the central biblical blessing, the Blessing of the Face (Numbers 6:22–27); Moses's veiling of his face (Exodus 34:29–35); God's hiding His face (Job 12: 24; Psalms 27: 8–9). The Hebrew word for "face," *panim*, has a dynamic connotation: it comes from the root *panah*, meaning "turn"—a turning to or away from.

of language. The subject is decentered, displaced, traumatized as ego; but this demand of otherness is precisely a claim and demand for *responsibility for the other* and leads to a metaphysical ex-cendence and inspiration. In Levinas, "difference" becomes non-indifference to the other (1981: 166).

How can the Subject be deconstructed, yet still remain ethically responsible? Neither Derrida nor Levinas, of course, are the first to attack metaphysics—Kant did that long before and laid out the subsequent course of modern philosophy. Will aesthetics or ethics, then, be the substitute or alternative left when transcendence is demolished? Or, instead of Heideggerian Being, is ethics as the "relation to the Other" the original structure of transcendence itself as Levinas tries to show.

For Levinas, "Already *ethics of itself* is an optics" (1969: 29), not simply a preparation for transcendence. Steven Schwarzschild notes that this is also the "one perennial differentia of all Jewish philosophical thought—what Kant calls 'the primacy of practical reason,' i.e., the metaphysical ultimacy of ethics and its constitutive and functional decisiveness even for the cognitive world" (1985: 252). Indeed Levinas writes, "If we retain one trait from a philosophical system . . . we would think of Kantism, which finds a meaning to the human without measuring it by ontology, . . . and outside of the immortality and death which ontologies run up against" (1981: 129). Since, however, Levinas sees "philosophical systems" as oppressive and totalitarian, he does not accept the call of the other as a universal law; the imperative is not categorical as it is for Kant.

In fact, Levinas's great attack on "totality" in Hegel, Heidegger, and phenomenology in *Totality and Infinity* itself has a strong Jewish origin: the work of Franz Rosenzweig whose first philosophical book was a critique of Hegel and whose masterwork, *The Star of Redemption* (1921) formulated a radically new Jewish philosophy. As Levinas writes at the beginning of *Totality and Infinity*, *The Star* "is a work too often present in this book to be cited" (1969: 28).[7] Levinas in general, however, avoids overtly mentioning or depending on Jewish sources for his arguments in his philosophical works: "My point of departure is absolutely non-theological. This is very important to me; it is not theology which I do, but philosophy" (1962: 110).

But what kind of philosophy? Writing of the relation between philosophy and life in Rosenzweig's work and the "end of philosophy"

7. In another interview with Salomon Malka, Levinas says that it is Rosenzweig's critique of the idea of totality in the *Star* "that I have purely and simply taken over" (Malka 1984: 105). Richard Cohen also thinks Levinas's use of the figure of "Face" may also come from the end of *The Star of Redemption* (personal interview, July 24, 1987).

which is "perhaps the very meaning of our age," he emphasizes: "The end of philosophy is not the return to an epoch where it had not begun, where one could not philosophize; the end of philosophy is the beginning of an era where all is philosophy, because philosophy is not revealed through philosophers" (1963: 124). "Theoretical man has ceased to reign" (Ibid.: 125)—that is theory as enchaining, totalizing system. But the result cannot be simple spontaneity or anarchic protest as in Kierkegaard and Nietzsche. Aristotle's "it is necessary to philosophize to not be a philosopher" defines the extreme possibility of the philosophy in the twentieth century, a statement with which Derrida agrees and indeed cites in his essay on Levinas (1978: 152).

Levinas also finds sources for his key idea of the otherwise than being within the history of non-Jewish Western philosophy, most paradigmatically in Plato's "Good beyond Being" in the *Republic*, in Plotinus's *Enneads* and in Descartes's "idea of the infinite" in the *Third Meditation*. In Descartes, this idea of the infinite is an excess, surplus, overflow in the finite mind as it conceives of "infinity" . . . i.e., an idea that comes from a beyond the finite mind, that the mind cannot contain.

As Levinas takes it up, then, the critique of metaphysics, reason, and theory does not become an intoxication with excess as the irrational, a worship of negativity, a fascination with the abyss or schizophrenic and psychotic states, a paralytic self-reflexivity or a political ideology as we have seen in much recent French theory and literature. For Levinas, as for other French theorists from Lacan to Barthes to Derrida to Foucault, the subject as self-enclosed, free, satisfied ego is deconstructed, made a *subject to*. But in Levinas this very movement constitutes the subject as irreplaceable, a unique self called upon to respond to the appeal of the other, constituted as responsible for the other.

In *Otherwise Than Being*, this idea of the subject is radicalized and further defined as the very *substituting of oneself* for the other. By this Levinas also means something as physical as "the duty to give the other even the bread out of one's own mouth and the coat from one's shoulders" (1981: 55). Substitution as one-for-the-other is also revealed as the basic structure of signification: A is for B or: A is instead of B. This mode of relation with the other cuts across both the logic of contradiction and dialectical logic where the same "participates in" or is reconciled with the other in the unity of system.

Levinas thus maintains an interhuman relation with the "other"; the subject is deconstructed but not dissolved into impersonal "systems" of signs or "discursive practices." These forms of impersonality, he claims, are as imperialistic as any other and subordinate the ethical relation. Unlike other French theorists, he does not relocate freedom in some autonomous or anthropomorphized power of "Language" nor is the antidote to totalizing systems the anarchic play of the signifier.

Thus while his work is a radical critique of being and philosophy, it is also "a defense of subjectivity" (1969: 26); the subject is dispossessed but in relation.

Subjectivity as Vulnerability

Precisely this dispossession enables language to found community because "it offers things which are mine to the other. To speak is to make the world common. . . . Language does not refer to the generality of concepts, but lays the foundation for a possession in common. . . . It abolishes the inalienable property of enjoyment."[8] Levinas here is pointing to the often unrecognized potential of language to be a gift, an offering, and welcome of the other. In this sense, language as the relation between me and the other as interlocutor presupposes every proof and every symbolism—and not simply because it is necessary to agree on that symbolism and establish its conventions. That is, the relation with the other *already* is necessary for a given even to appear as a sign, a sign signaling a speaker, regardless of what may be signified by the sign or whether it be decipherable. In other words, the one who signals himself by the sign is not the "signified" of the sign; rather, s/he delivers the sign and gives it (Ibid.: 92). Exposure and vulnerability then become the very conditions of communication. Communication can't be reduced to the manifestation of "truth" and saying is not a simple "intention to address a message" (1981: 48).

Contemporary theories of language, even those which are dialogical and social such as Bakhtin's, seem to neglect this essential point. Prior to cognition, there is a necessary solidarity of discourse; and that itself depends on a first dispossession of the self to even enable the movement toward the other in language. The primary level of communication, then, is not information or the giving of signs but the self as "the communication of communication, a sign of the giving of signs" (Ibid.: 119). Hence "metalanguage" is neither empty self-reflexiveness nor ideological demystification but openness and responsibility for the other and transcendence. This founds and makes possible the empirical ego who then thematizes, is conscious and cognizing. Communication would be impossible if it began with the ego as a "free subject to whom every other would only be a limitation that invites war, domination, precaution and information" (Ibid.: 119).

Levinas is reminding us that the "relationalism" of structuralism, (the idea that meaning is a function of relations between signs rather than referents to an external reality) is inadequate. Structuralism *synchronizes* all these relations in an atemporal horizontal whole; it is another form of totalizing system—and this critique, of course, has

---

8. For the relation of Levinas's ideas about language as performative action to speech-act theory, see Lyotard's essay on Levinas in Cohen (1986).

been made by many post-structuralists as well. But in Levinas there is an explicit ethical cast to this critique; it is not purely cognitive. "Difference," diachrony, and temporality as the disruption of synchrony and system are not merely other autonomous, neutral forces or linguistic "effects." Instead, these are constituted for Levinas in the relation behind all relations: the relation with the other and the *human* other is the place where the "other" passes, questions and interrupts being. Signs are *given* and Levinas takes this quite literally—before being given in impersonal systems, signs are given as offering between interlocutors. This giving is part of the ethical nature of language as relation of same and Other.

In much deconstructive criticism, the phrase "Everything is mediated through language" has become a way of denying connections to—or even the existence of—experiences beyond language and nontextual referents. Derrida in his interview with Kearney expresses frustration at the proliferation of critical commentaries on deconstruction which teach that "there is nothing beyond language, that we are submerged in words—and other stupidities of that sort. . . . It is totally false to suggest that deconstruction is a suspension of reference. . . . The critique of logocentrism is above all else the search for the 'other' and the 'other of language'" (Ibid.: 123). Deconstruction really shows, he continues, not that there is no referent but that "the question of reference is more complex and problematic than traditional theories supposed. . . . I totally refuse the label of nihilism . . . Deconstruction is not an enclosure in nothingness, but an openness towards the other. . . . My work does not destroy the subject; it simply tries to resituate it" (Ibid.: 125).

For Levinas also as we have seen, this openness toward the other is an overflow of the cognitive subject. But in contrast to Derrida, it is an overwhelming command and appeal such that the human ethical immediacy itself founds signification:

> It is not the mediation of the sign that forms signification, but signification (whose primordial event is the face to face) that makes the sign function possible. . . . *the being of signification consists in putting into question in an ethical relation constitutive freedom itself.* Meaning is the face of the Other, and all recourse to words takes place already within the primordial face to face of language. . . . [which is] society and obligation . . . the essence of language is the relation with the Other. (1969: 206–7)

Such a signification is "Infinite," an inexhaustible surplus, overflowing consciousness.

Ethics and Politics

In both *Totality and Infinity* and *Otherwise Than Being*, the asymmetrical relation of self and other also involves what Levinas calls the "third party," the "other of the other"—the third person who represents the political and social world beyond the pair of self and neighbor. Through the third party, the "whole of humanity" looks out from the destituteness of the face, appeals and commands. Thus discourse as relation with the other demanding justice for all humanity is also "sermon, exhortation, the prophetic word" (1969: 213). And prophetic in the classical biblical tradition of the cry for justice: "To hear his destitution which cried out for justice is not to represent an image to oneself, but is to posit oneself as responsible . . . the Other who dominates me in his transcendence is thus the stranger, the widow, and the orphan to whom I am obligated" (Ibid.: 215). Levinas's own style at this point becomes itself emphatically prophetic: "Speech is not instituted in a homogenous or abstract medium, but in a world where it is necessary to aid and to give" (Ibid.: 216).

This prophetic strain and the Jewish undercurrent are clearly evident in *Otherwise Than Being* which Levinas dedicates to the memory of those killed by the Nazis, both those "closest" among the six million Jews and the "millions of all confessions and all nations, victims of the same hatred of the other man, the same anti-semitism." The urgency of the question of the other comes not simply from the legacy of Hegel and Husserl and Western thought but from an attempt to combat the catastrophic hatred and violence in European history resulting from these philosophical systems. "Political totalitarianism rests on ontological totalitarianism," (1963: 257) for there is an "implicit metaphysics in the political thought of the West" (Ibid.: 221). Western philosophy has "mainly remained at home in saying being . . . the being at home with oneself, of which European history itself has been the conquest and jealous defense" (1981: 178).

In the margins of Western history, though, are the victims of these triumphs and "traces of events carrying another signification" (Ibid.: 178). One is reminded here of Walter Benjamin, another tortured modern Jew, whose solution to the catastrophes of contemporary history was an uncomfortable hybrid of Marxism and Jewish messianism, each of which furnished an eschatology which might recoup and redeem history's violence.

Levinas, however, did not follow the intellectual trends of post-war France in this respect as well; he was never attracted to Marxism. For him, ethics is irreducible and *prior* to politics just as it is prior to ontology. As Derrida puts it so well, Levinas's work is a "non-Marxist reading of philosophy as ideology" (1978: 97). Nevertheless, Levinas also recognizes the "ethical" intent and importance of

> Marx's critique of Western idealism as a project to understand the world rather than to transform it. In Marx's critique we find an ethical conscience cutting through the ontological identification of truth with an ideal intelli-

gibility and demanding that theory be converted into a concrete praxis of concern for the other. It is this revelatory and prophetic cry that explains the extraordinary attraction that the Marxist utopia exerted over numerous generations. (Cohen 1986: 33)

This prophetic cry and quasi-Marxist perspective also underlies much of the new "cultural materialism" in literary studies. J. Hillis Miller insightfully notes that, despite the differences in their reasons for attacking deconstructive linguistic theory, both the political left and the right "resort to moral or moralistic denunciation." The left claims it is immoral not to be concerned with history and society and only to indulge in the contemplation of language playing with itself; the right claims that the skepticism about language and humanistic tradition is immoral and nihilistic (1987: 283–84).

Levinas would not differ with the New Historicists or political critics about the need for political analysis or action but rather in the position given the political and material vis-à-vis the ethical. He defines the political as the realm of the "moral" as distinct from the "ethical," i.e., the moral as the rules of social organization, distribution and exchange of power, legislation and mediation of various "interests." Ethics, as extreme disinterestedness, vulnerability and sensitivity to the other then becomes "morality" when it moves into the political world of the "impersonal 'third,'" the other of the other—institutions, government, etc. The key point: "But the norm that must continue to inspire and direct the moral order is the ethical norm of the interhuman" (Cohen 1986: 29–30).

In other words, the realm of politics cannot be separated from its origin in the ethical structure of the one-for-the-other or else one justifies a "State delivered over to its own necessities" (1969: 159). This is not an authentic justice but another kind of manipulation of the masses. Without ethics as *first* philosophy, there is not even any way to discriminate among political systems. Moreover, "Equality of all is born by my inequality, the surplus of my duties over my rights" (1981: 159). Since responsibility is for what is precisely "other," i.e., non-encompassable, these obligations can never be satisfied but grow in proportion to their fulfillment; duty is infinite.

Levinas would then pose a question to all *materially based* movements for human freedom and justice: "The forgetting of self moves justice. [One must then know] if the egalitarian and just state in which man is fulfilled . . . proceeds from a war of all against all, or from the irreducible responsibility of the one for the all, and if it can do without friendship and faces?" (1981: 159–60). Without some primary act of withholding, of self-abnegation, of "passivity," of otherwise than being, all the alternatives still partake of the violent impersonal realm of being; that is, they are "egoisms struggling with one another, each against all, in the multiplicity of allergic egoisms which are at war with one another" whether the context is politics, psychology, sociology, linguistics (Ibid.: 4).

The Saying and the Said

Action, in other words, requires first a passivity, a trauma to the willing, enjoying, egoistic self. It requires an oscillation like breathing—between withholding and assertion; withdrawal and expulsion; philosophy and non-philosophy; soul and body; language and what is beyond representation and speech. This latter he will call the "Saying and the Said" (*le dire et le dit*). Thus his striking metaphor "that the subject could be a lung at the bottom of its substance—all this signifies a subjectivity that suffers and offers itself before taking a foothold in being," exposed and vulnerable (1981: 180).

In *Otherwise Than Being*, he drops the ontological vocabulary, refines and radicalizes his idea of language and changes the focus from the "face" to this idea of the "Saying and the Said." The saying is this "language before language" now defined as the unrepresentable, anarchic, unknowable aspect of the relation, which necessarily betrays itself into language as the "Said." This change is partially a response to the Derridean problem of finding, articulating the "other" of language in language. "Saying" is still a linguistic metaphor to describe a non-linguistic realm, thus acknowledging the complexity of our access to it. Levinas will then analyze this oscillation between the Saying and the Said as the very alternation between skepticism and philosophy.

Though the "saying" is non-thematizable, non-representable, beyond the gatherings of history and memory, "an-archic," (i.e., prior to all *arche*, origins and foundations), it still always must be "said," "betrayed" in the very language one uses to speak about it. The said, however, retains a "trace" of the saying and Levinas redefines the "phenomenological reduction" precisely as the movement back to the saying from the said. "In it the indescribable is described" (Ibid.: 53); philosophy is "indiscretion in relation to the inexpressible" (Malka 1984: 108).

While this line of thought seems to parallel deconstruction, it then veers away: though "saying" is antecedent to verbal signs, linguistic systems and semantic glimmerings, it "is not a game" and retains the ethical structure of what he now calls the "proximity of one to the other, the commitment of an approach, the one for the other, the very signifyingness of signification" (1981: 5). One of his essential theses is that the *orientation* of the terms takes precedence over their content: saying is a pre-original orientation, approach, nearness without abolishing distance between terms, the relation of responsibility. And this orientation, as we have seen, he considers the very ability of anything to signify, to give itself, to be not only itself but other—for something else.

Saying, then, is the "condition of possibility" of meaning. The subject here is "called," "chosen before choice," "hostage" to the other but in a positive way, ordered by the good beyond being. It is not, however, playful: this pre-original saying "sets forth an order more grave than being and antecedent to being. By comparison being appears like a game . . . without responsibility where every possibility is permitted." But play, Levinas notes, is not itself "free"—it, too, has its "interests" (Ibid.: 60).

Play still partakes of the egoistic structure of being; it is not "disinterestedness"—dis-inter- *esse,* the undoing of *esse,* of essence. Any game or play implies a "comic mask" and such a mask "always implies a self contemplating or expressing itself, playing" (Ibid.: 56). In contrast, the "otherwise than being" is a pure gratuitous disinterestedness, responsibility as substitution, hostage for the other—a giving of oneself over as a "complete gratuity which indicates an extreme gravity, and not the fallaciousness of play" (Ibid.: 60).

Whereas Derrida sees his task as eliciting alterity through a "gratuitousness" of miming, playing, dissimulation, equivocation, Levinas sees the task of philosophy as reducing or "unsaying" the dissimulation and betrayal of the said. This unsaying opens to exteriority, to the transcendence of the other. Yet he also recognizes the necessity of the said, of representation, for signification to show itself. This is not the grim necessity of the "prison-house of language" which one can only try to destabilize from within. Rather, the said, too, involves a positive ethical moment. For both responsibility and justice it is necessary that saying retain a reference to being; there can be no justice without measurement, comparison, correlation, synchronization, representation: "Essence has its time and hour" (Ibid.: 46) but "being must be understood on the basis of being's other" (Ibid.: 16).

This paradoxical necessity means that the other, the sincerity of saying will signify only through the *ambiguity* of every said (Ibid.: 152). Ambiguity, then, is not paralytic perplexity, dark undecidability, or an anonymous "effect of language." It is the "sign given of the giving of signs" (Ibid.: 151), the resonance of every language as inspiration, witness, and a kind of prophecy. Ambiguity here becomes the opening to the other, not an autonomous or indifferent self-reflexivity. Instead of turning on itself in emptiness, signification empties itself to turn toward and substitute for the other. And since by definition, the "infinite" or "transcendent" or other cannot be contained in the finite or same, signification will always show itself paradoxically. Indeed, it must interrupt its own demonstration to the point where it is "necessary that its pretension be exposed to derision and refutation" (Ibid.:

152). Skeptical critique is necessary—especially to prevent "ideology and sacred delirium" (Ibid.) from filling the space of this opening to the Other. But equivocations of signs in dissemination or parodic play do not constitute this opening. They are a "being otherwise"—but not an "otherwise than being."

When Levinas says that "language is already skepticism" (Ibid.: 170), he means that language can exceed thought by "letting be understood without ever making understandable," a meaning different from that which comes through sign system or logical concepts. But skepticism itself has an ethical structure and philosophy as critique has a double task, though not the doubleness of parodic ruse or playful displacement. Philosophy is both saying and said, indeed the very oscillation between them. It thus always gives birth to and is shadowed by skepticism and it both "justifies and criticizes the laws of being and of the city" (Ibid.: 165). There is, then, no end or closure of philosophical discourse; "Is not its interruption its only possible end?" (Ibid.: 200) "Logocentric, onto-theological" philosophy may have come to an end but speculative practice certainly has not. As Levinas ironically notes: "Indeed, the whole contemporary discourse of overcoming and deconstructing metaphysics is far more speculative in many respects than is metaphysics itself. Reason is never so versatile as when it puts itself in question" (Cohen 1986: 33).

Ambiguity and doubleness mark precisely the place of commitment and call of the other—not the spot of paralytic aporia. Thus the subject put in question by Levinas remains "rational," "responsible" and "inspired" even as it is "susceptible, vulnerable, wounded, traumatized, obsessed, hostage, persecuted."[9] If there is a folly of non-sense, it is not the play of frivolity but the "non-sense" of the one-for-the-other, suffering as gratuitous giving, "folly as the confines of reason" (1981: 50). The questioning of reason may appear as folly to the logic of identity and ontology but for Levinas, the result is another kind of reason—a prophetic or ethical reason, not delirium, madness, game, or will to power.

Such an exposed, inspired, subjected subject is by no means an ethereal Husserlian "Consciousness." "Only a subject that eats can be for-the-other, or can signify. Signification, the one-for-the-other, has meanings only among beings of flesh and blood . . . not a gift of the heart but of the bread from one's mouth" (Ibid.: 73). The biblical allusion is reinforced here by a direct quote from Isaiah 58. Matter, the material "is the locus of the for-the-other" (Ibid.: 77).[10]

9. As such, Levinas identifies the subject as psyche with the maternal body. Luce Irigaray responds to his thinking about the feminine in her essay in Cohen (1981).
10. Moreover, the body itself is a paradigmatic example of an exteriority not constituted by my consciousness; it permanently contests the prerogatives of con-

But the "place" of saying as "proximity" to the other is not spatial; it is a kind of Levinasian equivalent to Derrida's "non-site" and thought outside of ontology, cognition, recuperable historical time. In this sense, both the Levinasian and Derridean projects are thus also utopian.[11] This proximity is an "anarchic" relation, prior to all foundations and philosophical principles (Ibid.: 100), which is the very "anarchy of responsibility" (Ibid.: 26) and the "trace" of the Infinite. Thus Levinas's ethics have no epistemologically certain ground: "the ethical situation is not comprehensible on the basis of ethics" (Ibid.: 120). He does not give a set of prescriptions but rather calls the subject to responsibility, to the Other.

GreekJew/JewGreek

But the metaphors he uses to describe subjectivity and responsibility are disturbing: trauma, wound, exile, dispossession. They allude to the figure of the Jew in recent European history. On the other hand, the idea of substitution and suffering might appear Christian. But Levinas is opposed to any idea of suffering as "magically redemptive." The responsibility can be borne by no other; no one can act as a substitute *for me*, can relieve me of my responsibility. It is one-way. I am the unique, elected, chosen. "To say that the other has to sacrifice himself to the others would be to preach human sacrifice! . . . But it is I and no one else who am hostage" (Ibid.: 126).

The description of the subject in *Otherwise Than Being* culminates in the expression *me voici:* "The word *I* means *here I am* [*me voici*] answering for everything and everyone" (Ibid.: 114). Those familiar with the Bible recognize this as the oft-repeated Hebrew phrase *hineni*, the formulaic response of the Old Testament heroes when called by God. Abraham, for example, uses it in Genesis 22:1 when called to

---

sciousness to "give meaning." The body is the very mode in which a separated being exists—that is, a being in relation with another but distinct (1969: 168). Thus at the end of *Totality and Infinity*, Levinas engages in extended meditations on eros, the caress, fecundity, and the family.

11. When asked by Richard Kearney whether his search for a non-site or *u-topos* other than that of Western metaphysics can be construed as a prophetic utopianism, Derrida answers by affirming a positive moment in deconstruction as a response to the call of alterity and says that although he interrogates the classical ideas of *eschaton* or *telos*, "that does not mean I dismiss all forms of Messianic or prophetic eschatology. I think that all genuine questioning is summoned by a certain type of eschatology. . . ." Though he does not feel the kind of "hope" that would allow deconstruction to have a prophetic function—as "exodus and dissemination in the desert" it does have, he admits, certain "prophetic resonances" but as a search without hope for hope (Kearney 1984: 118–119). As Malka points out, there is a somewhat similar strain in Levinas, when he defines Judaism after Auschwitz as a "Faith which is also a fidelity without faith," a faithful ethic against the absent God (Malka 1984: 76).

sacrifice his son Isaac, as does Moses at the burning bush (Ex. 3:4). Levinas often contrasts Abraham to Ulysses: Abraham must depart his native land and go to a land of which he knows nothing (1966: 37); Ulysses, on the other hand "returns home" and symbolizes for Levinas the course of Western philosophy—that is, the identity, sameness, and egoism of the self which is ultimately protected—not exiled, called outside, broken up.

The "here I am" as the "I possessed by the other" is also the figure of inspiration, obsession, "a seed of folly, already a psychosis" (1981: 142); "for the order of contemplation it is something simply demented" (Ibid.: 113). At the same time it is a "reason" or "intelligibility" beyond the cogito. But the sickness Levinas refers to here in a footnote is a quotation from the Song of Songs, "I am sick with love" (6:8). This biblical text, of course, is a great erotic love song describing the quest of two lovers for each other. And this folly or sickness at the depth of the obligation for the other is "love"—a word Levinas has avoided using to this point. This, then, would be the most profound level of the ethical as first philosophy: "Philosophy is the wisdom of love at the service of love" (Ibid.: 161).

What, then, is the relation of Abraham and Ulysses or Jew and Greek here, the question Derrida perceptively asks at the end of his essay on Levinas. On the one hand, Levinas's philosophy is a kind of letter to the Gentiles. To subject the subject, put it under accusation is also to bring the philosophy of self, of consciousness and being, to trial—as Derrida puts it: "All the philosophical concepts interrogated by Levinas are thus dragged towards the agora, summoned to justify themselves in an ethico-political language. . ." (1978: 97). This trial is a prophetic indictment of Western philosophy.

Unlike Derrida, Levinas still speaks "Greek," i.e., philosophical language. He seeks to translate Jewish wisdom into Greek and to use Greek wisdom to understand Judaism: "The work of the 70 [the Jewish tradition of the 70 elders who translated the Bible into Greek 2,000 years ago] is not finished" (Interview in Malka 1984: 106). But this also because: "We have a great task to articulate in Greek the principles Greece ignored. Jewish singularity awaits its philosophy . . ." (Malka 1984: 81).

But who and what is a Jew? The subject as called, elected—the "chosen people" means for Levinas all human beings—not only the Jews. The very end of *Otherwise Than Being* claims that "each individual of all the peoples is a chosen one, called to leave the concept of the ego, *here I am,* to lose his place" (1981: 185): "I am for others. Nothing less is needed of the little humanity that adorns the world."[12]

12. In one of his Talmudic lectures, he writes: "I have it from an eminent master: each time Israel is mentioned in the Talmud, one is free, certainly, to understand

Levinas seeks to fight the violence—the violence of identity and totality and history—without more violence. He speaks to the smiters in their own language perhaps to purify philosophy, to bring it to account in its own terms. He and Derrida here again disagree about whether there is an ultimate possibility—even utopian—of peace and nonviolence in language and philosophy. Derrida will produce a philosophical style based not on metaphor, as is often thought, but on *catachresis*, the "violent production of meaning . . . an abuse . . . a violent writing . . . a monstrous mutation" (Kearney 1984: 123). And as Derrida also perceptively notes, *Totality and Infinity* is not a philosophical treatise; he calls it a work of *art*. Its thematic development "is neither purely descriptive nor purely deductive. It proceeds with the infinite insistence of waves on a beach, return and repetition of the same wave against the same shore" (1978: 312 n.7)

Again, I would term it less "art" than "prophetic appeal"; Levinas's style (which I have unfortunately had to reduce here to a set of propositions and do not have space to analyze in depth) itself resounds like that insistent call and appeal from the other that he understands as the essence of language. It comes across as an insistence, a battering, the demand of the alterity Levinas is trying to elicit. Its repetitiveness is a part of a lack of hierarchical ordering. But when waves break again and again, they repeat each time with a difference. In Derrida, repetition is a part of parodic doubling, an off-centering displacement; in Levinas, stylistic repetitiveness expresses the overflow of the Infinite.[13]

This prophetic appeal is not by any means an orthodox theology. "Theology would be possible only as the contestation of the purely religious" (1981: 196 n.19). Theological language belongs to the realm of the said and so "destroys the religious situation of transcendence. The infinite 'presents' itself anarchically, but thematization loses the anarchy which alone can accredit it. Language about God rings false or becomes a myth, that is, can never be taken literally" (Ibid.: 197 n.24). The other than being is not theological—"of the logos" or any "ology" or assertion of a God who is the Being behind or beyond beings. Though the Other "resembles God," the relation to the other

by it a particular ethnic group which probably really did fulfill an incomparable destiny. But to interpret in this manner would shrink the general aspect of the idea enunciated in the talmudic passage, would be to forget that Israel means a people who has received the Law and as a result, a human nature which has arrived at the fullness of its responsibilities and of its self-consciousness. The descendants of Abraham, Isaac and Jacob—that is a human nature which is no longer childish." I am grateful to Annette Aronowicz for this unpublished translation of "Judaism and Revolution" from *Quatre lectures talmudiques*.
13. I am indebted to Annette Aronowicz for this insight about repetition as an aspect of the idea of infinity in Levinas's style (personal interview, July 7, 1987).

and the assignation from the Good survive the death of God (Ibid.: 123).

On the other hand, Levinas does clearly use the name "God" as a name outside essence; "It precedes all divinity" (Ibid.: 190 n.38). In the very first pages of *Otherwise Than Being*, he states that "to hear a God not contaminated by Being is a human possibility no less important and no less precarious than to bring Being out of the oblivion in which it is said to have fallen in metaphysics and in onto-theology" [Heidegger's project] (Ibid.: xlii).

Furthermore, all of Levinas's key philosophical ideas are found in his Jewish writings. To what extent the philosophy "influenced" the Jewish writings or the Jewish writings "influenced" the philosophy is perhaps the wrong question. "Double reading" is perhaps the better term we can borrow from Derrida. Levinas sees himself as a philosopher in his approach to the Talmud, the Bible, the problems of modern Judaism; at the same time, his conception of philosophy as first of all and pre-eminently ethics and prophetic reason is very Jewish.

Not surprisingly, he defines that ethical appeal as the very essence of Judaism. Judaism is the "conscience of the world, justice, witness, martyrdom"—"as if Jewish destiny was a fissure in the shell of impenetrable being, and awakening to an insomnia where the inhuman is no longer covered and hidden by the political necessities it manufactures. . . . The prophetic moment of human reason . . . rupture of the natural and historical constantly reconstituted and, thus, Revelation always forgotten" (1982: 18). Or, in *Difficile liberté*, he writes that the fundamental message of Jewish thought consists in

> restoring the meaning of all experience to the ethical relation between men . . . to call on the personal responsibility of man, in which he feels chosen and irreplaceable, to realize a human society where men are treated as men. This realization of the just society is ipso facto an elevation of man to the company with God . . . is itself the meaning of life. To the extent of saying that the meaning of the real consists in the function of ethics; this is to say the universe is sacred. But it is in an ethical sense that it is sacred. Ethics is an optical instrument to the divine . . . The Divine can only manifest itself in relation to one's neighbor. For the Jew, incarnation is neither possible nor necessary. (1963: 187)

Levinas does not reject philosophy for Judaism or vice versa. In his view, the modern western Jew must approach Judaism with all the resources of Western tradition—independently judge and question Judaism: "resay it in the language of the University: philosophy and philology" (Ibid.: 75). Yet he has passed through assimilation and through the collapse of European culture in the Holocaust and must bring this culture, too, to judgment.

Here, perhaps, is one answer to Derrida's question of why Levinas continues to use philosophical language. Levinas is a Jew, a Jew and a Greek who lives both interpretations at once; he prophetically calls Judaism to philosophy and philosophy to Judaism. He can do so because his call comes ultimately from the primary and irreducible interhuman relation to the other. On another level, Judaism is the "other" of philosophy and philosophy is the "other" of Judaism. The call is a call of one form of reason to "an other." In this way, he interrogates and redefines both the sacred and the secular; he writes neither philosophy nor theology in their traditional senses; nor is he a Greek or Jew in any simple or familiar way. Like Derrida, his work is an uncategorizable hybrid, an often dissonant doubling.

Indeed he describes the interhuman relationship, the relation to the other, with a metaphor of doubleness: "interface."

> The interhuman is thus an interface: a double axis where what is "of the world" qua *phenomenological intelligibility* is juxtaposed with what is not "of the world" *qua ethical responsibility*. It is in this ethical perspective that God must be thought and not in the ontological perspective. . . . as the God of alterity. (Cohen 1986: 20)

Biblical thought, in this sense, has

> influenced my ethical reading of the interhuman, whereas Greek thought has largely determined its philosophical expression in language. . . . philosophy can be at once both Greek and non-Greek in its inspiration. These two different sources of inspiration coexist as two different tendencies in modern philosophy, and it is my own personal task to identify this dual origin of meaning—*der Ursprung der Sinnhaften*—in the interhuman relationship. (Cohen 1986: 21) [14]

Moreover, his idea of the "saying" as the otherness which is the excess of meaning in all language and the very *prophetic dignity of language*—implies that all secular literature is related to Scripture. The religious essence of all language may be concretized in the Scriptures but it is something that "all literature awaits or commemorates, that it celebrates or profanes" (1982: 8). This otherness as opening is a call to exegesis. For the book as the "said" retains the trace and call of this saying. Thus the ethical nature of reading and interpretation are not restricted to the reading of "sacred" texts. For language is not merely

---

14. The reasons for this double reading and double attachment are complex, as we have seen. Levinas's thought is unique in many ways but also shares trends with other modern Jewish thinkers such as Hermann Cohen in stressing the rational and ethical character of Judaism. Nathan Rotenstreich attributes this trend in part to the influence of Kant. Ethics could remain a realm unchallenged by Kant's critique, as we have noted. But also, "The ethical interpretation of Judaism makes possible a further, more radical interpretation, that the ethical teaching of Judaism may be meaningful and binding apart from religious attachment. Thus the ethical interpretation can be placed historically on the borderline of the religious attitude and the secular transformation of Judaism" (Rotenstreich 1968: 3–4).

instrumental or cognitive, but "coordinates me with another to whom I speak; it signifies from the face of the other" (Ibid.: 9) and thus calls me to responsibility. Reading itself, then, partakes of the ethical structure of the other than being.

This aspect of reading is missed, for example, in de Man's mode of deconstruction. He appropriated the epistemological critique of Derrida as mainly a cognitive problem and thus understood the problem of interpretation as undecidability or impossibility. Perhaps for him, that marked the site of the "otherness of language" and one could go no further; there is no "excendence" and certainly no "good beyond being." Thus there can be no positivity but only impossible aporias. Rhetoric became the "other" of philosophy for de Man but lost its classical sense of language as an *action* or effect on a public audience. Rhetorical tropes are negative epistemological challenges to grammar and logic and must be separated from "peformative speech acts" and the "pragmatic banality" of psychology (1982: 19). Similarly, the model for teaching is "not primarily an intersubjective relationship between people but a cognitive process in which self and other are only tangentially and contiguously involved" (Ibid.: 3). Despite these rather chilling words, J. Hillis Miller reports that all de Man's agonies over undecidability and impossibility should not be misunderstood: "I remember de Man looking me in the eye and saying, 'For me, the most important questions are religious questions.' So much for 'nihilism'" (Campbell 1986: 48).

In contrast, the "other" or double of the text for Levinas, what he calls its "second sonority" (1982: 137), is not parody or aporia but "inspiration," the "more in the less." Inspiration is the very fact that language can say more than it says; at the hour of its ethical truth, language is prophecy—not prophecy as some type of individual genius or frenzied possession but an "ability of human speech in overflowing the first intentions which bear it," the very spirituality of the spirit (Ibid.: 141).

Inspiration as this "otherness" or other sense (the "tearing of the Same by the other") (Ibid.: 138 n.11) is also the ethical beyond of conscience. A critical point here is that the other voice in the voice is *without* any "organized content." The content is the "meaning of meaning" awakening the listener to the proximity of the other—not stopping at self-reflexiveness. Revelation thus calls to exegesis and "inspiration is the exercise of reason itself" (Ibid.: 141) requiring the participation of the reader.

The Final Responsibilities of Reason and Play

What can be said, in summary, of the conflict of rabbis and poets, parodic play and prophetic reason? One key issue is heteronomy and autonomy of the subject, an issue also at the center of contemporary literary theory. The rupture with the egoistic realm of cognition and being in Levinas signifies the relation to the other as heteronomous but not as an enslavement; instead it is a "difficult liberty," the "paradox of responsibility": "To be free is only to do what no other person can do in my place" (Ibid.: 172); "human autonomy rests on a supreme heteronomy" (1963: 24–25). But for Derrida, the poet (and by extension philosopher-poet or critic) needs to break the Tablets of the Law to elicit the "other" of language, the play of the text; poetic autonomy thus liberates an otherness which can put philosophy in question.

Yet as Derrida writes, we are both "rabbis" and "poets," free and unfree, caught always between philosophy and its other. We live both interpretations simultaneously. For Levinas, Judaism and philosophy are the pair that put each other in question; for Derrida, that pair is "literature" and philosophy. Both Derrida and Levinas interrupt philosophy by soliciting its other. But they differ in defining the "call" that originally engenders this putting into question—and the kind of response it requires. As Derrida writes at the beginning of his essay on Levinas, however, the question itself is what they share: philosophy is now a "community of the question about the possibility of the question" (1978: 79).

For Levinas, the very "awakening by the Other of the same" is, finally, "revelation" and opening to transcendence. More than any specific content, isn't revelation precisely "to think this awakening," asks Levinas, now sounding Derridean, "to put in question the rationality of reason and even the possibility of the question"? This is revelation as an "incessant questioning of quietude and priority of the Same . . . burning without consummation of an inextinguishable flame." "Isn't the prescription of Jewish revelation in its priceless obligation this very modality?" (1982: 180). Yet here is the step beyond Derrida: "Otherwise said, the traditionality of the rupture isn't it practical reason? Isn't the model of revelation ethical?" (Ibid.: 176)

For Levinas, then, philosophy is ultimately the servant of the non-philosophical, the good beyond being or as Richard Cohen prefers to explain it, the "better than being." Levinas nevertheless remains a philosopher; for the truth is found neither in philosophy or its refusal but in the alternation or oscillation of "Concept and refusal of concept" (1981: 126). For this oscillation as ambiguity is the opening of the other.

As Cohen also notes, though, Derrida's idea of the play of meaning in his differential theory of signs lays waste both transcendence and immanence (Cohen 1983: 245) and in Cohen's view, the reason/play opposition is too simple. Cohen argues that the answer to the crisis of philosophy is not the opposition between play and reason but a recognition of the bond uniting them; they are both forms of privilege.

The privilege of reason is not the metaphysical privilege of presence "which is rightfully subverted by play, but rather the privileging exigency of *responsibility*." Reason is not solely the rational but a form of responsibility and "play is reason's necessary companion if reason is to remain reasonable. Reason has a sense of humor," and play is responsive to this (Ibid.: 251).

In the end, perhaps, the real challenge to metaphysics is best summed up by the Frankfort school luminary, Max Horkheimer: "I do not know how far metaphysicians are correct; perhaps somewhere there is a particularly compelling metaphysical system or fragment. But I do know that metaphysicians are usually impressed only to the smallest degree by what men suffer" (1972: 232).

References

Bakhtin, M. M.
  1981 *The Dialogic Imagination*, edited by Michael Holquist, translated by Caryl Emerson and Michael Holquist (Austin: University of Texas Press).
  1984 *Rabelais and His World*, translated by Helene Iswolsky (Bloomington: Indiana University Press).
Bernasconi, Robert
  1985 "The Trace of Levinas in Derrida," in *Derrida and Difference*, edited by D. Wood and R. Bernasconi (Coventry, Eng.: Parousia Press, University of Warwick), 17–44.
  1987 "Deconstruction and the Possibility of Ethics," in *Deconstruction and Philosophy*, edited by John Sallis (Chicago: University of Chicago Press), 122–139.
Blanchot, Maurice
  1986 "Our Clandestine Companion," see Cohen, *Face to Face With Levinas*, 41–52.
Burggraeve, Roger
  1986 *Emmanuel Levinas: Une bibliographie primaire et secondaire (1925–1985)* (Leuven, Belg.: Center for Metaphysics and Philosophy of God).
Campbell, Colin
  1986 "The Tyranny of the Yale Critics," *New York Times Magazine* (February): 20–48.
Cohen, Richard A.
  1983 "The Privilege of Reason and Play," *Tijdschrift voor Filosofie* 2: 242–255.
Cohen, Richard A., ed.
  1986 *Face to Face With Levinas* (New York: SUNY Press).
De Man, Paul
  1982 "The Resistance to Theory," *Yale French Studies* 63: 3–20.
Derrida, Jacques
  1976 [1967] *Of Grammatology*, translated by Gayatri Spivak (Baltimore: Johns Hopkins University Press).
  1978 [1967] "Violence and Metaphysics: An Essay on the Thought of Emmanuel Levinas," in *Writing and Difference*, translated by Alan Bass (Chicago: University of Chicago Press), 79–153.
Descombes, Vincent
  1980 *Modern French Philosophy*, translated by L. Scott-Fox and J. M. Harding (Cambridge: Cambridge University Press).
Foucault, Michel
  1977 "Nietzsche, Genealogy, History," in *Language, Counter-Memory, Practice:*

Selected Essays and Interviews, edited and translated by Donald F. Bouchard and Sherry Simon (Ithaca: Cornell University Press), 139–164.

Frank, Joseph
1986 "The Voices of Mikhail Bakhtin," *New York Review of Books* 23 (October): 56–60.

Jay, Martin
1972 "The Frankfurt School and the Genesis of Critical Theory," in *The Unknown Dimension: European Marxism Since Lenin*, edited by Dick Howard and Karl Klare (New York: Basic Books), 225–247.

Kearney, Richard
1984 "Jacques Derrida," in *Dialogues With Contemporary Continental Thinkers: The Phenomenological Heritage* (Manchester: Manchester University Press), 105–126.
1986 "Dialogue with Emmanuel Levinas," see Cohen, *Face to Face With Levinas*, 13–25.

Levinas, Emmanuel
1962 "Transcendance et Hauteur," *Bulletin de la Société française de Philosophie* 56: 89–101.
1963 *Difficile liberté: Essais sur le Judaïsme* (Paris: Albin Michel).
1963 "'Entre deux Mondes,' Biographie spirituelle de Franz Rosenzweig," in *La Conscience Juive. Données et débats*, edited by Éliane Amado Lévy-Valensi and J. Halpérin (Paris: PUF), 121–149.
1966 "On the Trail of the Other," translated by Daniel Hoy, *Philosophy Today* 10: 34–46.
1967 "Martin Buber and the Theory of Knowledge," in *The Philosophy of Martin Buber*, edited by Paul Arthur Schilpp and Maurice Friedman (LaSalle, IL: Open Court), 133–150.
1968 *Quatre lectures talmudiques* (Paris: Minuit).
1969 [1961] *Totality and Infinity: An Essay on Exteriority*, translated by Alphonso Lingis (Pittsburgh: Duquesne University Press).
1978 [1947] *Existence and Existents*, translated by Alphonso Lingis (The Hague: Martinus Nijhoff).
1978 "Signature," edited and translated by Adrian Peperzak, *Research in Phenomenology* 8: 175–189.
1981 [1974] *Otherwise Than Being or Beyond Essence*, translated by Alphonso Lingis (The Hague: Martinus Nijhoff).
1982 *L'au delà du verset: Lectures et discours talmudiques* (Paris: Minuit).
1985 *Ethics and Infinity: Conversations With Philippe Nemo*, translated by Richard A. Cohen (Pittsburgh: Duquesne University Press).

Malka, Salomon
1984 *Lire Levinas* (Paris: Cerf).

Megill, Allan
1985 *Prophets of Extremity: Nietzsche, Heidegger, Foucault, Derrida* (Berkeley: University of California Press).

Miller, J. Hillis
1987 *The Ethics of Reading* (New York: Columbia University Press).
1987 "Presidential Address, 1986: 'The Triumph of Theory, the Resistance to Reading, and the Question of the Material Base,'" *PMLA* 102: 281–291.

Ponet, James
1985 "Faces: A Meditation," *Orim: a Jewish Journal at Yale* 1: 58–76.

Rose, Margaret
1979 *Parody/Meta-Fiction* (London: Croom Helm).

Rosenzweig, Franz
    1971 [1930s] 2nd German ed. *The Star of Redemption*, translated by William W.
        Hallo (New York: Holt, Rinehart and Winston).
Rotenstreich, Nathan
    1968 *Jewish Philosophy in Modern Times: From Mendelssohn to Rosenzweig* (New York:
        Holt, Rinehart and Winston).
Schwarzchild, Steven S.
    1985 "An Introduction to the Thought of R. Isaac Hutner," *Modern Judaism* 5:
        235–278.

Death in the Ethnographic Present

Renato Rosaldo

My central question is: How should ethnographies talk about death and bereavement? Ethnographic discourse on death tends to ignore the cultural practices and lived experiences characterized by improvisation, subjectivity, and particularity. Instead it concentrates on formality, externality, and generality. Aside from being inhumane, the result is superficial social analysis. My hope is that a diagnosis of the problem will lead to better studies in the future.

Ethnographic representations of death can be characterized by formality, externality, and generality. *Formality* refers to the practice of describing human events as if they were normal, highly codified, and always repeated in precisely the same manner. Such accounts eliminate significant variations in timing and tempo, sources of disturbance and particular struggles or goals. *Externality* refers to the distance at which ethnographers write. This distance presumably confers objectivity but it also objectifies by producing descriptions that fail to consider the subjectivity of the people described. *Generality* refers to the way many accounts stress not particular agonies of grief but general recipes for mourning rituals. Perhaps the notion of shared culture leads analysts to suppose they should explore only identical forms throughout a group.

Following their discipline's norms of writing, ethnographers tend to flatten their accounts, distancing themselves from the tears and agony, as they seek out the lowest common denominators that make all funerals not different from one another but the same. Yet the emotional tug of death derives less from the brute generalized abstract fact than from a particular intimate relation's permanent rupture: "Dad just died"–not just anyone's dad but my own dad.

Consider a few examples chosen at random to lend texture to these general assertions. Most ethnographies consider death under the rubric of ritual rather than bereavement. The subtitles of many books on death make the emphasis on ritual explicit. William Douglas's *Death in Murelaga* is subtitled *Funerary Ritual in a Spanish Basque Village*; Richard Huntington's and Peter Metcalf's *Celebrations of Death* is subtitled *The Anthropology of Mortuary Ritual*; Peter Metcalf's *A Borneo Journey into Death* is subtitled *Berawan Eschatology from Its Rituals*. Ritual itself is defined by its formality and routine; it is virtually a program for action, rather more like a recipe or book of etiquette than an actual event or a human process.

I have selected these examples not because they are so egregious (indeed a number are quite good) but because because they are so representative. My quarrel with them is that they follow the discipline's descriptive norms which are particularly well suited to accounts of social structure and cultural patterning. They do less well in applying a theory of practice, particularly with reference to politics (another story) and emotions (in this case, bereavement).

Consistent with an emphasis on formal ritual, case histories from ethnographic studies of death have been selected with an eye to maintaining a fiction of orderly routine. Such cases can range from deaths of prominent individuals to gradual and expected deaths. In the former, the deceased are of such high status that relatively elaborate funeral procedures should be strictly followed. In the latter, the deceased often are old, and usually they are women dying a slow death. Neither men nor women who died in childbirth, by accident or violence tend to appear in case histories. Most ethnographic descriptions thus preserve a sense of programmed unfolding which enables the subject of analysis to remain mourning rites rather than bereavement.

In his book *Kwaio Religion*, Roger Keesing follows the tactic of using a high status person's death for his case history. His initial remarks are sensitive to bereavement:

> Death of an adult profoundly disrupts the community; it usually leaves a spouse and children, as well as natal kin, bereaved. Unless it has been preceded by a long, wasting illness, it has usually left them unprepared for the shock of loss. (1982: 143–144)

Keesing then licenses his slighting bereavement by proposing the following rough rule-of-thumb ratio between the deceased's age and the socio-religious elaboration of funerary rites:

> But if the shock of premature loss lessens as a life runs full course, the sociological and religious impact of death may increase with age. (Ibid.: 144)

In the end his detailed case history follows the death of a descent group's priest and concentrates on details of ritual. The account is written in the distanced normalizing discourse of the ethnographic present:

> When the priest of the descent group dies, the body—unbound—must be taken up to the men's house, if death has not occurred there. The taboos that descend on the community begin the evening before burial.   (Ibid.: 148)

Evidently, Keesing is not describing a particular death but a set of formulas that apply to any such death. Surely ethnographies should include such formulas, but they should not rely on them to the exclusion of bereavement.

Consider another example, Peter Metcalf's work on a Borneo society, where the author follows the tactic of using a case history of a woman who died after a long illness:

> At the end of December 1973, not long before I left the village, a middle-aged woman died at Long Teru. Her name was Utan Nin. She had been sick for many years with a degenerative disease that was readily recognizable as tuberculosis.   (1982: 33)

The following paragraph begins: "It was a slow death" (Ibid.: 33). After her death there is a moment of spontaneous emotion which social regulation quickly eclipses:

> I joined the other longhouse members rushing to the deathbed. There I found a scene of apparent chaos, with people running around aimlessly, or keening uncontrollably. The emotional out-pouring was intense, and I found myself fighting back tears. But after a few minutes, I began to observe that a pattern was emerging in the activity in the room, and that there was a division of labor between the men and the women, the immediate kin and others. The expression of grief also varied.   (Ibid.: 38)

Evidently overcome by the people's initial reaction, Metcalf quickly recovered his anthropologist's poise when he noticed emergent social differentiation. Sobbing, ululation, hair thrown forward, all become part of the systematic variation in expressions of grief.

Metcalf's sentence, "The expression of grief also varied," occurs so frequently in ethnographies of death that it could be called the "it varies with" trope, as illustrated by the following:

> The number as well as the scale of the funerary rites vary with the age, sex, and status of the deceased.   (Nadel 1970: 122–123)

> How deep the shock, how dramatic the subsequent events, depend on the age and identity of the decedent, and the circumstances of death. We shall first look at these axes of variation, then turn to their outcomes.   (Keesing 1982: 143)

> As I shall discuss later, the role of the living in the rituals varies according

> to sex as well as degree of relationship to the deceased. (Goodale 1971: 241)

Although differently phrased, Jack Goody's argumentation has the same sense:

> Having reviewed these various methods of distinguishing the classes of mourners, I shall now return to a consideration of the three main categories of bereavement: parent-child, conjugal, and sibling bereavement. (1962: 90–91)

Not unlike generalized formulas, these kinds of observations are apt but should not (as they usually do) exclude exploration of bereavement within each category. In books about bereavement in our own culture, such dimensions of variations usually are the points of departure for analysis, not its end point.

Ethnographers write more as witnesses to a visual spectacle than as people who converse with the participants. They notice not what the bereaved say about their experience but externally observable differences in mourning behavior by members of different social categories (calculated relative to the deceased). Such accounts are even marked by scepticism about the authenticity of sentiments expressed.

The Berawan of Borneo, by Metcalf's account, appear rather uneven, sometimes sincere and sometimes not, though the total impression remains that emotions are expressed because they are obligatory and not because they are felt. The key description is as follows:

> Most of the women were wailing in a formalized way, beginning on a high note and descending the scale in a jerky staccato fashion until they ran out of breath. Then they drew in air in a great sob, and began the ululation over again. Some knelt with their long hair thrown forward to cover their faces, and seemed lost in grief. Others were more restrained and wove a kind of recitative into their wailing. . . . These dirges are a verbal art form, and proficiency at them is admired. (1982: 38)

Curiously, the description dwells most on those least involved. The chief mourner, the dead woman's husband, receives only half a sentence:

> Tama Aweng sat by the corpse motionless, looking drawn and haggard, and the adult men looked on, solemn but dry-eyed. (Ibid.)

Readers see the husband only momentarily and from the outside, as in a snapshot. What he had to say about his experience is left in silence.

The relative silence about the chief mourner is maintained as the account proceeds. Instead there is a detailed account of what happens to the dead woman's body. Indeed over the next six pages she is mentioned by name twelve times as contrasted with the husband's three times. The husband initially appears as follows:

Tama Aweng first lay beside the corpse of his wife in a posture of sleep, then he sat up and was handed a cigarette of local manufacture, i.e., home-grown tobacco rolled in a leaf. He took a few puffs, and then held it to his wife's lips as if she too would draw upon it. The same acts were mimed out by their daughter and adoptive son.   (Ibid.: 41)

Again, the husband remains silent, although Metcalf asserts that his being mimed by his daughter and adoptive son expresses "the shared residence and commensality of the now-disrupted family" (Ibid.). Why, one wonders, wasn't the husband consulted about the signifi-cance of the miming practice?

Ethnographic writing concentrates, in short, on routine expressions of grief and programmed ways of handling the corpse immediately after death. Thus the central subjects become the least involved and the deceased rather than the chief mourners. In all cases, the ethnog-rapher stands as spectator, witnessing events from the outside and not asking people about their subjective experiences. Most ethnographic accounts see grief in partial and mechanistic ways and even remain sceptical about the emotional experience of grieving. They (implau-sibly) maintain that the work of mourning occurs only in connection with formal rituals.

Consider an example of how bereavement could be described in our culture. Just a few passages from my diary, the first from November 5, 1981, after my wife Shelly's accidental death on October 11:

Up early. Feeling out of control; dispersed, like I'm swimming through molasses. All kinds of things taking too long and filling days.

Another passage from November 23 reads as follows:

Today I feel worse than yesterday when I felt worse than the day before . . . I feel worn down, diminished capacity; able to do so little and so inadequate at just being. My lethargy appalls me, and I can do no other; I feel restless and searching for Shelly, for anything that will cheer or move or even comfort me. Nothing, nothing. No sexual impulses; no desire to work; a sense that I want to draw but no will to do anything about it yet; wanting to see friends but no energy to arrange things.

Bereavement, of course, was complex, varied, and long lasting. The funeral and other rituals were significant but hardly encompassed the experience.

Yet I found that the bereavement of others both diverged from and significantly overlapped with my own experience. In *A Grief Observed*, for example, C. S. Lewis describes his state after his wife's death in this manner:

And no one ever told me about the laziness of grief. Except at my job— where the machine seems to run on much as usual—I loathe the slightest

> effort. Not only writing but even reading a letter is too much. Even shaving. What does it matter whether my cheek is rough or smooth?   (1961: 8)

In this and other respects his grief seemed like mine; yet at other times it appeared as something from another cultural universe. His world was one of stiff-upper-lips and religious convictions alien to mine; his wife's death was slow, not sudden.

Perhaps I felt closer to the child, Peggy Laird, who described her initial reactions as follows:

> When Mom told me that Dad had died, it was so painful that I could feel my chest hurting, like somebody had hit me. I screamed and remember my sister Alletta screamed too and it was kind of like letting all the anger out. (Krementz 1981: 29)

I wrote:

> I felt like in a nightmare, the whole world around me expanding and contracting, visually and viscerally heaving. Going down I find a group of men, maybe 7 or 8, standing still, silent, and I heave and sob, but no tears.

The first tearless sobs, as I realized even then, were mixed sorrow and anger.

Yet these diary extracts could seem far from most societies studied by ethnographers. We have a tradition of autobiography in high culture from Augustine through Rousseau to the present. In the Protestant Reformation people learned to keep diaries as they scrutinized their daily lives to learn whether they were among the saved. Christianity itself had a longer tradition of public and then more private confession, and those of us with middle class financial support and more secular folk beliefs can practice introspection in psychotherapy. Perhaps such factors even account for the capacity of American children to describe their feelings about a parent's death.

Surely there will be differences but consider simply the following passage from Godfrey Wilson's account of Nyakyusa burial customs:

> "This war dance (*ukukina*)," said an old man, "is mourning, we are mourning the dead man. We dance because there is war in our hearts. A passion of grief and fear exasperates us (*ilyyojo likutsila*)." (1939: 13)

The expression of bereavement seems well worth exploring, and it surely would lead to a deeper understanding of bereavement than most accounts written in the ethnographic present.

Arguably, the problem with ethnographic writing on death resides not only in distanced normalizing discourse, but also in an excessive reliance on a metaphoric rather than a metonymic analysis of culture in general and ritual in particular. Let me sketch these two contrasting views.

The *metaphoric* view treats cultural phenomena as highly condensed reflections of larger totalities. Whether a ritual, a form of play or a classificatory system, the cultural phenomenon under analysis is treated as if it were internally coherent and capable of being understood in its own terms. Often such phenomena are regarded as microcosms of larger macrocosms; sometimes as but aspects of larger totalities. In both cases, they contain meaning, encompass significant sets of relations, or display order.

A more sophisticated version of this view becomes dialectical, as in Clifford Geertz's "model of" and "model for," or the way particular cultural phenomena both reflect and shape larger totalities (Geertz 1973: 93–94). Richard Huntington and Peter Metcalf, for example, in their synthetic anthropological work on death, cite Geertz in support of their argument that "[D]eath and its rituals not only reflect social values, but are an important force in shaping them" (1979: 5). Even in the more sophisticated version of the metaphorical view, rituals are regarded as coherent arenas within which cultural wisdom can be explored.

Lest it appear that I have overstated my case concerning the conflation of ritual, coherence, and wisdom, consider the following passage in which Huntington and Metcalf introduce their work:

> This study is about the rituals by which people deal with death, and hence celebrate life. Anthropologists have no special understanding of the mystery of death. We can but recount the collective wisdoms of many cultures, the wisdoms that have been acted, sung, wailed, and danced at funerals through the ages.   (1979: 1)

In other words, funerary rituals are the wisdom distilled from generations of cultural experimentation with bereavement. Indeed, Huntington and Metcalf go on to phrase the position in the strongest possible terms: "Whatever mental adjustments the individual needs to make in the face of death he or she must accomplish as best he or she can, through such rituals as society provides" (Ibid.: 44). Their notion is that what is not pre-packaged in ritual containers is not culturally available to the individual.

It probably comes as no surprise to discover that people from other disciplines, such as the psychologist Beverley Raphael, take what they read in ethnographies literally. Thus they contrast Americans versus members of other cultures, asserting that "we" have a hard time coping with grief and "they" make the best of what their cultures provide in the way of formal rituals. We go through agony and they don't, but [a tacit "but"] we're psychologically conscious and they're unconscious; we process our private bereavment and they unthinkingly follow their social norms. Under the rubric "longer-term adjustments," for example, Raphael asserts that "Some cultures may have rituals and ceremonies that facilitate transition, while others, such as many Western cultures, may leave the bereaved uncertain and perhaps stressed because of this" (1983: 57). Raphael's view accurately reflects the ethnographic literature but the literature itself should be questioned.

Perhaps at this point it is useful to recall Edmund Leach's explicitly metaphoric view that rituals "involve comparable multiple condensations"

> When we take part in such a ritual we pick up all these messages at the same time and condense them into a single experience, which we describe as "attending a wedding," or "attending a funeral," and so on.   (1976: 41)

In a passage worth citing at length, Leach contrasts his metaphoric view with what he regards as a mistaken metonymic view:

> Because the analysis is bound to take a verbal metonymic form, with one thing following after another, the overall impression is one of enormous complexity and total disjointedness. But what actually *happens* is that the participants in a ritual are sharing communicative experiences through many different sensory channels simultaneously; they are acting out an ordered sequence of metaphoric events within a territorial space which has itself been ordered to prove a metaphoric context for the play acting. Verbal, musical, choreographic, and visual-aesthetic "dimensions" are all likely to form components of the total message.   (Ibid.)

I do not wish to deny the possibility that people can, as Leach so lucidly argues, say the same thing through different channels (such as music, dance, and speech). The analytical usefulness of the metaphoric view has often been demonstrated, but its validity in opposition to (or in conjunction with) alternatives has more often been assumed than explored. In what follows I will explore the avenue Leach rejects by asserting that rituals can be heterogeneous events of "enormous complexity and disjointedness" where one thing follows another.

The metonymic view of culture, as contrasted with the metaphoric view, stresses that rituals are part of larger processes. Rather than being a self-contained whole, a ritual in this view is like a busy intersection through which a number of different processes happen to pass. In the case of funerals, one could imagine, among other processes, both bereavement and the social differentiation of the deceased, the chief mourners, and others. This metonymic view can lead to two broader shifts in social analysis.

First, the unit of analysis is no longer the ritual or even the system of rituals, ordered spatially or temporally. Instead it is a set of processes people undergo. One studies not rituals of mourning but the process of bereavement. A ritual is but one step in a larger process, which could include spontaneous outbursts, dreams, conversations with family, and other encounters. The process includes the factors conditioning as well as the consequences resulting from each phase. They are united, as the structuralists used to say, by their contiguity and not their similarity.

Second, the temporal perspective becomes analytically significant. Cultural practices and lived experience come to the forefront of any analysis, and we want to know how things work out for the participants over the long run, not simply during the confines of any particular ritual. The time lapsed between events or the tempo within an event can prove significant. Pierre Bourdieu has put the matter in this way:

> The detemporalizing effect (visible in the synoptic apprehension that diagrams make possible) that science produces when it forgets the transformation it imposes on practices inscribed in the current of time, i.e., detotalized simply by totalizing them, is never more pernicious than when exerted on practices defined by the fact that their temporal structure, direction, and rhythm are *constitutive* of their meaning.   (1977: 9, his emphasis)

Although cumbersome to the Anglo-Saxon ear, his phrasing corresponds with the contrast between metaphoric ("synoptic apprehension") and metonymic ("temporal structure") modes of analysis.

Perhaps brief homespun examples can illustrate the general notions about temporality. A timeless theory of exchange could ignore the vast differences between returning a dinner party invitation the next day (frighteningly soon), after three months (perhaps about right), or a decade later (astonishingly late). Consider what could happen if dinner guests either were not fed until midnight or ushered through their entire meal and told to go home within half an hour of arriving. In addition, dinner parties are not self-contained. They intersect with daily life in myriad ways. Sometimes they warm friendships, other times they cool them. In one case, two dinner guests, meeting for the first time at my house, became lovers a few hours after their commensal union. In another extreme case, I recall the Berkeley philosopher who had dinner at my home and 45 minutes later, at a public event, introduced himself to me as if we'd never met.

In contrast with Leach I find the heterogeneity of ritual less apparent than real. Multiple processes can occur together within a single ritual and each can be followed along different pathways. Their coming together within a specific setting can be motivated (due to underlying coherence), accidental (more coincidental than not), or somewhere in between. Hence ethnographic works purporting to study death should include processes of bereavement along with the social and symbolic organization of funerary rites.

References

Bourdieu, Pierre
1977 *Outline of a Theory of Practice* (New York: Cambridge University Press).

Douglas, William A.
  1969 *Death in Murelaga: Funerary Ritual in a Spanish Basque Village* (Seattle: University of Washington Press).
Geertz, Clifford
  1973 *The Interpretation of Cultures* (New York: Basic Books).
Goodale, Jane C.
  1971 *Tiwi Wives* (Seattle: University of Washington Press).
Goody, Jack
  1962 *Death, Property and the Ancestors* (Stanford: Stanford University Press).
Huntington, Richard and Peter Metcalf
  1979 *Celebrations of Death: The Anthropology of Mortuary Ritual* (New York: Cambridge University Press).
Keesing, Roger
  1982 *Kwaio Religion* (New York: Columbia University Press).
Krementz, Jill
  1981 *How It Feels When a Parent Dies* (New York: Alfred A. Knopf).
Leach, Edmund
  1976 *Culture and Communication: The Logic by Which Symbols Are Connected* (New York: Cambridge University Press).
Lewis, C. S.
  1961 *A Grief Observed* (New York: The Seabury Press).
Metcalf, Peter
  1982 *A Borneo Journey Into Death: Berawan Eschatology from Its Rituals* (Philadelphia: University of Pennsylvania Press).
Nadel, S. F.
  1970 *Nupe Religion* (New York: Schocken Books).
Raphael, Beverley
  1983 *The Anatomy of Bereavement* (New York: Basic Books).
Wilson, Godfrey
  1939 *Nyakyusa Conventions of Burial* (Johannesburg: The University of Witwatersrand Press).

The Challenge of Poetics to (Normal) Historical Practice

Robert F. Berkhofer, Jr.

Among the challenges to the historical profession, few seem more important—and less heeded—than those concerning the poetics of normal historical practice. Contemporary literary theory defies the very intellectual foundations of current professional historical practice by denying the factuality that grounds the authority of history itself. That the past is not the same thing as history creates the methods as well as the methodology of historical practice. That the history produced is not the same thing as the past itself creates the crisis of that practice given contemporary poetics. The extent to which the past and history can be said to be quite different poses the problems of poetics for historical practice.

Why poetic analyses achieve such devastating results in the eyes of so many historians today can be understood best if we follow the process by which historians create written history from past evidence according to what we might call "normal" history, borrowing Thomas Kuhn's older terminology for the stable paradigmatic exemplar in a discipline. What, in other words, must professional historians predicate about the past in their practices so as to represent it and thereby conceive it, according to what we today call a history in specific practice and history in general.

At the heart of normal historical practice is presumed to be the processes for obtaining facts about the past from evidence or remains from the actual living past, but the combination of those facts into a coherent narrative or synthesis is even more important in actual historical practice. Thus from sources presumed to be about as well as from (past) history the historian creates generalizations assembled into a synthesis that is once again in the present called (a) history. The ambiguity of the word *history* is deliberate, for the written history is supposed to reconstruct or portray past events, behaviors, thoughts, etc., as they once occurred. In diagram, therefore, the predicated idealized process of normal history looks like this. Solid lines designate what historians generally consider "empirically grounded" conclusions while the dotted line represents "inference" according to normal historical practice.

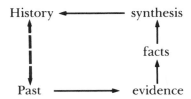

The presupposition grounding normal or traditional, historical practice is, therefore, that the historian's work is an accurate representation of an actual past, much as a map is to its terrain or a photograph to its subject. Thus the historian's written history acts as if it were a transparent medium, to use a linguistic analogy, between the past and the reader's mind, although both historian and reader would deny such an easy equation if raised to their consciousnesses. Nevertheless, the central presupposition of idealized, normal history production is transparency of medium, in which the exposition conveys or at least parallels factuality. Expository representation equals referentiality, to use other terms, because the truthfulness or validity of such normal history productions is tested supposedly by reference to the actual past itself—a past presumed, however, to be more than the sources or remains from which it is derived.

Given this image of normal historical practice(s), then, historical methods designate the ways the historian gets from past evidence or sources to the discovery or creation of facts and then from those facts to their larger expository synthesis. The standard handbooks discuss how to validate sources as evidence and how to derive valid facts from such evidence. These standard handbooks tell little about how to connect those validated facts into a coherent narrative or synthesis beyond some propositions about style and rhetoric.[1] Since today historians be-

1. Compare chapters 8–11 with chapters 3–7 in Louis Gottschalk (1969). See also parts two and three in Jacques Barzun and Henry F. Graf (1957). An exception to this generalization is Savoie Lottinville (1976).

lieve moral and political judgments shape these steps whether in the selection of topics, synthesis of facts, or otherwise and that historians' images of basic human nature, etc., also influence these steps, let me modify the above diagram to reflect the two-way process involved in normal history production. Once again the solid lines indicate supposed empirical method and the dotted line shows inference according to normal historical practice.

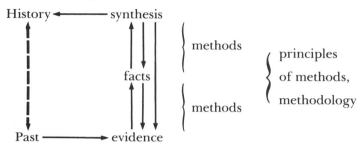

Professional historians theorizing about the nature of their task usually end their discussions at this point, because the past is not problematical beyond this point in practice. It is here that the poetics theorists begin. In other words, poetics raises issues that force a reconsideration of the entire left side of the diagram as I have represented the process.[2]

Such a conception of the historian's tasks still neglects the question we posed earlier: what must the normal historian presume about the past to conceive or represent it as history? To consider sources as evidence of the past, historians must predicate that they remain from past real events and behaviors and bear such a relationship to those past actualities that the historian can reconstruct those past events and behaviors from them. Whether documentary or other kinds of sources stand in indexical, iconic, or other semiotic relationship to the past (White 1982: 284–286) is less important to my argument at the moment than the general presupposition that present day remains and sources, no matter how numerous, are but a small part of what was once produced and, even more significant, reveal only a minute portion of full living past reality, regardless of how they are construed semiotically or otherwise.

Normal historians, as a consequence, worry about "capturing" the past in its full complexity or plenitude. Even the historical sociologist Charles Tilly argues, for example, that historical practice cannot analyze or connect all the experiences in past times, because "it is not

2. Perhaps no better proof of this point may be offered than a comparison of my diagrams (1969) and the ones that follow. Readers familiar with that book will discover that some of its arguments and even some of its premises are quite different from—even contradicted by—many in this article.

humanly possible to construct a coherent analysis of the history of all social relationships; the object of study is too complex, diverse, and big" (1985: 12). Regardless of its difficulty, Henri Marrou makes just this effort the chief goal of normal history.

> This brings us to the essential point: explanation in history is the discovery, the comprehension, the analysis of a thousand ties, which, in a possibly inextricable fashion, unite the many faces of human reality one to another. These ties bind each phenomenon to neighboring phenomena, each state to previous ones, immediate or remote (and in like manner to their results). (1966: 192)

One need not agree with the philosophical premises of these scholars to see that each, like other historians, postulates the past as plenitude as well as real. In one sense, then, we can borrow Clifford Geertz's term "thick description" for this version of normal historical practice.[3]

For the historian the notion of "context" is both a way of comprehending past plenitude and portraying it according to thick description. It is therefore both an empirical method and a methodological premise for normal historical practice.

Contextualism is a—some would say *the*—primary method of historical understanding and practice. As a strategy it is both relational and integrative. The premise behind the strategy has been termed "colligation" by the philosopher W. H. Walsh:

> The historian and his reader initially confront what looks like a largely unconnected mass of material, and the historian then goes on to show that sense can be made of it by revealing certain pervasive themes or developments. In specifying what was going on at the time he both sums up individual events and tells us how to take them. Or again, he picks out what was significant in the events he relates, what is significant here being what points beyond itself and connects with other happenings as phases in a continuous process. (1974: 136)

The principle of historicism underlies this premise of historical practice, because what happened is described and therefore explained or interpreted in terms of when it happened and what happened around it at the same time or over time. Hayden White describes well what such an approach entails:

> The informing presupposition of contextualism is that events can be explained by being set within the "context" of their occurrence. Why they occurred as they did is explained by the revelation of the specific relationships they bore to other events occurring in the circumambient historical

---

3. This term, borrowed from Gilbert Ryle and popularized in the human sciences by Clifford Geertz, has its own context and therefore meaning in (1973: chapter 1).

space. . . . [T]he Contextualist insists that "what happened" in the field can be accounted for by the specification of the functional interrelationships existing among the agents and agencies occupying the field at a given time. (1973: 17–18)

Whether historians achieve true explanation by such a method(ology) is a matter of philosophic debate, but normal historians believe that they establish a pattern that is more than mere contiguity or contingency.[4]

Contextualism in the end copes with plenitude through seeking "unity in diversity," to use Walsh's phrase (1974: 143). As Walsh says,

> The underlying assumption here is that different historical events can be regarded as going together to constitute a single process, a whole of which they are all parts and in which they belong together in a specially intimate way. And the first aim of the historian, when asked to explain some event or other, is to see it as part of such a process, to locate it in its context by mentioning other events with which it is bound up.   (1967: 23–24)

The methodological assumptions of contextual analysis tend to individualize the unit of study in terms of an overall uniqueness as the primary way of understanding history. By placing past events, behaviors, etc., in an ever-larger context—be it cultural, social or otherwise—their similarities are reduced in favor of their dissimilarities. As the context is enlarged, the overall pattern of meaning among the elements emphasizes the individuality of the total network of relationships. This principle applies to units within societies and cultures as well as between societies and cultures themselves studied as units. In all cases, the unit of study and its context become the same or coincident whether the historian posits contextualism as the basis for deducing facts from evidence or for synthesizing those facts into a written history.[5] This approach to contextualism does not raise the spurious issues of whether or not historians use generalizations, abstract from "reality," or even consume comparisons. They do. Rather contextualism presumes and produces uniqueness as its chief explanatory or interpretive mode, hence it also predicates that the past can be

---

4. The argument over the nature of explanation in history and whether historical explanation achieves a true or proper explanation was a phase of a debate among philosophers and was associated with the names of Carl Hempel, William Dray and others. Many of the important articles are reprinted in Patrick Gardiner (1959: 344–475). Just as professional historians thought this argument irrelevant to their actual practices, so too do they feel that the New Historicism pertains to controversies internecine to the literary theory crowd and not pertinent to historians. In fact, they come away from examples of the New Historicism feeling that these scholars establish homologies at best rather than any real (causal?) interconnections.

5. That is why the phrase "comparative history" seems an oxymoron to so many historians.

comprehended as a story whether on the level of synthetic exposition or as a way of evidentiary inference.

To context as plenitude, therefore, we must add the idea of narrative if we are to understand what historians presuppose about the past as history so as to produce current historical practice. The "return to narrative" discussion oversimplifies current conceptions of narrativity as applied to historical productions, because it equates all of narrative logic with simple story-telling. Thus for Lawrence Stone, who introduced the topic into the profession, "Narrative is taken to mean the organization of material into a single coherent story, albeit with sub-plots" (1979: 3). Thus, for him, narratives are "descriptive," not "analytical." The central focus is "on man, not circumstances." The historian deals with the "particular and specific rather than the collective and the statistical" (Ibid: 3–4). Narrativity embraces more forms and pervades more aspects of history doing than Stone allows but his emphasis on the singularity of the story holds important implications for conceiving of the past as history.[6]

Just how narrative should be conceived as a form in historical practice is less important to my argument at the moment than considering at which points in the process of historical understanding the normal historian applies narrative logic. Historians apply plot and narrative logic (no matter how defined) not only to their synthetic expository efforts but also, I would argue following the reasoning of Louis Mink (1978: 129–149; 135–141), to the past itself as history. It is through postulating the past as a complex but unified flow of events organized narratively that enables normal historians to presume that their sources—as created by a past so conceived—allows (helps?) them to "reconstruct" the story of that past according to some narrative structure. Historical methods can operate only if historians conceive of contextual plenitude as a continuum of structured events organized according to the same narrative logic they employ in their own synthetic expositions, which supposedly mirror the past as homologously structured. Modern historical practice therefore only makes sense if historians predicate that the living past as contextual plenitude can be comprehended as a unified flow of events which in turn can be organized into some kind of unified exposition or story. Once again, the exposition as story and the flow of once actual events are presumed map-like or at least homologous. Whether the past is actually structured as we conceive narrative or only our understanding is struc-

6. Compare another historian on narrative, Hayden White (1984: 1–33). That historians might have grounds for confusion on the nature of narrative, see Wallace Martin (1986).

tured in that manner,[7] we can see through a simple diagram how such predication of narrative structure affects historical practice and methodology. (In this and succeeding diagrams, the solid lines designate what I take to be empirically based in normal historical practice and the dotted lines represent connections made through presupposition in my opinion.)

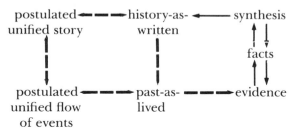

From the diagram, we can see that normal historical practice uses narrative structuring in two ways to transform the past into history. First, the paradigm of normal history presumes that there existed a total past that can be understood and constituted as history, even if only in the mind of God or an Omniscient Historian, according to narrative logic in some form. Second, each partial version of history can be organized according to the same logic both as synthesis of factuality and as the actual partial past it supposedly resembles. If we recall Stone's definition of narrative and Walsh's description of colligation, we see that they apply to both the partial and total versions of history. Only by predicating that the plenitude and context of (past) history is comprehended from the viewpoint of a third-person, omniscient narrator can normal history practice be understood: first, as the partial histories historians produce and, second, as the total historical context from which they are said to be part.

To suggest this multiple application of narrative organization to the postulated actual past as total and partial and to the representations of those pasts, I would add the notion of the "Great Story," (or what others might call the "Meta-story," the "Meta-narrative" or the "Meta-Text") of the total past that justifies the synthetic expositions of normal historians and the idea of the "Great Past" (or what others again might term the "Meta-past," "Ur-text" or "Meta-source,") that narrativizes the source material for all of the past as history.[8] Once again in diagram:

7. Compare Paul Ricoeur (1984), with F. R. Ankersmit (1983) on this matter.
8. I owe these insights to Louis Mink more than to any other scholar but see Peter Munz (1977: chapters 7–8). My use of the "Great Story" is not meant to be a translation of *grand récit*. While all *grand récits* presume a great story, the great story need not presume any one master interpretive code.

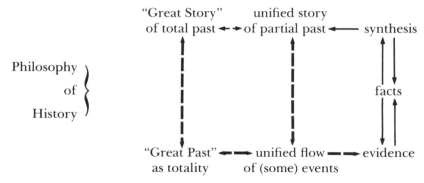

I have chosen to designate the left side of this diagram the philosophy of history to indicate, first, that the nature of the Great Story was the province of classic or older philosophy of history and, secondly, that the presuppositions of historical practice are the subject of the newer analytical philosophy of history in Anglo-American practice (as well as in later metahistory).

Such a view of normal historical understanding raises some obvious questions about the relation of partial stories or histories to the total or overall story of HISTORY itself. How many stories are there in the Great Story or Meta-narrative? How many pasts in the Great Past or "Ur-text"? How are variant versions or interpretations of the same partial past time period to be understood? Are variant interpretations to stand alongside each other as valid, autonomous synthetic expositions, or should all variants be reconciled by reference to the single Great Story? But, since the Great Story is nothing but a postulation of the paradigm of normal historical practice, what decides the validity of one version over another? Does measurement against the Great Past conceived as Ur-text decide between the variants? But, once again, the Great Past seems as much a paradigmatic presupposition as its synthetic equivalent, the Great Story.

To explore such questions about variant interpretations, we must turn to the issues of representation and referentiality as presumed in historical practice. The issues of representation and referentiality—or structure of interpretation as embodied in the process of synthesis versus the structure of factuality presumed as the basis of the synthesis —underlie some of the dichotomies considered basic to the historical discipline: abstraction versus concreteness, fiction versus factuality, art versus science, interpretation versus empiricism, construction versus reconstruction. The effect the normal historians try to achieve in their (re)presentations is the fusion of the structures of interpretation and factuality to impress the reader that the structure of interpretation *is* the structure of factuality, thereby reconciling and transcending the various supposed dichotomies endemic to the discipline. Rather than showing the reader how the (re)presentation is structured to *look like* total factuality, the normal historian's job is to make it appear *as though* the structure of factuality itself had determined the organizational structure of his or her account. The narrative organization, no matter what its mode or message, usually (re)presents its subject matter, in turn, as the natural order of things, which is the illusion of realism.[9]

Because normal historians try to reconcile variant interpretations by *reference* to facts rather than by arguments over the nature of narratives as such, they must presume in practice that factuality possesses some sort of coercive reality in their expositions of the partial past and their understanding of the Great Past. How can the profession's normal activities in meetings, books, and reviews be explained otherwise? If historians assumed with Roman Jakobson (1960: 350–377) or Roland Barthes (1974) that referentiality is just one mode of coding communications, just one part of a text's complex structure, then normal historical reviews, meetings, and books would take quite different forms than they do now.

According to my argument so far, history is distinguished from the past in normal disciplinary practice because historians need to divide representation from referentiality to make factuality the supposed test as well as the supposed basis of synthetic exposition in their profession. Rather than arguing this case further here, let me show what such a presupposition means in terms of an extended diagram. Without duplicating all parts of previous diagrams, I will indicate the relationship between representation and referentiality, basic to normal historical practice in general, by showing their connection to narrativity and factuality in particular. In brief, I link methods and history-as-written with the postulated unified stories through synthesis as historical construction and as narrative. Representation, then, concerns both the mode of presentation as embraced in that linkage and the nature of what that mode covers in the whole process of doing normal history. In terms of the diagram, representation covers the whole upper half of normal history practice, for it embraces both the synthesis pro-

9. On the presumption of realism in historical productions, see Lionel Gossman (1978: 3–40); Robert Anchor (1983: 107–119); and Martin (1986: 57–80). I have chosen not to distinguish between story and discourse in general, or between what is told and how it is told or between the order of events etc., as they are presented in the text as opposed to the order in which they supposedly occurred in time as represented in the text. Important as these distinctions are to historical productions, I feel they only complicate my argument without greatly affecting its main points.

duced and the way it is understood as "history." I also connect methods and pasts, partial and Great, as sources through evidence as historical reconstruction and as (f)actuality. Referentiality designates the mode of understanding presumed by the recourse to (f)actuality and supposedly achieved through historical reconstruction. In diagrammatic terms, once again, referentiality therefore covers the entire lower half of the process of doing normal history.

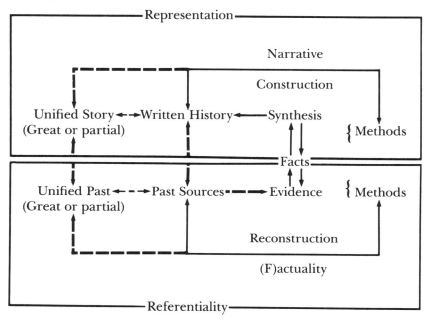

The paradigmatic presuppositional framework of normal history connects representation and referentiality through the transition from the derivation of facts from evidence to the synthesis of those facts into an exposition, as the diagram shows. Hence the statements so customary in the profession that history is both science and art, both a reconstruction and a construction. The two realms are postulated as connected but separated so that produced history can claim to be both empirical and factual but also literary in its larger sense—factual because of reference to (f)actuality, literary because of its synthetic (re)presentation of the partial and Great Stories.

It is this strict separation of representation and construction from referentiality and (re)construction that poetics, or the general theory of literary works, and contemporary literary criticism question and, therefore, in turn, challenge the basic paradigm of normal historical practice portrayed in the above diagram. In fact, poetics of history and criticism of history as literature (once again in its largest sense) take the lack of such separation as one of their basic premises.[10]

The core question that causes all the problems is quite simple: just what is the referent for the word "history"? It cannot be the past as such, because that is absent by definition. If linguistic analysts define words as signs or signifiers that denote objects in their stead, then "history" certainly fits the definition twice over. Normal history exists as a practice because of the very effort needed in the present to imagine (predicate) in the present an absent past actuality presumed to have once existed, but for that reason no one can point to the past in the same way that one can point to a horse or a tree (or even a picture of them) as the objects to which the words "horse" and "tree" refer.[11] The historian, at best, can point to actual remains that supposedly come to us from the past or to the sources historians use as evidence for their historical reconstructions. But as we know from the paradigm of normal history, those sources are employed to create pasts, whether partial or greater, that are larger than the sources themselves. Those pasts, however, depend upon still another predication or construction as observed by those interested in the poetics of historical practice.

The only referent that can be found for "history" in the eyes of such critics and theorists is the intertextuality that results from the reading of sets of sources combined with (guided by?) the readings of other historians of these same or other sources as synthesized in their expositions. "History" refers in actual practice only to other "histories," in the eyes of these critics. Thus they fail to see much, if anything, in the distinction drawn by normal historians between fact and fiction, for factual reconstruction is really nothing but construction according to the working "fictions" of normal history practice, which, in turn, are the premises of both historical realism and realistic mimesis.

10. Revealing is the entry under "Hi/story" in ed. A. J. Greimas and J. Courtés, trans. Larry Crist and Daniel Patte et al. (1982: 143–144). We do not have a work specifically aimed to help historians in their everyday production of history written from the perspective of poetics or semiotics, but see the provocative book by Sande Cohen (1986).
11. To use Ferdinand de Saussure's two examples (1970) to explain sign, signifier, and signified, reprinted conveniently in Michael Lane (1970: 43–45). The terms *signifier, signified* and *referent* are used differently by scholars depending upon their premises, but I believe my use here is both consistent and useful for the argument at hand. See Robert Scholes (1981: 200–205). Compare the entries under "sign" and "reference" in Oswald Ducrot and Tzvetan Todorov (1979); and Greimas and Courtés (1982) as well as "signifier," "signification" and "signified" in the latter. Just as complicated as the relationships among these terms are the relationships involving "author" and "audience." See, for example, Michel Foucault, (1979: 141–160); the anthology edited by Jane P. Tompkins (1980); and William Ray (1984). Once again, I have decided not to develop these possibilities in the interest of keeping my argument to its main points.

Such an analysis of historical productions and practices stands normal history on its head, so to speak. Much, if not all, of what normal history presents as factuality becomes subsumed into the synthetic side of historical practice and therefore questioned as to just what it does represent. In terms of our last diagram, representation embraces the entire process of doing history with referentiality referring to, at best, the actual documentary and other remains in the present presumed to come from a past postulated passed. According to this view, then, most (all?) of what is presented as (f)actuality is a special coding of the historians' synthetic expository texts, designed to conceal their highly constructed basis.[12] In our previously used terms, the partial stories are represented as if they mapped or mirrored the partial pasts themselves.

That normal historical practice attempts to make its representations appear to present information as if it were a matter of simple referentiality indicates that the premises of realism are basic to the paradigm. Realism enters historical practice to the extent that historians try to make their structure of factuality seem to be its own organizational structure and therefore conceal that it is structured by interpretation represented as (f)actuality. This is as true of analytic as narrative expositions: art is presented as a science quite literally in the former while a supposed historical science is transformed into an art in the latter.[13]

Many contemporary scholars under such an impression of historical practice see history as just another mode of coding words and texts according to conventional presuppositions about representing the past as history. That such coding is conventional also means it is arbitrary in a technical sense to many literary and other scholars today, because they argue realism is a cultural and not a natural category of representing things. In the end, such beliefs about realism and the arbitrary

12. Regardless of how an historian might view the relationship between language and extra-linguistic phenomena, the factuality of an overall synthesis is not of the same order as that of the individual facts constituting it. As a result, this argument about the constructed nature of the synthesis holds, I believe, independent of one's philosophy of language. See, for example, Jerzy Topolski (1981: 47–60), who agrees with this conclusion about factuality of and in an historical production but holds quite another view of the relation of language to the world than those who advocate what we might call a radical constructionist position in historical practice. For a sample of the debate on constructionism, see "The Constitution of the Past," *History and Theory*, XVI (no. 4 [Beiheft 16], 1977).
13. On the artistry of scientific history, see the interesting article by Donald N. McCloskey (1985: 1–22). That social science historians and traditional historians need not differ in their basic premises about the nature of historical "reality" is shown in Robert W. Fogel and Geoffrey R. Elton (1983). Even a so-called hard social science can be read poetically: see, for example, Donald N. McCloskey (1985).

coding of the past in the present as history collapse all distinction between representation and referentiality, for the latter can only be the
former. The signified (the past) is naught but the signifier (history);
no referent exists outside the history texts themselves (Barthes 1970:
145–155).[14]

Ultimately, the Great Past is the Great Story and nothing but the
Great Story according to this view. As with the partial stories and
pasts, the Great Past is coded according to the same paradigmatic
presuppositions of realism. But the Great Story is no less a predication
or presupposition of the historical practice paradigm than the Great
Past. Its referent can no more be pointed to than that of the Great
Past. It exists in the mind of God or the Omniscient Historian to
test and organize the variant versions of partial stories as (hi)stories.
In practice, the Great Story is extrapolated from the many partial
(hi)stories and they must, in effect, be the referent for the Great Story,
if it can even be said to have one apart from its own wishful predication
in normal history itself.[15]

Now we can modify our previous diagrams to indicate the place
of meta-understanding in historical practice from the viewpoint of
the poetics of history. The presuppositions that ground the synthetic
constructions of historical production or the coding of the past as
narrativity in its most general meaning can be labelled "meta-story,"
"meta-narrative" or perhaps, in some sense, "meta-text." The phrases
"meta-source" and "ur-text" would seem to do the same for the presuppositions necessary to interpret sources as intertextual evidence
of the story of the past as history, as might "meta-past" to designate
the premises behind the narrativization of the Great as well as partial
pasts. Meta-narrativity, in its most general sense, pervades therefore
the paradigmatic presuppositions of normal history both through the
connection of referentiality to representation and through the link
between the partial and larger pasts. Metahistory embraces the whole
paradigm of presuppositions that create normal historical practice, so
we replace the philosophy of history with that term on the left of the
diagram.

14. That *res gestae* equal *historia rerum gestarum* in normal historical practice is also
the point of Munz (1977: chapter 8).
15. Even if the historians could recreate the actual past in its totality, such would
still not be history as we conceive it today; historians would still have to select
their themes and understandings of the past from the bewildering multiplicity of
phenomena confronting them. Compare the conception of the "ideal chronicle" in
Arthur C. Danto (1985: 149–182). To revert to the terms used in this article, even
if the total past were reconstructed for historians, it would still not be the Great Past
let alone the Great Story, without analysis and interpretation by historians—and
professional ones at that—because the past as history cannot even be predicated
without interpretation according to some customary presuppositional framework.

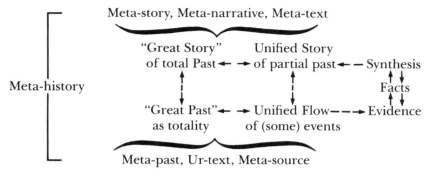

Metahistory equates meta-story with meta-past, that is, it collapses the presuppositional framework underlying representation with the one underlying referentiality, because the latter is considered primarily a postulation of the former in the paradigm of normal historical practice. Given this picture of the place of metahistorical premises in normal history, small wonder some theorists of historical poetics see history, historiography, the philosophy of history and metahistory all integrally (inter)related, even coincident to the horror of normal historians.

One challenge of poetics to history lies in the implications of this equation of representation and referentiality, of the collapse of meta-past into meta-story. Normal, that is, traditional, history is shown to be but a conventional, hence arbitrary, mode of coding communication as factuality by presenting the representation as if it were entirely referential and realistic. The transmutation of so much—some would say all—of the referential side of history into the representational and narrative side destroys the effect of overall factual authority claimed for historical productions. Demystification of the historical enterprise, therefore, also delegitimizes it as a discipline in this view.

Demystification of normal history probably also denies that any single meta-narrative organizes either the partial or Great Stories. Thus the story of the past cannot be read simply as a history of progress or as decline, as cycles or as catastrophes, as class conflict or as consensual pluralism, or even as change or continuity alone. No longer can any single master interpretive code be privileged over another as if one were somehow more correspondent to the (a?) "real" past than another. The denial of a single meta-narrative Great or partial story to organize history eliminates the omniscient viewpoint, probably the third person voice, and maybe the ethnocentrism so evident so long in history productions.[16]

16. The ethnocentrism, indeed cultural hubris, of contemporary industrial societies as embodied in normal historical practice was the main target of the well

Demystification therefore frees the historian to tell many different kinds of "stories" from various viewpoints, with many voices, emplotted diversely, according to many principles of synthesis. By denying the traditional meta-narrativity presuppositions, the historian liberates the ways of coding the past as history as well as how it is represented. For Hayden White, the demystification achieved through metahistory was intended to free the historian to emplot his narrative according to choice—or will—and therefore to move beyond the modernist stance of irony (1980: 433–34). To many normal historians, however, such a radical demystification appears to be the "end of [normal] history,"[17] because it implies that historical discourse refers to little or nothing outside itself. After all, they would ask, of what use are maps or photographs if one cannot be sure what they represent according to the usual realistic or mimetic criteria or even if they represent anything beyond their own surface configurations? By opening history construction therefore to greater possibilities of story-telling and interpretive coding than normal history allows, one appears to have eliminated the legitimating authority of factuality for history itself according to traditional premises.

But why is this a problem? Because normal history orders the past for the sake of authority and therefore power over its audience. Such power is asserted through voice and viewpoint in the paradigm of normal history. What is suppressed (repressed?) in normal historical narratives no matter what the mode of exposition, whether in so-called new or old histories, conservative, liberal or radical histories, is the personal production of the history which is claimed to map or mirror the past. By assuming a third person voice and an omniscient viewpoint, authors, be they left or right or in between politically, assert their power over their readers in the name of REALITY.

Authorial power over the reader is also asserted through the normal history presupposition of a single meta-story to organize the synthetic, representational side of history doing. Left and right seem to take similar positions on this matter. Those historians inspired by Karl Marx are no different in this search for a single metastory than those who follow Leo Marx, just to pick another Marx out of the historical hat. Those who follow Karl Marx seek a single interpretive code or

---

known last chapter, "History and Dialectic," of Claude Lévi-Strauss (1966). That the discipline is organized by national histories and professional associations illustrates how deeply such ethnocentrism pervades the profession and how natural it seems to the discipline as organized academically. See the classic article by David M. Potter (1962: 924–950).

17. As some French intellectuals proclaimed for various reasons two or more decades ago. Vincent Descombes, *Modern French Philosophy*, trans. L. Scott-Fox and J. M. Harding (1980: 27–32, 180–86) places the "end of history" and the "death of man" in an interesting philosophical and political context.

master story, although they may disagree among themselves as to just what the key may be in interpreting the ur-text according to Marx himself (Jameson 1979: 46). As with radical historians so too with liberal and conservative historians, for all must prove their cases by a single metastory, a single interpretive coding of the past; otherwise, the arbitrary nature of the produced history becomes easily evident to the audience and THE history loses its intended natural effect.

We could accept the death of normal history without declaring the death of history doing itself. Historical practice could be transformed with important implications for how the profession reads, produces, teaches and reviews what it calls "history." Poetics presents the profession with a plurality of possibilities. Rather than refusing to explore the many exciting possibilities in order to preserve old ways in the name of some meta-narrative about the true nature of professional history doing, we might explore the many ways in which Clio can be clothed in garb less transparent to our humanistic colleagues and more in fashion with our late twentieth-century audience.

References

Anchor, Robert
> 1983 "Realism and Ideology: The Question of Order," *History and Theory* 22(2): 107–119.

Ankersmit, F. R.
> 1983 *Narrative Logic: A Semantic Analysis of the Historian's Language*, Vol. 7 (The Hague: Martinus Nijhoff).

Barthes, Roland
> 1970 "Historical Discourse," in *Introduction to Structuralism*, edited by Michael Lane (New York: Basic Books), 145–155.

> 1974 *S/Z*, translated by Richard Miller (New York: Farrar, Straus and Giroux).

Barzun, Jacques and Henry F. Graf
> 1957 *The Modern Researcher* (New York: Harcourt, Brace and World).

Berkhofer, Robert F., Jr.
> 1969 *A Behavioral Approach to Historical Analysis* (New York: The Free Press).

Cohen, Sande
> 1986 *Historical Culture: On the Recoding of an Academic Discipline* (Berkeley: University of California Press).

Danto, Arthur C.
> 1985 *Narration and Knowledge*, expanded ed. of *Analytical Philosophy of History* (New York: Columbia University Press), 149–182.

Descombes, Vincent
> 1980 *Modern French Philosophy*, translated by L. Scott-Fox and J. M. Harding (Cambridge: Cambridge University Press).

Ducrot, Oswald and Tzvetan Todorov
> 1979 *Encyclopedic Dictionary of the Sciences of Language*, translated by Catherine Porter (Baltimore: Johns Hopkins University Press).

Fogel, Robert W. and Geoffrey R. Elton
> 1983 *Which Road to the Past: Two Views of History* (New Haven: Yale University Press).

Foucault, Michel
   1979 "What is an Author?," in *Textual Strategies: Perspectives in Post-Structuralist Criticism*, edited by Josué V. Harari (Ithaca: Cornell University Press), 141–160.
Gardiner, Patrick, ed.
   1959 *Theories of History* (Glencoe, IL: Free Press).
Geertz, Clifford
   1973 *The Interpretation of Cultures* (New York: Basic Books).
Gossman, Lionel
   1978 "History and Literature: Reproduction or Signification," in *The Writing of History: Literary Form and Historical Understanding*, edited by Robert H. Canary and Henry Kozicki (Madison: University of Wisconsin Press), 3–40.
Gottschalk, Louis
   1969 *Understanding History: A Primer of Historical Methods*, 2nd ed. (New York: Alfred A. Knopf).
Greimas, A. J. and J. Courtés, eds.
   1982 *Semiotics and Language: An Analytical Dictionary*, translated by Larry Crist and Daniel Patte, et al (Bloomington: University of Indiana Press).
Jakobson, Roman
   1960 "Closing Statement: Linguistics and Poetics," in *Style in Language*, edited by Thomas Sebeok (Cambridge, MA: MIT Press), 350–377.
Jameson, Fredric
   1979 "Marxism and Historicism," *New Literary History* 11 (Autumn): 41–73.
Kuhn, Thomas S.
   1970 *The Structure of Scientific Revolutions*, 2nd ed., enl. (Chicago: University of Chicago Press).
Lévi-Strauss, Claude
   1966 *The Savage Mind* (Chicago: University of Chicago Press).
Marrou, Henri-Irénée
   1966 *The Meaning of History*, translated by Robert J. Olsen (Baltimore: Helicon).
Martin, Wallace
   1986 *Recent Theories of Narrative* (Ithaca: Cornell University Press).
McCloskey, Donald N.
   1985 "The Problem of Audience in Historical Economics: Rhetorical Thoughts on a Text by Robert Fogel," *History and Theory* 24 (1): 1–22.
   1985 *The Rhetoric of Economics* (Madison: University of Wisconsin Press).
Mink, Louis
   1978 "Narrative Form as a Cognitive Instrument," in *The Writing of History: Literary Form and Historical Understanding*, edited by Robert H. Canary and Henry Kozicki (Madison: University of Wisconsin Press), 129–149.
Munz, Peter
   1977 *The Shapes of Time: A New Look at the Philosophy of History* (Middletown, CT: Wesleyan University Press).
Nadel, George H., ed.
   1977 "The Constitution of the Past," *History and Theory* 16 (4) Supp. 16.
   1980 "Metahistory: Six Critiques," *History and Theory* 19 (4) Supp. 19.
Potter, David M.
   1962 "The Historian's Idea of Nationalism and Vice Versa," *American Historical Review* 67 (July): 924–950.
Ray, William
   1984 *Literary Meaning: From Phenomenology to Deconstruction* (London: Basil Blackwell).

Ricoeur, Paul
1984 *Time and Narrative*, Vol. 1, translated by Kathleen McLaughlin and David
Pellauer (Chicago: University of Chicago Press).
Saussure, Ferdinand de
1970 "Course in General Linguistics," in *Introduction to Structuralism*, edited by
Michael Lane (New York: Basic Books), 43–56.
Scholes, Robert
1981 "Language, Narrative, and anti-Narrative," in *On Narrative*, edited by
W. J. T. Mitchell (Chicago: University of Chicago Press), 200–208.
Stone, Lawrence
1979 "The Revival of Narrative: Reflections on a New Old History," *Past and
Present* (Oxford) 85: 3–24.
Tilly, Charles
1985 "Retrieving European Lives," in *Reliving the Past: The Worlds of Social History*,
edited by Olivier Zunz (Chapel Hill: University of North Carolina Press),
11–52.
Tompkins, Jane P., ed.
1980 *Reader-Response Criticism: From Formalism to Post-Structuralism* (Baltimore:
Johns Hopkins University Press).
Topolski, Jerzy
1981 "Conditions of Truth of Historical Narratives," *History and Theory* 20 (1):
47–60.
Walsh, William H.
1967 *An Introduction to the Philosophy of History*, 3rd ed. (London: Hutchinson).
1974 "Colligatory Concepts in History," in *The Philosophy of History*, edited by
Patrick Gardiner (Oxford: Oxford University Press), 127–144.
White, Hayden
1973 *Metahistory: The Historical Imagination in Nineteenth-Century Europe* (Baltimore: Johns Hopkins University Press).
1982 "Method and Ideology in Intellectual History: The Case of Henry Adams,"
in *Modern European Intellectual History: Reappraisals and New Perspectives*, edited
by Dominick LaCapra and Steven L. Kaplan (Ithaca: Cornell University Press),
280–310.
1984 "The Question of Narrative in Contemporary Historical Theory," *History
and Theory* 23 (1): 1–33.

The Inevitability of Stereotype: Colonialism in *The Great Gatsby*

Michael Holquist

As ever more work is done in the name of Dialogism, it is increasingly necessary to specify a particular period of Bakhtin's activity when invoking his name. Reading Fitzgerald's *The Great Gatsby* in the light of Dialogism, a task that will constitute the latter half of this paper, requires us to keep in mind the first two phases of Bakhtin's career: the very first, in which he writes such philosophical texts as "Author and Hero in Aesthetic Activity" and "Towards a Philosophy of the Deed," and the phase immediately following, when he produces texts bearing on social theory, such as *Marxism and the Philosophy of Language*. Roughly speaking, the first period may be characterized as a phenomenological meditation on the subject in general; the second as a meditation on the work of ideology as it produces, and is produced by, the subject through language and in society.

I wish to address the general problem of what a dialogic historiography might look like by reading *The Great Gatsby* as an example of how speech genres over long stretches of time shape and are shaped by change. Although I will be reading Fitzgerald's novel, I am not attempting to appropriate it as a self-enclosed text (were such a thing possible). Rather, *Gatsby* will be used as a means for examing the role played by otherness in giving shape to the past. More particularly, this reading will want to consider certain formal features of the novel to consider some of the historical effects wrought by the memory of colonization. Reading *The Great Gatsby* in this way will, I hope, help to illustrate the central place in Dialogism occupied by Bakhtin's phenomenological biology, the degree to which ontogeny's relation to philogeny may be appropriated as a model not only for the individual subject's relation to society but as a structural metaphor for conceiving the otherness of the past.

Both alterity and historiography are now common topics across a broad range of scholarship. But it has been groups with urgent political agendas that have been most acute in analyzing the role of otherness in history and historiography: feminist critics such as Luce Iragaray, anti-colonialist critics such as Edward Said or engaged black theorists such as Henry Louis Gates, Jr. Said has called these critics "libertarian," recognizing, as most of them do, that the theoretical moves they make have much in common. He is, he writes, engaging not only Orientalism but "similar issues raised by the experiences of feminism or women's studies, black or ethnic studies, socialist and anti-imperialist studies. . . ." (Said 1986: 213). It is arguably the case that the most comprehensive work in this area has been done by analysts of colonialism such as Said himself or by Homi K. Bhabha, to whom we shall have occasion to return. Most of these groups are currently rereading Derridean or Lacanian appropriations of linguistics in an effort to initiate new and "deeper" analyses of political repression.[1] The practice and agendas of these groups differ from each other in significant ways, but they have in common the need to rethink an otherness that always founds its effects on a binary opposition, whether it be of "imaginative geography" (Occident/Orient), gender (male/female), race (white/black, non-Jew/Jew) or of a power alignment that assigns privilege according to whether the subject is either a colonial-izer or one of the colonialized. I believe that insofar as this proposition holds, there are certain parallels between Bakhtin's attempts to the-orize his way out of dialectical habits of thought—"dialectical" being his way of generalizing the host of problems that cluster around bi-narism, teleology, and closure—and the attempts of blacks, feminists, and anti-colonialist thinkers to rethink the categories of alterity.

Bakhtin's early work is concerned not so much with the self/other distinction as it is usually conceived—a tradition that has led certain of his readers to misconstrue his project as a covert strategy to resurrect a transcendence for the ego—as it is with otherness as such (I say lamely,

---

1. For an illuminating example of some of the problems that must be confronted by theorists who wish to use Deconstruction as a means for politicizing their prac-tice of reading extra-canonical (in this case Black) texts, see the exchange between Joyce A. Joyce, Houston Baker Jr., and Henry Louis Gates, Jr. in *New Literary History*, vol. 18, no. 2 (Winter 1987), pp. 335–384.

aware at the same time that there cannot be any "as such" in Dialogism). A Bakhtinian *à priori* is that self cannot coincide with itself. It is less a static locus of privilege than it is a specifically structured worksite for the dynamic and all-encompassing activity of alterity. It cannot be over-emphasized that it is only one of *several* ways in which a general otherness specifies itself in particular practices. But the dialogic self has certain characteristics that make it differ from other instances of alterity, characteristics that derive from neccessity, but which have an appearance that can mislead the unwary into assuming they constitute a privilege.

To grasp the reality of the necessity and the appearance of privilege, it will be useful to remember that Dialogism is essentially a post-Kantian theory of knowledge. Dialogism in its first phase begins by assuming a cut-off between what is perceived and the mechanism by which perception takes place: it is a version of constructivist epistemology that takes for granted our inability ever to penetrate to a level where things would be in themselves. Self in this sense is similar to the Kantian "I think," the point at which apperception occurs and back to which experience relates for the categories that can shape it into perceptible meaning. In his second phase, Bakhtin complicates this gnoseological scenario by adding to it a linguistic dimension. Kant had posited that experience was organized through activity of twelve categories and two forms of intuition, time and space, which were prior to any actual event. We knew not the world but what the categories constructed of the world.

While each of Bakhtin's first two periods is distinctive, they nevertheless articulate with each other at important points, as can be seen in the way Bakhtin assumes this essentially Kantian epistemology in both. But in the twenties, Bakhtin radicalizes the Kantian *à prioris* by grounding them in linguistics rather than metaphysics. Russians had been quicker than most to see the radical implications first of Wilhelm von Humboldt's work and then of Saussure's; thus it is perhaps not surprising that Bakhtin (immediately following on the appearance of the *Cours* in Russia in the early twenties) in his second phase posits language as the vehicle used by the categories dominating perception to legislate their specific effects: the fuel of knowing may remain the categories, but its engine is now seen to be language. Making words —if I may metaphorize the proccess in another way—the police of perception's categorical rulers had the effect of making colonization a problem not only for Africans and Indians but for all speaking subjects. Dialogism suggests we become selves only when we enter language; in other words, our ability to say "I" is a form of subjugation, for it results from our organism's being invaded by language, the only means by which we can become subjects able to interact with other subjects in a community. Insofar as we are in this sense subjects in society, we are subjects *of* language:

> Although the reality of the word, as is true of any sign, resides between individuals, a word, at the same time, is produced by the individual organism's own means without recourse to any equipment or any other kind of extracorporeal material. This has determined the role of [the] word as *the semiotic material of inner life—of consciousness* (inner speech).

And he adds, in a sentence fraught with consequences for any consideration of colonial discourse, in which the physical aspect of bodies plays so major a role, "Indeed, consciousness could have developed only by having at its disposal material that was pliable and expressible by bodily means" (Bakhtin 1986: 14).

Insofar as consciousness is a function of language, we become conscious—that is, become subjects—only when we acquire language. Language is both the benefactor of subjectivity and the means by which it will always be alienated from any "self" that is not striated by the otherness of signs: *"experience exists even for the person undergoing it only in the material of signs.* Outside that material there is no experience as such" (Bakhtin 1986: 28). The progenitor of my "I" is not I, and in that gap is the epistemological structure grounding the perceptual gap between colonizer and colonized. In what follows we shall have occasion to pursue language acquistion and the subjects it produces in comparison with the political effects of imperialism, i.e., colonization and the subjects produced by it.

Bakhtin, of course, is not alone in positing a subject produced by language. However, his insistence on the *responsibility* entailed by subjectivity of this kind sets him apart from most other twentieth-century figures who, like Lacan, have also assumed a language-centered (and thus language-*de*centered) ego. When we are invaded by language, or as we might more hopefully say, when we enter language—both descriptions being accurate under different conditions—it is not Language as such we enter. Rather, at a particular time and a particular place each of us makes an entrance into a matrix of highly distinctive economic, political, and historical forces—a unique and unrepeatable combination of ideologies, each speaking its own language, the heteroglot conglomerate of which will constitute the world in which we act. It is only in that highly specific, indeed unique placement that the world may address us: in a very real sense it is our "address" in existence, an address expressed not in numbers but by our proper name. It is only from that site we can speak. Bakhtin concludes from this that none of us has an "alibi in existence," for we cannot be excused from being in the place that the world as heteroglossia assigns us, and which only we will ever occupy. The subjectivity whose placement is determined by the structure of addressivity requires us then to be answerable for that site, if only in the sense that the subject occupying that particular place (who *is* that place) will be the source of whatever response called forth from it by the physical forces of nature and the discursive energy of society. What the self is answerable *to* is the environment; what it is responsible *for* is authorship of its responses.

Because Dialogism assumes that otherness is at work everywhere, including the self, a major problem for the subject it proposes is how to see itself. Whether in a rigorous phenomenological attempt to achieve an eidetic intimation of myself or in the most banal daydream, Bakhtin maintains "It is precisely I myself I cannot see." Much like the relation of an author to his heroes, the subject for itself is "the main character who is on a different plane from all the other characters" s/he constructs. (1979: 27) The term Bakhtin uses for this "different plane" is transgredience, or "outsidedness" (*vnenaxodimost'*), a position outside the other that lets the perceiver see things about the other that s/he— as a subject—cannot see him/herself. The subject perceives the other from a "surplus of seeing" (*izbytok viden'ja*), a surplus that begins with the exterior features that are the other's physical sign of identity, the signature, as it were, of his body, but a body cannot be seen from the placement of the other's own subjectivity. However my surplus of seeing also extends to a completeness in my perception of the other's total image that encompasses it as a totalized meaning, giving to the other a finished quality I reject as appropriate to myself as subject. The subject differs from the others it perceives—constructs—in terms of the fundamental building blocks of all knowing: time and space. The subject operates as if its environment were open, unfinished (*nezaveršën*), existing in an "absolute future" so long s/he is conscious, whereas the other is perceived as if s/he were finished off (*zaveršën*) insofar as he/she can already be known as s/he *is*. This fundamental doubling in perception is a function of the duality of the sign itself: as Karcevskij pointed out long ago,

> In a 'complete' sign (a word as opposed to a morpheme) there are two opposed centers of semiotic functions, one for formal values, the other for semantic values. The formal values of a word (gender, number, case, aspect, tense), represent aspects of signification known to every speaking subject which are more or less safe from any subjective interpretation on the part of interlocutors; they are assumed to remain identical to themselves in all situations. The semantic part of a word, in contrast, is a residue resistant to any attempt to decompose it into elements as 'objective' as formal values. (1982: 52)

Inner and outer speech are both composed of signs, but there are important differences between the two nevertheless. These differences can be traced as a kind of geological fault line dividing formal from semantic properties of the linguistic sign, which is "both static [formal] and dynamic [semantic] at the same time . . ." (Ibid.: 50). While much of structuralist theory has been toppled by the various schools nominated as *post*-structuralist, this fundamentally structuralist principle continues to be affirmed. Lacan, for instance, speaking of the subject's relation to the simultaneous stasis and dynamism of the signs says:

> The signifier, producing itself in the field of the Other, makes manifest the subject of its signification. But it functions as a signifier only to . . . petrify the subject in the same moment in which it calls the subject to function, so to speak, as subject. (Lacan 1979: 207)

The master distinction of self/other is the mechanism language drives through ceaseless slippage from static to dynamic, formal to semantic, to produce the subject. And just as the self's time, the activity of the dynamic aspect of language, is never exhausted by the present "now," the space of the self's placement, in his/her own subjectivity like that of the constantly sliding aspect of the sign, is never completely "here." It must be transgredient and not completely coincidental with *this* environment if it is to have the wider perspective needed to do its work in the ceaseless dialogue with the static and formal elements of language, modelled in the subject's drive to constitute a finished whole out of the other and his placement. But the other is seen by me as completely *here* insofar as I equate his subjectivity, his body and his environment as a unified totality—insofar as I architectonically complete him.

The site to which language assigns us as subjects is unique but never ours alone. The subject determined by language is never singular: like language itself, which has simultaneously a canonical, *langue* aspect and a freer, performative or *parole* aspect, the subject is organized by both an abstract, normative category—the other, and a specific, more open category—the self. It has always been recognized that language can work only if it exists between subjects, i.e., only if it belongs to more than one speaker. But this has usually reflected itself in no more than a mere subject/object distinction, as reflected in the gross features of most grammars which deploy nominative, accusative, and dative cases as if one speaker were an active sender and the other no more than a passive receiver. Bakhtin goes further: he insists that language can work only if it belongs to more than one aspect of self *within* the subject. By making language the framing condition for Kant's *a priori*s of perception, Bakhtin was thus impelled to double the forms of intuition: there is one time/space organizing perception of the subject by the subject; and there is another time/space that shapes the subject's perception of others. Bakhtin calls this model of intuition an "architectonics of responsibility," because it is the algorithm that structures responses made from the site where subjectivity is addressed. In other words, the structure of addressivity is a process of subjectification.

It is precisely here, at the heart of Dialogism, that we begin to en-counter parallels with some of the more interesting work being done in the analysis of colonial discourse, particularly with the analysis car-ried out in recent essays by Homi K. Bhabha (Bhaba, 1983, 1986). In one of the earlier of these (1983), he takes an epigraph from one of Derrida's early essays: "To concern oneself with the founding concepts of the entire history of philosophy . . . is probably the most daring way of making the beginnings of a step outside of philosophy." The presumption is that Bhabha is going to attempt to step outside colonial discourse by concerning himself with its founding concepts. Of these, none for Bhabha is more foundational of colonial discourse than the specific kind of otherness we call a stereotype. Unlike many other theorists who invoke rhetorical reading strategies to do political or historical analysis of sexism or racism, Bhabha begins by assuming the need not to deconstruct but rather to *"reconstruct"* colonial discourse. He argues that colonialist practice has never been codified, it has no manifesto beyond desire. It has always been a *set* of extremely various practices that has never been theorized, either by imperialists or their victims. Bhabha begins by trying to think his way out of "determinis-tic or functionalistic modes of conceiving of the relationship between discourse and politics [that do not go beyond merely] dogmatic and moralistic positions on the meaning of oppression and discrimination" (1983: 18). His means for doing so is to "shift from the *identification* of images as positive or negative, to an understanding of the *processes of subjectification* made possible . . . through stereotypical discourse" (Ibid.). In other words, stereotyping is not in its ground a moral or political affect. It is rather a discursive phenomenon rooted in "pro-cesses of subjectification." Bhabha's particular analysis of stereotyping appeals to an essentially Freudian/Lacanian model, which is powerful so long as it is used to explain the perceptual bases of a global subjec-tivity. But the model loses some of its strength, I believe, when Bhabha uses it to specify stereotyping as a *special case* in subject formation.

For, to understand any particular stereotype, we must examine forms of perception that constitute the fundamental conditions en-abling all stereotypes. A more common term for what Bhabha is call-ing "colonial discourse" is racism, as Bhabha's frequent and honorific appeals to Frantz Fanon make clear. With this in mind, Dialogism's gloomy assessment of both Bhabha and Fanon would be that they parochialize the structure of perception. What they take to be the dis-tinctive feature of stereotyping is the finished-off quality of the images it produces. Bhabha begins by remarking that "An important feature of colonial discourse is its dependence on the concept of 'fixity' in the ideological construction of otherness" (Ibid.: 18). And Fanon says of the colonialist's behavior that it ". . . betrays a determination to objectify, to confine, to imprison, to harden" (1970: 44).

But so does the activity of perception itself: stereotyping is a global activity, in all the senses of the word global. It is not just something that whites do to blacks, but which is also done by blacks to whites. Moreover, it is done by blacks to other blacks. It is also done by whites to other whites, who perceive (or *pre*-ceive) each other as being from a different part of the country, a different nationality, a different social class, a different gender, etc., where different in each case means other than the self. The stereotype so understood realizes the presence of force in the Latin—or in the context of imperialism perhaps it is better to call it the Roman—etymology of "perception," with its prefix "per-" that intensifies the violence of the root "capere," to seize: Stereotyping is a universal strategy for seizing the other. It is a way that subjects colonialize each other as different kinds of subjects, different not merely in features such as those of class or the body: such distinctions are merely incidental compared to the difference between the way each subject conceives them as bearing on other subjects and the way s/he conceives them as relating to his or her *own* status as a subject.

In effect, Bhabha argues that stereotyping is pathological, because it is fetishistic behavior: "The construction of colonial discourse is then a complex articulation of the tropes of fetishism—metaphor and metonomy—and the forms of narcissistic and aggressive identification available to the Imaginary" (1983: 29). By Imaginary he means, of course, that primitive level of desire Lacan posits as interacting with the more complex layers of the Symbolic and the Real. In Bhabha's reading of the Lacanian schema,

> The Imaginary is the transformation that takes place in the subject at the formative mirror phase, when it assumes a *discrete* image which allows it to postulate a series of equivalences, samenesses, identities, between the objects of the surrounding world. However, this positioning is itself *problematic,* for the subject finds or recognises itself through an image which is simultaneously alienating and hence potentially confrontational. This is the basis of the close relation between the two forms of identification complicit with the Imaginary—narcissism and aggressivity. It is precisely these two forms of "identification" that constitute the dominant strategy of colonial power exercised in relation to the stereotype.   (Ibid.: 29)

I quickly pass over the obvious point that Bhabha himself has here been guilty of stereotyping Lacan—as I, of course, am guilty of stereotyping him but then the inevitability of stereotypes is part of my point. Powerful as Bhabha's analysis of colonial discourse undeniably is, I believe it goes astray when it assumes a distinction between mirror phase and stereotyping (stereotyping while "like" the mirror phase, differs from it): narcissism and aggression are not merely "complicit" but *necessary* aspects of subjectivity. Many things get mirrored in the mirror stage; among these there is a reflection of the nature of the linguistic sign itself. Thus it is imperative for those using Lacan to discriminate between the multiple aspects of what gets represented in specular subjectivity. It is particularly important that hierachization among the reflected be observed, so that, for instance, the paradoxical nature of the linguistic sign is not confused with the ambivalence of its more local effects. I believe something like this occurs in Bhabha's argument when he writes that "Fixity, as the sign of cultural/historical/ racial difference in the discourse of colonialism, is a paradoxical mode of representation," and then goes on to identify this paradox as an ambivalence that is "one of the most significant discursive and psychical strategies of discriminatory power—whether racist or sexist . . ." (Ibid.: 18). That is, instead of a part being taken for the whole, the whole (the ambivalent nature of the linguistic sign as such) is taken by Bhabha for a part (the particular way the signs's mode of being is articulated as the ambivalence of colonial discourse). When talking about "the stereotype," Bhabha is quite often—and particularly at the most abstract level of his theorizing—talking about the sign.

The subject understood as born in a recognition scene of its own otherness, whether as in Lacan, that recognition originates in a mirror phase, or as in Bakhtin (or Vygotsky), described as initiated through entrance into language as the child learns to speak, is not just "threatened" with "lack," it *is* "lack." Lacanian entrance into the symbolic, like Bakhtin's account of language acquisition, assumes the power of signs to shape the subject. And like Bhabha, a dialogical thinker would be compelled to recognize the central role of stereotyping in racist, sexist, and all other forms of "colonial discourse." But the Freudian base of Bhabha's Lacanian analysis compels him to assume that stereotyping *as such* is pathological ("fetishistic") behavior. I submit that for all its rigor, such a conclusion is a subtle effect of desire; it is a version of optimism, for it presumes that it stands opposed to another mode of perception that is "normal," i.e., not diseased in the sense that it is not stereotypical. Dialogism, on the other hand, suggests a more lugubrious possibility: it argues that stereotyping is not an aberration among strategies available to the subject in his/her efforts to think the other. On the contrary, stereotyping *is* perception's normal mode of operation.

The stereotype is then not a category so much as it is an event, one that has three steps: the subject seeks to finalize the other in a fixed identity; events dramatize to the subject that the other may elude or exceed such an identity; but "finally" the subject finds a way to stitch both lack and stereotype into a unified perception that governs his actions with regard to the other. If Bakhtin is correct, this process describes the normal functioning of perception, structured as it is by the instability of the I/Other dichotomy, mandated by the sign/referent dichotomy governing the language that produces the subject in the first place. Although we have spoken of stereotyping as a sequential proccess up to this point, it is perhaps more accurately characterized as a proccess that unfolds in a time less sequential in any normal sense (it is not chronological in any significant way), than it is neo-platonic.

Stereotyping gives fixity a value in itself, much as neo-platonism is a tendency to assume phenomena associated with stasis are "more real" than those characterized by change: in metaphysics this tendency is familiar in the division between the level of ideas that have the permanence of mathematical logic (the concept of a three-sided geometrical shape) and the lower level of reflections or shadows of ideas (a particular drawing of a triangle). In theology this tendency is present in the cut-off between the high status of a durative God who "was, is, and shall be" and the low status of mortals, subject to the punctual indignities of change and death. The valorization of stasis vs. change, an uncomplicated opposition of "real" vs. "less real," or high vs. low, in most neo-platonisms, is, like everything else, ambivalent and doubled in dialogism: stasis as the source of the only identity not only others but I myself can have, carries a plus sign. It is the source of a possible order, no matter how constructed its status; without it, the world would give itself as sheer flux, a perceptual chaos. But stability as an exclusivist, monologizing category carries a negative sign: it leads to psychic disorder in the individual subject and is the source of prejudice in society, a prejudice that is not blind but rather a special way of seeing. In either case, the difference between positive and negative stereotyping is dialogic, not binary. Colonial discourse is less a pathology in its own right than it is an extension of normal apperceptual activity.

By assuming so much I in no way wish to diminish the force of protest in the analyses of those working against racism, sexism, or any other version of suppression that Bhabha globalizes as colonialist discourse. There is of course a difference between stereotypes that rigidify the teeming heterogeneity of effects we call a country so that we may, for instance, perceive its variety and complexity as the unified concept "India" and the stereotype that fixes Indians as "wogs." The body of practices of which "wog" is an element should, of course, be resisted—among other ways by being subjected to theorization. But attempts to read racism as a pathology whose name is stereotype can get us only so far. For insofar as the subject is produced by language, and one of the fundamental axes of language works by making "solid impressions" of all signs, stereotyping as such is unavoidable, and therefore knowledge of it cannot—in itself—serve to liberate. Stereotyping cannot be extirpated; its effects can only be ameliorated.

One way, perhaps, to do this would be to recognize both the universality of stereotyping as a semiotic funciton, while simultaneously attending to the particularity of its effects. To proceed in this way would permit us to use some of the undoubted strength advocatory critics have generated in their accounts of colonial discourse as an aid in reading works not normally included in the anti-canon of colonialist texts. If such a move can be made, it would perhaps help us see canonical texts in a somewhat new perspective, while at the same time reflecting a different light on colonialist discourse itself. As an illustration of what I mean, I turn now to *The Great Gatsby*.

I choose this text first because it would appear to be "canonical" not only in the sense that it is securely established in university curricula as a classic of American literature but in the sense that its racial and social ambience is also "canonical" insofar as its major figures are all white and all ruling class. I need a "classic," because I wish to argue that many of the issues and formal features frequently said to be characteristic of anticanonical works are not confined to anti-colonialist, black, or commitedly feminist texts. *The Great Gatsby* is a text that is no less generated by stereotype, ambivalence, and the lack that diffuses subjectivity as many that are cited as examples of such tendencies in anti-canons. Another reason for choosing *The Great Gatsby* is that it textualizes its own stereotyping with the clarity of a paradigm: in large measure it is "about" the suppression of difference and change required to maintain the (stereotypical) illusion of identity and stasis. It is "about" Gatsby's **stereotype** of Daisy, of Nick's stereotype of Gatsby, and the stereotype of themselves fashioned by all these characters. And, at a higher level of thematics, it is "about" the stereotype of that country of the mind called "America." The novel attempts to chronicle (in the technical, historiographic sense of that word) the fate of these stereotypes, each of which is treated with great social and historical particularity, as they are broken down or intensified in their conflict with each other.

Before examining the relation between the text's formal aspects and colonial discourse, it will be useful to keep in mind its gross narrative features. *The Great Gatsby* gives itself as a memoir, written down in 1924 in the Midwest by Nick Carraway, as he seeks to make sense of events that unfolded two years earlier, when Nick's neighbor on Long Island, Jay Gatsby, is murdered by a crazed mechanic whose wife has been killed in a hit-and-run accident. Although Gatsby was in the car, it had actually been driven by Daisy, the great love of Gatsby's life. After Gatsby's death, Daisy returns to her husband and Nick to his birthplace in the Midwest, where, after an interval, he writes "a history of that summer." While the main body of the narrative is compressed in time to a few months in 1922 and in space to a small area of the east coast, this time/space is complicated both by its own pastness and thereness to the moment of its being put into writing by Nick, and by the pastness and thereness of the major characters prior to the events of 1922. In each case the relation of here and now to then and there is enacted as an incongruity, a discordance modelled in the constant inadequacy and breakdown of stereotypes.

The ambivalence and lack that characterize the stereotype are manifest in the novel as a complex series of contradictions and incommensurabilities. There are so very many of these and they are of such a variety, it may be said that the text is governed by the trope of oxymoron. It is first of all the most characteristic feature of Nick's narrative voice; the novel contains page after page of locutions such as I was "that most limited of all specialists, the 'well-rounded man'" (4); "the rock of the world was founded securely on a fairy's wing" (100); the First World War (which is, of course called "the great war") is a "delayed Teutonic migration" (3), ceilings have "Presbyterian nymphs" (70) on them, and characters eat their food with "ferocious delicacy" (71).[2] But the oxymoronic nature of the narrator's epigrams and descriptions is not merely stylistic. A dramatized incongruity characterizes virtually every aspect of the text. The title of *The Great Gatsby* is itself an oxymoron, an eponymous gap between its honorific adjective and the proper name of the sentimental gangster. Incongruity is at work in the novel's most obvious and superficial thematic level, the gap between Gatsby's image—his stereotype—of Daisy and Daisy as she is outside Gatsby's "riotous dream" of her as quest object. Incompatibility legislates the novel's basic narrative pattern, which is articulated as a rupture between events as they unfolded in 1922 and Nick's act of chronicling the same events two years later. This break between event and representation as present disfigures all attempts in the novel to make past and present cohere, as in the gap between the point in 1917 in Louisville when Gatsby and Daisy first meet and the struggle each undertakes to continue that moment when they encounter each other on Long Island five years later. A grotesque incommensurability is a dominant of all the incidental features of the narrative as well, such as a vagrant selling stray dogs on the streets of Manhattan whose name is Rockefeller. This incommensurability is particularly bizarre in its mapping of America: when asked what part of the middle west he is from, a character replies, "San Francisco" (65). Another character has been assigned the task of finding "a small town" and, when queried on his choice, answers "Detroit" (95). These are trivialities that would not bear mentioning if not that they double the radical incongruity present in the formal feature of oxymoron that shapes the text's pro-

---

2. All references are to the trade paper edition of the novel: F. Scott Fitzgerald, *The Great Gatsby*. New York: Charles Scribner's Sons, 1925 (copyright renewed).

found meditation on the unavoidable incongruities in its own status as a text, the gaps between stasis and change that pock its surface as a work, as it fails to exceed the stereotyping that is the fate of all representation and writing most ineluctably.

The narrative voice keeps insisting on its "honesty": "Every one suspects himself of at least one of the cardinal virtues, and this is mine: I am one of the few honest people that I have ever known" (60). But the particular form this "cardinal virtue" assumes is "mid-western" plainness (for all Nick's habit of turning fancy metaphors), as opposed to "eastern" corruption and excess. This is just one of the ways complexities of geography and social force are reduced by the narrator to stereotype, raising questions that put his claims to accuracy in doubt. At the level of work, *The Great Gatsby* is controlled by Nick's perception, a virtual paradigm for "a form of multiple and contradictory belief, [that] gives knowledge of difference and simultaneously disavows or masks it. . . ." On the one hand, Nick is a tireless chronicler of the different identities rumor assigns Gatsby (that he is related to Hindenburg, that he is a German spy, that his house is really a boat that detaches itself from the shoreline to cruise as a rum runner, that he is related to Kaiser Wilhelm II, that he has killed a man, etc.—all associations that, as in colonial stereotypes, stress his exotic otherness). In addition, he is aware of the difference between Gatsby's account of himself (Oxford graduate, scion of inherited wealth, etc.) and Gatsby's activity as a bootlegger and dealer in stolen securities. Nevertheless, his whole activity as narrator is directed toward constituting a unified, finished-off image of Gatsby.

It is not by chance that the image he constructs is one almost precisely the opposite of that he manufactures for his own persona: Nick comes from a large, old, closely knit family; Gatsby has no family in the most radical sense that he gives birth to himself (when he transforms himself from James Gatz to Jay Gatsby); Nick values solidity, being a careful vs. a careless driver (a recurring figure in the text), Gatsby is absolutely reckless and is as much killed by the careless driving of his great love as the victim Daisy runs over. Nick works at the Probity Trust; he deals in "securities," whereas Gatsby specializes in stealing bonds. The oppositions are too obvious to dwell on. More often than not in the critical literature they have been treated at a characterological or psychologistic level, strategies that obscure the implications of such programmatically precise binarization for the process of subject formation. Subject formation not just for this or that individual actor in the novel but at the non-trivial level where it is a problem in the kind of representation that language will permit. At that level, the differences begin to appear less capable of articulating a uniqueness for any of the individual characters, least of all those that are deployed by Nick to set himself off from Gatsby. In their representation of each other and their representation of their selves to themselves, both (as well as Fitzgerald in his representation of them as characters) are ventriloquated by the same extrapersonal force. It is the necessity that mandates perception be accomplished through the simultaneous interaction of stasis and flux. This is a semiotic *ukaz* that language imposes on producing subjects. From the point of view of our topic, the most important consequence is that not only do Nick and Gatsby perceive the other as a stereotype, but each is guilty of perceiving himself as a stereotype as well.

That is, each operates from a site in addressivity that is assumed to be not only unique but stable. As such, it can globalize the meaning of the other. Invoking parallels with neo-Platonism again, we may say that the subject's assumption of his fixed identity is similar to the claim godhood makes when it intones "I am that I am." And like a god-figure, the subject assumes he can, with respect to the other, see all and know all, completely exhausting the other's capacity to elude the subject's categories. Thus Nick, the teller of this tale, makes explicit his desire to have a panoptic point of view: looking out of a tall New York building, he says ". . . high over the city our line of yellow windows must have contributed their share of human secrecy to the casual watcher in the darkening streets, and I was with him too, looking up and wondering. I was within and without, simultaneously enchanted and repelled by the inexhaustible variety of life" (36). But his vaunted honesty is based not on the enchantment of variety. Rather, it is based on a truth that is guaranteed by its stability. Thus, after his initial doubts about Gatsby's account of his past at Oxford, he is easily convinced when a photograph is produced showing a group of young men in blazers "loafing in an archway through which were visible a host of spires." As if this were not enough to establish the degree to which his sense of truth is based on clichés (a form of stereotyping), Nick adds, "There was Gatsby, looking a little, not much, younger—with a cricket bat in his hand. Then it was all true" (67). I emphasize not only the photograph's ability to metaphorize Nick's willingness to regard fixity as a condition of truth but the mind-bending banality of the stereotypes he is prepared to accept.

Gatsby's self-stereotyping is caught in one of the least remarked formal features of the text, its punctuation. I mean the place in the text where Jay Gatsby is printed in quotation marks. On the night Daisy runs over Myrtle Wilson, after she has returned to her husband Tom, Gatsby tells Nick the story of his past, particularly about that point in his past when he ceased being just James Gatz and told Dan Cody, the millionaire yachtsman who adopts him, that he is Jay Gatsby. Nick writes: "It was that night he told me the strange story of his youth with Dan Cody—told it to me because 'Jay Gatsby' had broken up like glass against Tom's hard malice, and the long secret extravaganza was played out" (148). "Jay Gatsby" is James Gatz's attempt to fix a meaning for the subjectivity nominated by that name.

I wish to dwell on those quotation marks for a moment because they both frame the stereotype in which Gatz/Gatsby has sought to inscribe himself, and at the same time they ironize the fixity of such an identity. Before looking at the specific instance of these quotation marks, we should keep in mind the peculiar textualizing role that punctuation plays in general. Punctuation is an appropriate vehicle for dramatizing stability, for it belongs to the formal, static pole of language activity, it is (in its dictionary definition) "the use of standard marks and signs in writing and printing in order to clarify meaning." Like that most rigid of all linguistic phenomena—grammar—punctuation is, then, a formal means that seeks to contain the volatility of semiotic operations. It is thus not merely an appropriate way to enact the fixity of identities but an ironic one as well, for of course no matter how florid or complex, punctuation is never completely able to harden a single meaning in the words it diacritically seeks to govern. Of all punctuation marks, none is more radical than those that fix the borders between speakers, for in doing so they double the function of pronouns, i.e., they assign responsibility for words.

Thus, when the site of Gatsby's place in the structure of addressivity is put into quotation marks, what gets foregrounded is the degree to which he has shaped that site in his own image: he is responsible for the identity Jay Gatsby names, just as he is responsible for other words ascribed to him by quotation marks that establish it is he who is speaking. It is here that the crucial role of narrative to the process of subject formation makes itself felt: "Jay Gatsby" for all its author's attempts to make it so, is less a name than it is a story. Insofar as it is a name for a story, "Jay Gatsby" is structurally similar to mythic names, insofar as Hercules cannot be thought without his labors or Odysseus without his voyages, etc., "Jay Gatsby" as a name that is a story dramatizes the central role of stereotyping in formation of the individual subject on the one hand, and on the other, the role of stereotyping as a dynamic in social and historical formation. Gatsby is the story of his career; in it we can see how history uses stereotypes to form the subject as a link in the social chain.

To do this in more detail, it will be helpful to keep in mind the bases of the argument so far; these may be stated as a number of theses: the nature of the linguistic sign is synergistic, a constant struggle and cooperation between the necessity to be static and repeatable and the opposed but no less imperative neccessity of the same material to be open to constantly new and changing circumstances; the individual subject is constituted by his entrance into the world of signs, therefore the asymmetric dualism of the sign governs the perceptual activity of subjects; this universal condition is reflected in our inability to eradicate stereotypes, since they are a function of the nature of the sign itself and precede any particular subject or experience; but this general condition is specified into particular stereotypes in different times and places. In other words, the universality of stereotypes is imposed by language; their particularity derives from history.

Since the narrative shape of Gatsby's career is important evidence for this view, let us remember its gross outlines. As Jimmy Gatz, he is born to a family of unsuccessful farmers in the midwest, "but his imagination had never accepted them as his parents at all" (99). He leaves home early to wander the Great Lakes, he changes his name to Jay Gatsby when he encounters a wealthy miner whose travelling companion he then becomes; the First World War sees him in training outside Louisville, where he meets Daisy. They fall in love, Daisy assuming Gatsby is as wealthy as she; before the deception can be discovered, Gatsby is sent to France. After some time, Daisy is persuaded to marry the Chicago millionaire Tom Buchanan, and they move to his estate on Long Island. Gatsby has in the meantime had a spectacular war, decorated by several governments and after the armistice permitted to enroll in Oxford, spending five months there before returning to the States where he becomes associated with the underworld boss Meyer Wolfsheim. He makes immense amounts of money selling bootleg liquor and stolen securities, buys a mansion across the bay from Daisy and Tom. All his labors have been in the service of recapturing Daisy; they meet again, Daisy is involved in a hit-and-run accident, Gatsby is shot by the victim's husband.

The poverty of this account will be obvious to anyone who has read the book, but I hope enough of an outline has been provided to establish *The Great Gatsby* as a quest romance. At the level of work, it is the quest of Gatsby for his dream of Daisy, a dream specified in terms that make it clear it is also the distinctively American dream of going from rags to riches; for beautiful as Daisy may be, it is her voice that sings the siren song to Gatsby, the voice that is not only full of promise but "full of money," as Gatsby himself once says (it is the only memorable thing he says). Gatsby is first perceived standing on his shore, reaching out in the night to a green light shining across the bay, the green light at the end of the pier belonging to Tom Buchanan's estate, the light that is Daisy, and whose greenness is not only the yea-saying of green as a signal but of green as the sign of money. The quest has more to do with Horatio Alger than with Chrétien de Troyes. It is further elaborated with associations of Frontier: Gatsby's first patron, whose name evokes Buffalo Bill, and who is "a product of the Nevada silver fields, of the Yukon, of every rush for metal since seventy-five . . . [a] pioneer debauchee who during one phase of American life brought back to the Eastern seaboard the savage violence of the frontier brothel and saloon" (100–101). The association of violence with money that is so much a part of the dream of rapidly acquired wealth is maintained in Gatsby's second patron, Meyer Wolfsheim, who fixed the World Series of 1919, wears human teeth for cufflinks, is associated with several murders, and says of his relation to Gatsby that he not only started him off in business but that he "made him" (172). Gatsby is a composite figure, then, who incorporates a number of key American stereotypes extending to his childhood bible, a western novel about a cowboy named Hopalong Cassidy. Inside this book, the young Gatz writes rules that savor of Benjamin Franklin, a reminder that "the West" was once a frontier in "the East." The rules ("No wasting time. . . . Bath every day, Study electricity, etc." [174]) are those of self-improvement and point to the degree to which Gatsby seeks to make his self.

Unlike Jimmy Gatz, the self that chance has assigned him and which is prey to every contingency, "Jay Gatsby," the self he lusts to produce for himself, is one that will be improved in the sense that it will be liberated from chance, free of intervention from the other, characterized by the absolute stasis of identity that guarantees the higher reality of a god. In this, I tried to suggest earlier, he is simply manifesting the pattern of subject formation that language-produced subjects are condemned to, given the nature of the linguistic sign. What is particular about the way Gatsby goes about this task is determined by American history, not only in the apparent features of frontier, dreams of success, invention, etc. but by the very temporality that governs all its major moves. I have argued that, if I am at all right about the nature of stereotyping, its mode of activity must be understood as neo-platonic. A major reason why *The Great Gatsby* is so paradigmatic a text for any attempt to understand the relation of stereotyping to history is that it works out not only the surface features of stereotyping as they are particularized in a specific history, but at the more basic level of temporality as well.

Gatsby, remember, is someone who is seeking to erect his own selfhood, an identity that is whole, immaculate and lasting; bluntly stated, what he needs is a biography free of changes, thus a narrative without time. This is, like the sign or the stereotype, an absurd condition, one that is literally oxymoronic; which is why, at the level of text, the oxymorn dominates *The Great Gatsby*. The Americanness of Gatsby's dilemma is caught in the general term for what he seeks to become: a self-made man. Thus, like Henry Ford, he must believe that "history is bunk." America is the sort of place where you can get a "Jazz History of the World" with no discrepancy felt between the improvisatory nature of jazz and the linear nature of history—the irony being compounded by the composer's name—"Tostoff." The chronotope of "self-made" men is one that must be split-level: it requires change and radical change, very rapid change, to move from the contingent space of rags into which such men are thrust by the accident of birth to the absolute space of riches that is all invested with their intention, and thus must be free for contingency and change. Thus they need time at one stage and must deny it at another stage. This double bind determines the dual asymmetry organizing the narrative shape of biographies appropriate to self-made men. I will quickly pass over the parallels between such a temporal asymmetry in the lives of Horatio Algers, Henry Fords, and Thomas Edisons and the temporal asymmetry in the lives of Christian saints who, like St. Augustine, undergo conversion experiences, to emphasize the American peculiarities of such a life narrative.

It should come as no surprise that Gatsby has great trouble with time. This is especially true as time relates to Daisy, the icon of his individual appropriation of the American dream. As he is about to meet her for the first time after his return from the Army and her marriage, he becomes anxious and says to Nick, who is hosting the meeting, "It's too late!" But Nick points out that it is in fact early for the meeting: "It's just two minutes to four" (85). He is out of synchrony with the time of his dream, a point reinforced when he almost knocks over the clock on Nick's mantle. Even at this first meeting, there are hints of a rupture between Gatsby's stereotype of Daisy and Daisy's capacity to be adequate to the stereotype, a problem expressed in temporal terms: "He had been full of the idea so long, dreamed it right through to the end, waited with his teeth set, so to speak, at an inconceivable pitch of intensity. Now, in the reaction, he was running down like an overwound clock" (93).

Gatsby has trouble with clocks because of his need to deny time. When Nick tells him not to expect too much of Daisy, because you cannot repeat the past, Gatsby, as a good American neo-platonist, is outraged: "'Can't repeat the past?' he cried incredulously. 'Of course you can!'" (111). And of course, as someone who gave birth to himself in the past, he must take such a position. It is the American version of stereotyping, captured as well in the careers of other self-made men, like the brewer who originally built the great mansion Gatsby has bought, a monument to the proposition that you *can* repeat the past, at least architecturally: it "was a colossal affair by any standard—it was a factual imitation of some Hotel de Ville in Normandy" (5). But it is an eclectic repetition of the past: it has "Marie Antoinette music rooms and Restoration salons," and its books are kept in "the Merton College Library" (92), a location the text gives, like Gatsby's name, in quotation marks. But such radical attempts to repeat the past, to make time stop, have consequences for the future. The brewer who built Gatsby's house had wanted to imitate the past so badly he had "agreed to pay five years' taxes on all the neighboring cottages if the owners would have their roofs thatched with straw." But men who spring from themselves, who resist continuity, pay the price in their own genealogies: the brewer goes into decline and "his children sold his house with the black wreath still on the door" (89). Stereotyping history, relating to the past as if it could be packaged and bought and then rearranged not in time but in the fixed space of "period rooms," has the effect of catapaulting Americans back into flux and change so rapid, that "historical" houses are sold "with the black wreath still on the door." The symbol of ultimate stasis, death, is transformed by such haste into a sign of change and movement: new owners come, as Gatsby does, to repeat the dream of fashioning history with a fixed identity, only to fall back into a transcience beyond the power of human categories to arrest.

In conclusion, we may say that the house where Gatsby's corpse lies at the end of the novel is his true home insofar as it is an architectural monument to the architectonics of his place in existence, the place at which he has been addressed by the dual mandate of language's requirement for a fixity that always fails. It is the situation in which history in America has been stereotyped into the American dream. No one has put it better than Fitzgerald in the great last lines of the novel, where what we have been calling otherness gets nominated as "the past":

> Gatsby believed in the green light, the orgiastic future that year by year recedes before us. It eluded us then, but that's no matter—tomorrow we will run faster, stretch out our arms farther . . . And one fine morning——
> And so we beat on, boats against the current, borne back ceaselessly into the past." (182)

References

Bakhtin, Mikhail
1979 "Avtor i geroj v esteticeskoj dejatel'nosti ('Author and Hero in aesthetic activity')," in *Estetika slovesnogo tvorcestva* (*The Aesthetics of Verbal Creation*) (Moskva: Iskusstvo), 5–180. An English translation of this work will be published next year by the University of Texas Press.
1986a *Marxism and the Philosophy of Language* trans. Ladislav Matejka and I. R. Titunik (Cambridge, MA: Harvard University Press).
1986b "K filosofii postupka ('Towards a Philosophy of the Act')," in *Filosofija i sociologija nauki i texniki* ('*Philosophy and Sociology of Science and Technology*'), edited by N. T. Frolov et al. (Moskva: Nauka), 80–160.
Bhabha, Homi K.
1983 "The Other Question. . . ," *Screen* 24 (6): 18–36.

1985 "Signs Taken for Wonders: Questions of Ambivalence and Authority under a Tree Outside Delhi, May, 1817," *Critical Inquiry* 12 (1): 144–165.

Fanon, Frantz
1970 *Black Skin, White Masks* (London: Paladin).

Gates, Henry L., Jr.
1987 *Figures in Black: Words, Signs, and the 'Racial self'* (New York: Oxford University Press).

Irigaray, Luce
1985 *Speculum of the Other Woman*, translated by Gillian C. Gill (Ithaca: Cornell University Press).

Karcevskij, Sergej
1982 "The Assymetric dualism of the Linguistic Sign," in *The Prague School: Selected Writings*, edited by Peter Steiner (Austin: University of Texas Press).

Lacan, Jacques
1979 *The Four Fundamental Concepts of Psychoanalysis*, translated by Alan Sheridan (Harmondsworth: Penguin books).

Said, Edward
1978 *Orientalism* (New York: Pantheon).
1986 "Orientalism Reconsidered," in *Literature, Politics, and Theory* edited by Francis Barker, et al. (London: Methuen), 210–229.

Vygotsky, Lev
1986 *Thought and Language*, translated by Alex Kozulin (Cambridge, MA: MIT Press).

Index

Notes on Contributors

Houston Baker is Albert M. Greenfield Professor of Human Relations at the University of Pennsylvania. He is the author of *Blues Ideology and Afro-American Literature* (1985) and *Modernism and the Harlem Renaissance* (1987). He is also a poet whose most recent volume is *Blues Journeys Home*.

Robert F. Berkhofer, Jr. is Professor of History and American Studies at the University of Michigan. He is the author of *A Behavioral Approach to Historical Analysis* and *The White Man's Indian: Images of the American Indian from Columbus to the Present*. He is currently writing a book-length essay on some of the implications of modern literary theory for conceiving, reading, and writing history.

Jonathan Culler, Director of the Society for the Humanities at Cornell University, is the author of *Framing the Sign* and other works of literary theory. His essay comes from a book-length project on Baudelaire.

Terry Eagleton teaches at Wadham College, Oxford. His books include *Literary Theory: An Introduction* (1983) and *The Function of Criticism* (1984).

Susan Handelman is Associate Professor of English at the University of Maryland, College Park. She is the author of *The Slayers of Moses: The Emergence of Rabbinic Interpretation in Modern Literary Theory* and of articles on Freud, Shakespeare, Woolf, Jabes, midrash, and literary theory. She is currently working on a book on contemporary Jewish thought and literary theory discussing Walter Benjamin, Gershom Scholem, Emmanuel Levinas, and Edmond Jabes.

Paul Hernadi teaches English and Comparative Literature and directs the Interdisciplinary Humanities Center at the University of California, Santa Barbara. He is the author of *Beyond Genre: New Directions in Literary Classification* and *Interpreting Events: Tragicomedies of History on the Modern Stage*. He also edited *What is Literature?*, *What is Criticism?*, and *The Horizon of Literature*.

Michael Holquist is Professor of Slavic and Comparative Literature at Yale University. He is the author of *Dostoevsky and the Novel* and (with Katerina Clark) *Mikhail Bakhtin*.

Martin Jay is Professor of History at the University of California, Berkeley. His books include *The Dialectical Imagination* (1973), *Marxism and Totality* (1984), *Adorno* (1984), *Permanent Exiles* (1985), and *Fin-de-Siècle Socialism and Other Essays* (1988). He is currently working on the theme of vision in twentieth-century French thought.

Dominick LaCapra is Goldwin Smith Professor of European Intellectual History at Cornell University. His recent books include *Rethinking Intellectual History* (1983), *History and Criticism* (1985), and *History, Politics and the Novel* (1987).

Richard Ohmann teaches in the English Department at Wesleyan University. He is the author of *Politics of Letters* (1987) and works on the board of *Radical Teacher*.

Edward Pechter is Associate Professor of English at Concordia University in Montreal. He is the author of *Dryden's Classical Theory of Literature* and essays on Shakespeare and Renaissance dramatic and non-dramatic texts.

Renato Rosaldo is Mellon Professor of Interdisciplinary Studies and Director of the Stanford Center for Chicano Research. He is the author of *Ilongot Headhunting, 1883–1974: A Study in Society and History* (1980) and *Culture and Truth: The Remaking of Social Analysis* (1989).

Hayden White is Presidential Professor of Historical Studies at the University of California, Santa Cruz.